Readers will have to range far and
spirituality of the Acts of the Apost
Dr. Smith has highlighted and eluci   ...vugnout Acts, but
she has enriched and expanded them with a remarkable array of insights
gleaned from twenty centuries of the Christian quest to live out their faith.
Well-framed questions at the end of each chapter will inspire and stimulate
the continuing life of faith in today's world.

—E. Glenn Hinson
author of *A Serious Call to a Contemplative Lifestyle*

This highly accessible commentary on Acts is a trove of insights enabling
readers to develop their spiritual formation through deep reflection on
the biblical text. Karen Smith is a knowledgeable guide, adeptly sharing
her familiarity with the terrain. Her probing questions at the end of each
section enable every reader to engage personally with the texts discussed,
applying them to their own contexts. The volume will be invaluable for
preachers and laypeople alike. Strongly recommended!

—Dr. Christine E. Joynes
Fellow in Theology and Director of the Centre for Baptist Studies
Regent's Park College, Oxford

Drawing on her years of experience in preparing people for Christian
ministry, Karen Smith has provided us with a reading of Acts that allows
us all to grasp what it means to be formed and to mature as Christian
disciples. Her gentle sensitivity as a pastor, together with her evident love
of Scripture, shines through this book. Karen explores such vital themes as
the experience of conversion, life in community, the importance of waiting,
attentiveness to God Spirit, and the cost of discipleship. And throughout
she draws on the riches of the Christian traditions to deepen our understanding and enrich our spirituality. It is a book to guide all of us who are
"on the Way."

—The Revd. Graham Sparkes
President, Luther King Centre for Theological Education
Manchester, England

Similar to Luke's engaging story as penned in the Book of Acts, Karen
Smith has written a well-suited companion for that narrative journey for all
followers of Christ. Like a map for faithful discipleship, *Following on the Way*

offers insight, instruction, direction and encouragement, pointing readers toward growth in Christ through the community of faith, the church. The various chapters of this spiritual formation commentary provide readers with the foundation and also the tools needed in their journey of faith—following the contours of the book itself. This commentary is a rich resource for any follower on the way.

—Scott M. Gibson, D.Phil
David E. Garland Chair of Preaching
George W. Truett Theological Seminary
Baylor University

With passion, depth, skill, and imagination, Karen Smith's creative commentary on Acts encourages today's Christian disciples to embark on a quest of discovery alongside the first followers of Jesus, as together we are spiritually formed into the body of Christ. Through spiritual themes such as remembering, waiting, and journeying—together with whole-hearted reliance on the Holy Spirit—we are urged to grow into the likeness of Christ, as individuals and communities. A thoughtful and challenging book, brimming with faith, wisdom, and lived experience.

—The Revd. Catherine Williams
Anglican Priest, Writer and Spiritual Director

FOLLOWING ON THE WAY

Smyth & Helwys Publishing, Inc.
6316 Peake Road
Macon, Georgia 31210-3960
1-800-747-3016
©2022 by Karen E. Smith
All rights reserved.

The cover photograph is of an ancient wayside marker along one of the pilgrimage roads in France that medieval pilgrims followed on the way to Santiago de Compostela. This marker is located southeast of Fresnay-sur-Sarthe, Pays de la Loire, France.

Library of Congress Cataloging-in-Publication Data

Names: Smith, Karen E., 1957- author.
Title: Following on the way : the Acts of the Apostles as a guide to
spiritual formation / by Karen E. Smith.
Description: First. | Macon, GA : Smyth & Helwys Publishing, 2022. |
Includes bibliographical references.
Identifiers: LCCN 2022024302 | ISBN 9781641733946 (paperback)
Subjects: LCSH: Bible. Acts--Criticism, interpretation, etc. | Spiritual
formation--Biblical teaching.
Classification: LCC BS2625.6.S64 S65 2022 | DDC 226.6/06--dc23/eng/20220720
LC record available at https://lccn.loc.gov/2022024302

KAREN E. SMITH

FOLLOWING
ON THE
WAY

The Acts of the Apostles as
A Guide to Spiritual Formation

Also by Karen E. Smith

Christian Spirituality

With Gratitude and Thanksgiving to God
for the Life and Witness
of

Dorothy Walters Smith (1927–2020)
W. Ches Smith III (1927–2013)
Jessie Goodship Harris (1928–2019)
Norman L. Harris (1927–2017)

Family, Friends, and Followers of the Way

Acknowledgments

Commentaries on biblical texts are written for different purposes and different audiences. Many biblical commentaries offer insight and understanding by approaching the text verse by verse. Others take a more thematic approach. Some commentaries are written with the preacher or teacher in mind, while others are aimed at those involved in academic study. This volume is written as a spiritual formation commentary. As such, it takes a very different approach to the text as it seeks to draw out and reflect on themes related to spiritual growth and discipleship. Taking this approach to examine the Acts of the Apostles offers us an opportunity to reflect not only on Luke's understanding of being a follower of Jesus, but also on the meaning of being a disciple of Christ in the present day. I am grateful to Smyth & Helwys for commissioning me to undertake this project, which has been richly rewarding for me.

In writing this book, I have been enlightened in my own understanding of Acts through reading the commentaries and articles of New Testament specialists. I have tried to note my dependence on these works in the footnotes and in the bibliography, but I am sure that I could never indicate fully how much I have learned and benefited from the scholarship of others.

While writing the book, I had the privilege of visiting the Collegeville Institute as a scholar in residence. I register my thanks to Carla Durand, director of programs, for the hospitality that was offered, and to the Benedictine community at St. John's Abbey, Collegeville, Minnesota, who welcomed my husband and me to worship with them during our stay. I have also greatly appreciated the more recent opportunity for regular worship at Tewkesbury Abbey, another community that has Benedictine roots. The music, prayers, and recitation of the creed have been a balm to my soul and a reminder that by the grace of God, I am united in Christ with a wide community of saints on earth and in heaven. I also gladly register my thanks to the communities where I taught for twenty-seven years, South

Wales Baptist College and Cardiff University, Cardiff, UK. Both the college and the university have offered me access to research materials and libraries for which I am very grateful.

Many years ago, I read a book by David H. C. Read titled *Preaching About the Needs of Real People*. In his discussion of sermon preparation, he said that when preparing a sermon he found it helpful to have what he called "controls."[1] That is to say, he claimed that while writing a sermon, one should always imagine that certain people are looking over your shoulder and asking, "What do you mean by that?" Or perhaps looking at what you are saying about a text and asking, "Is there anything there for me?"

Over the years, in preaching and in writing, I have always tried to follow that advice. My "controls" for this book are numerous. Some, like my parents, parents-in-law, and grandparents, have now departed this life and joined the wider communion of saints. Still others are dear friends from my home church in South Georgia. Then, of course, there is the fellowship of believers in Orchard Place Baptist Church in Neath, South Wales, UK, where I served as pastor for twenty-five years. These are the people who graciously and patiently put up with me and who, in the "to and fro" of community life, taught me much about trying to follow in the way of Christ. In thinking of all of these and so many others, I acknowledge my debt to them. They have all had a rich input into this book.

My greatest thanks, of course, is to my husband, Paul Harris. He not only read the manuscript and discussed it with me but also offered many suggestions for improving the text and helped formulate questions for further reflection, which are provided at the end of each chapter. As always, his comments and suggestions have sharpened my thinking about the texts. I am so grateful to God for life together with him and within the wider fellowship of believers.

Soli Deo gloria!

K.E.S.
Tewkesbury
September 2020

---

1. David H. C. Read, *Preaching about the Needs of Real People* (Louisville, KY: Westminster Press, 1988), 12.

Contents

Preface

New Testament scholars studying Luke-Acts have wrestled with issues such as authorship, dating, purpose, and audience and have explored textual, literary, sociological, cultural, and economic concerns. As a result, there are many fine scholarly works on both the Gospel of Luke and what is generally accepted as the companion volume, the Acts of the Apostles. Yet there is still no agreement by scholars on how Acts should be approached. Early studies treated Acts as a history of the church and tried to use it to reconstruct the development of the church in the apostolic era. Later, studies of Acts asked questions about the provenance of the volume, including possible sources: Who was Luke and why was he writing to Theophilus? When were the Gospel and Acts written and why? What was Luke's purpose in writing the Gospel and Acts? What was the Græco-Roman world like at the time of early Christianity, particularly as it relates to Luke's work? Ranging from approaches that have focused on scrutinizing form and analysis of textual variants to those that have engaged with literary concerns and theological themes, Acts has been looked at from many different angles in recent scholarship.

The amount of study focusing on Acts has resulted in a vast array of books and articles. Some commentaries have been written for the preacher. These present verse-by-verse exegetical analysis of the text or offer themes that one might tackle usefully in a sermon or Bible study. Others are written by and for the specialist with particular attention to an examination of word studies and textual problems. Still other works focus on particular themes ranging from the geographical, cultural, historical, or socioeconomic to the theological and doctrinal. All of these approaches have their place. While some of these approaches and themes in Acts will be noted, the purpose of this study, is to try to go beyond a textual or merely devotional reading of Acts in order to explore issues specifically relating to spiritual formation. In doing so, we will try to note the way that scholars have interpreted the text and think about how the text may have shaped perspectives on Christian faith. While some attention will be given to hermeneutical and exegetical issues (as they relate to the study and interpretation of the text), the primary aim of this book is to encourage readers to enter into the stories in Acts in a rather different way, so as to reflect on what it means both to be a follower of Jesus Christ and to be bound in Christ in fellowship with other believers. Throughout this book, I have used the New Revised Standard Version (NRSV) of the Bible, and for ease of reading I have incorporated quotations of some verses into the commentary itself. At other times I have paraphrased the text. Sometimes this has meant a slight change in the use of capital letters and punctuation, though the text itself is as given in the NRSV.

From the perspective of Christian faith, spiritual formation is God's work. For Luke, the author of Acts, there is no suggestion that individuals may come to faith or grow in the spiritual life by making choices to be better people or trying, in their own strength, to adopt a particular lifestyle or keeping spiritual disciplines. Christian formation is never an individual task but takes place within a community of faith. We are formed as individuals within community, just as the church is truly formed as believers work together, pray together, and share life in Christ together. This emphasis on "life together in Christ," as we shall see, is central to understanding Luke's vision of the church.

Throughout this spiritual formation commentary, it is assumed that, at a basic level, the primary purpose of the two-volume work Luke-Acts was both to assure readers of the continuing work of God in the world and to encourage them to respond with constancy and faithfulness to the call to follow Christ. In writing these volumes, Luke makes it plain that to claim that Jesus Christ is Lord means that both individuals and communities of faith no longer desire to conform to the image of the world but are seeking to be formed and transformed by God more and more into the likeness of Christ.

Given Luke's own approach, and since the overall focus of this commentary is on spiritual formation, this volume was written with the idea that the reader intends to embark on a study of the whole of Acts. In other words, unlike commentaries written as exegetical works or for the purpose of preaching on a single text, this spiritual formation commentary assumes that the reader will use it as a tool on a journey of spiritual formation. This means that the commentary is most effectively used as a guide while one works through the entire text. In doing so, the reader will discover that the early chapters of the commentary set the grounding for the discipline of spiritual formation in community, and the later chapters focus more on the challenges to the individual embarking on a pilgrimage of faith. I believe that this was the pattern that Luke himself set when he wrote the Acts of the Apostles. By following this pattern, we will first engage with what it means to be a follower of Christ in community, and then we will move on to discern some of challenges faced by those who are on the Way.

Introduction

Anyone reading Acts for the first time will be struck by the fact that the author was a magnificent storyteller. Acts is an action-packed drama from beginning to end! Twentieth-century Baptist scholar Edgar Johnson Goodspeed (1871–1962) described activity in Acts in this now oft-quoted way:

> Where within eighty pages will be found such a varied series of exciting events—trials, riots, persecutions, escapes, martyrdoms, voyages, shipwrecks, rescues—set in that amazing panorama of the ancient world—Jerusalem, Antioch, Philippi, Corinth, Athens, Ephesus, Rome? And with such scenery and settings—temples, courts, prisons, deserts, ships, seas, barracks, theaters? Has any opera such variety?[1]

Where else, indeed, could one find what Jaroslav Pelikan calls "a tale of adventure" with "frenetic action" and with more than a few "touches of humor"?[2] The inclusion of so many stories has influenced the way interpreters view the purpose of Acts. The fourth-century historian Eusebius (c. 260–339) treated Acts as a historical account and focused on the stories as a way of trying to reconstruct the development of the church. However, most scholars today agree that Luke was not intending to write a history of the church; they argue that he wove together stories of Jesus and his followers and of the early church in order to preach, teach, evangelize, and encourage.[3] While it is difficult to pinpoint a primary purpose for Acts, it

---

1. E. J. Goodspeed, *Introduction to the New Testament* (Chicago: University of Chicago Press, 1937), 187–88.

2. Jaroslav Pelikan, *Acts, Brazos Theological Commentary* (Grand Rapids, MI: Brazos Press, 2013), 23–24.

3. I. Howard Marshall argues that it is possible to see Luke as both a historian and a theologian and that "he used his history in the service of his theology." See I. Howard Marshall, *Luke, Historian and Theologian* (Exeter: Paternoster Press, 1970, 1979), 19.

is evident that the writer's artful use of storytelling enables the reader to think more deeply about what it means to be a follower of Jesus Christ. Put simply, in the Gospel of Luke the author tells stories that introduce the reader to the birth, life, death, resurrection, and ascension of Jesus. In the sequel to that story, the Acts of the Apostles, the author encourages the followers of Jesus to focus on discipleship or, perhaps better, to focus on how a Christian may "move toward maturity."[4]

Who Wrote Acts and When?

Since the Gospel of Luke and the Acts of the Apostles are addressed to Theophilus, the earliest studies of Acts accepted the tradition that both the Gospel according to Luke and the Acts of the Apostles were written by the same person. While the author is not identified within the text, most scholars today continue to refer to Luke as the author of both. But who was Luke, and what do we know about him? Scripture suggests that Luke, who was referred to as "the beloved physician" (Col 4:14), may have also been a travel companion of the Apostle Paul and was with him when Paul was imprisoned in Rome.[5] Scholars have also noted that Luke was called a "follower of Paul" by an early Christian writer, Irenaeus (c. 130–202).[6] The suggestion that Luke may have been a travel companion of Paul is supported further by what are now sometimes called the "we passages" in Acts (Acts 16:10 17; 20:5-15; 21:1-18; 27:1–28:16).[7]

For many years, those who studied Acts suggested that Luke was probably a Gentile who sought to write to other Gentiles about the gospel that was to be proclaimed to all people. Emphasizing the work of God as Holy Spirit, Luke certainly gives attention to the movement of the Spirit and to the inclusion of both Jews and Gentiles in the church. Yet it may not be assumed that Luke's sole purpose was to tell the story of an "unhindered"

---

4. This emphasis on spiritual development is from Charles Talbert, "The Way of a Lukan Jesus: Dimensions of a Lukan Spirituality," in *Perspectives in Religious Studies* 9 (1982): 237–49. For a discussion of Talbert's emphasis on a "move toward maturity," see Mikeal Parsons and Joseph B. Tyson, eds., *Cadbury, Knox and Talbert: American Contributions to the Study of Acts* (Atlanta: Scholars Press, Society of Biblical Literature, 1992), 151ff.

5. See Philemon 24 and 2 Timothy 4:11. For a discussion of manuscript evidence from the second and third centuries, see David G. Peterson, *The Acts of the Apostles: The Pillar New Testament Commentary* (Grand Rapids, MI: Eerdmans, 2009), 1ff.

6. See Irenaeus, *Against Heresies* 3.1.1; 3.14.1 as cited in Peterson, *Acts of the Apostles*, 1.

7. Charles H. Talbert, *Reading Acts: A Literary and Theological Commentary* (rev. ed.; Macon, GA: Smyth and Helwys, 2005), xii.

gospel.[8] New Testament scholars have suggested that perhaps Luke was not a Gentile primarily focusing on the Gentile mission but instead a Jew writing to other Jews who had become Christians, in order to encourage them and explain why many others rejected the faith.[9] Taking this line of thought, it is possible that Luke may have been a priest who knew Paul and perhaps even travelled with him, which would have given him more authority to interpret the faith to others.[10] In the introduction to the third Gospel, the writer claims that the information he was recording had been handed down to him from "eyewitnesses and servants of the word" (Luke 1:2). On that basis, it is possible that he was a second-generation Christian whose native tongue was Hellenistic Greek and that he was well educated in the Græco-Roman tradition.[11]

While the exact dating of Acts is uncertain, it seems likely that it may have been written between AD 70 and AD 90, which would have been after the appointment of Festus as Procurator of Judea (AD 59/60) and before Acts is cited in second-century writings.[12] Most scholars assume that Luke used the Gospel of Mark as a source and so date Luke-Acts after AD 70. F. F. Bruce suggested that the writing of Acts may have taken place over a period of time.[13]

---

8. Acts ends with a reference to the "unhindered" or "unfettered" word. Frank Stagg emphasized this reference in *The Book of Acts: The Early Struggle for An Unhindered Gospel* (Nashville: Broadman, 1955).

9. David Garland, *Acts, Teach the Text Commentary Series* (Grand Rapids, MI: Baker Publishing, 2017), 3.

10. Rick Strelan, *Luke the Priest: The Authority of the Author of the Third Gospel* (Farnham, UK: Ashgate Publishing, Ltd., 2008/2013), 103. This would also explain the "we" passages toward the end of the book when the writer is obviously speaking as a fellow traveller with Paul. However, Pervo suggested that it is unlikely that Luke was a companion of Paul; more likely he was a writer of the third Christian generation. See Richard I. Pervo, *Luke's Story of Paul* (Minneapolis: Fortress Press, 1990), 13. Jacob Jervell claims that the author was an artist and narrator rather than a systematic theologian (*The Theology of Acts* [Cambridge: Cambridge University Press, 1996], 10).

11. Ben Witherington III, *The Acts of the Apostles: A Socio-Rhetorical Commentary* (Grand Rapids, MI: Eerdmans, 2001), 52. Witherington notes Luke's knowledge of Græco-Roman rhetorical practices.

12. Procurator was the title of the governors (first over Judea and later over much of Palestine, appointed by Rome during the years ad 6–41 and ad 44–46). Some of the procurators were hostile to the Jewish population, though Porcius Festus made some attempt to improve the conditions of the people. See David Solomon, "Procurator," in *Jewish Virtual Library*, https://www.jewishvirtuallibrary.org/procurator.

13. F. F. Bruce, "The Acts of the Apostles," in D. Guthrie et al., *The New Bible Commentary Revised* (London, 1970), 968f., as cited in I. H. Marshall, *Acts, Tyndale New Testament*

Although we do not know a great deal about Luke's background, it is clear that he was a skilled writer. Over the years, Luke has been described in many ways: preacher, historian, and theologian.[14] He was also a storyteller par excellence.

Why and How Was Acts Written?

In order to develop his premise of the overarching story of God's longing to be in relationship with all people, in Acts Luke weaves together travelogues, trial and courtroom scenes, farewell speeches, maxims, proverbs, and stories of miracles. The inclusion of speeches in particular points to his familiarity with Græco-Roman literary styles. Scholars have debated the way that these should be interpreted and understood. While it has been argued that Luke may have included summaries of actual speeches, it seems likely that the speeches merely reflect the teaching that had been handed down and underscore the themes that he felt were appropriate for his day and time.[15] It is enlightening to compare the speeches made in other contexts in that era. In doing so, it appears that speeches were often used as a literary device in order to convey certain ideas of the author.[16] Charles Talbert noted that Thucydides in *History of the Peloponnesian War* claimed that it was impossible to remember the exact words spoken, so he had summarized the sentiments of the speakers in his own words.[17] Other early writers used speeches as a way of trying to display their own rhetorical style. Talbert emphasized that the author of Acts would have constructed each speech "so that it conforms to what he thought was appropriate to the individual, to the time, the place, and the circumstances."[18]

For our purposes, it is helpful to consider the way that the speeches function. What is Luke trying to convey to the reader? One answer is that Luke was trying to teach, so he drew on familiar approaches to writing in

---

Commentaries (Grand Rapids, MI: Eerdmans, 1980/1983), 48.

14. Gasque noted the emphasis on Luke as theologian. See W. Ward Gasque, "A Fruitful Field: Recent Study of the Acts of the Apostles," in *Interpretation, The Journal of Bible and Theology* 42/2 (April 1988): 123–24.

15. Janusz Kucicki, *The Function of the Speeches in the Acts of the Apostles* (Leiden: Brill, 2018), 4.

16. Marion L. Soards, *The Speeches in Acts: Their Content, Context, and Concerns* (Louisville, KY: Westminster/John Knox Press, 1994), 9.

17. See the discussion by Talbert, *Reading Acts*, 29ff.

18. Talbert, *Reading Acts*, 30.

order to put the stories about the faith in a memorable pattern. Moreover, rather than simply compiling a narrative of events, in both the Gospel and in Acts Luke was interested in recording his understanding of the Christian faith.[19] Indeed, by engaging the reader in this narrative account, it appears that the writer was not seeking primarily to compile a history or to explain what happened. Nor is this a work that was written merely to teach Christian doctrine or to explain the role of God as Holy Spirit. It was not written simply to give an account of the development of the church. Nor was it written just as an *apologia* or defense of the Christian faith.

While Luke may have had a pastoral desire to provide the readers with "surety" or "certainty" in uncertain times,[20] he was not suggesting that life would be trouble free or that, indeed, Christian faith should not be seen as a threat to the status quo. Rather, Acts is what Frances Young described as a "culture-forming narrative."[21] Those who follow Christ are not simply to adapt to culture but to seek to transform it. Hence, Luke points out that those who follow Jesus Christ can expect to face suffering, even as they experience peace, joy, and hope beyond compare. Indeed, for those who are followers of Jesus, the world will be turned upside down. C. Kavin Rowe describes Acts as a "political document that aims at nothing less than the construction of an alternative way of life—a comprehensive pattern of being—one that runs counter to the life-patterns of the Græco-Roman world."[22]

Luke chose to communicate his message through story. While he was obviously aware of the power of story as a means of communication, he also knew that storytelling is not simply a matter of relating occurrences. Rather, storytelling is about seeking to communicate a truth that is behind or perhaps points beyond the story itself.[23]

---

19. Fred B. Craddock, *Luke*, Interpretation: A Bible Commentary for Teaching and Preaching (Louisville, KY: Westminster/John Knox, 1990), 8.

20. This is suggested by Rubén René Dupertuis in "The Acts of the Apostles, Narrative, and History," in the *Oxford Handbook of Biblical Narrative*, ed. Dana Nolan Ferwell (Oxford: Oxford University Press, 2016), 331.

21. Frances M. Young, *Biblical Exegesis and the Formation of Christian Culture* (Cambridge: Cambridge University Press, 1997), 12.

22. C. Kavin Rowe, *World Upside Down: Reading Acts in the Graeco-Roman Age* (Oxford: Oxford University Press, 2009), 4.

23. For a discussion of story and Christian spirituality, see K. E. Smith, *Christian Spirituality* (London: SCM Press, 2007), 40–53.

Stanley Hauerwas has suggested that narrative accounts bind "events and agents together" in an understandable pattern.[24] He also claimed, "Good and just societies require a narrative . . . that helps them know the truth about existence and fight the constant temptation to self-deception."[25] For Luke, the main overarching, organizing story for the formation of Christian community consists of the stories he includes in his Gospel account: the stories of Jesus and his birth, life, death, and resurrection. In Acts, we have the stories about the way people, prompted by God as Holy Spirit, moved out into the world in order to share the story of Christ with others. We have stories of people meeting together and praying together, stories about people who struggled to be followers of the Way, and tales of transformation and conflict with culture. In reading Acts, we discover people who, in responding to the call to follow Christ, found that they had to seek to discover what it means to love God with all their heart, soul, mind, and strength; we learn of the joys and temptations as well as the trials and difficulties the early believers faced.

Given the fact that the very nature of stories means that they communicate and function at different levels, it seems probable that in telling the stories in Acts, Luke had more than one purpose in mind. It has been suggested that in addition to teaching and encouraging the early followers of Jesus, perhaps there was a more specific theological purpose. Hans Conzelmann argued that Luke-Acts was written in order to deal with the disappointment of the followers of Jesus over the delay of the *parousia* or the return of Christ.[26] While Conzelmann's theory has been largely rejected, Luke still may have had theological objectives as well as pastoral ones. It has been suggested that Acts could easily be renamed "Acts of God" because Luke focuses on the power of God made known through the Holy Spirit at work in the lives of believers and the church. Was Luke interested in pointing to the church as the "fulfillment of the Old Testament promises"?[27] Rather than seek to encourage Jews to become Christians, was Luke's purpose to explain to those who are Christian why so many Jews had not

---

24. Stanley Hauerwas, *The Hauerwas Reader*, ed. John Berkman and Michael Cartwright (Durham, NC: Duke University Press, 2001); and *Truthfulness and Tragedy* (Notre Dame, IN: University of Notre Dame Press), 8, as cited in George W. Stroup, *The Promise of Narrative Theology* (London: SCM Press, 1981), 79.

25. Hauerwas, *Reader*, 178.

26. Hans Conzelmann, *The Theology of St. Luke* (Los Angeles: Harper, 1961).

27. Garland, *Acts*, 5.

become believers? If Luke was a priest, was his focus on Israel rather than a Gentile mission?

Reflecting on Luke's theological purpose for Acts, Willie James Jennings writes movingly that Acts "beckons us to a life-giving historical consciousness that senses being in the midst of time that is both past and present and that pulls us toward a future with God in the new creation."[28] This is what happens when one enters into a story or, perhaps better, when one enters into a story with an openness to transformation under the power of the Holy Spirit. Since the Spirit "blows where it chooses" (John 3:8), this transformation may happen at many different levels and in different ways, individually and collectively. Hence, Luke's narrative approach was not simply for the purpose of telling a good story. Because he chose to communicate in story, it may be that his narrative functions pastorally and theologically in different ways for different people. Goodspeed recognized the multifaceted objectives reached by narrative when he suggested,

> Acts may appear at first little more than a storybook of the early Christian movement, but this means only that the writer has skillfully concealed his didactic and left the intrinsic interest of his materials to carry the reader on. Each story has a point of its own, but the whole has a larger meaning of its own too, which the writer has not spoiled by elaborating but has left to the intelligence of his readers.[29]

Whatever Luke's original purpose for writing may have been, those who read the Gospel and Acts will find that Luke's narrative approach, and particularly his use of storytelling, engages the reader not only intellectually but spiritually, too. Indeed, Richard Longenecker claimed that in Luke-Acts, we find that the theme of discipleship is "more extensively developed, more radically expressed and more consistently sustained" than in other New Testament books.[30] This was so because Luke wanted his readers to respond to the question "Who is Jesus?" but also to answer the question "What does it mean to be a follower of Jesus?"[31] Spiritual formation is

---

28. Willie James Jennings, *Acts*, Belief: A Theological Commentary (Louisville, KY: Westminster, 2017), 4.

29. Goodspeed, *Introduction to the New Testament*, 188.

30. Richard N. Longenecker, "Taking Up the Cross Daily: Discipleship in Luke-Acts," in Richard N. Longenecker, ed., *Patterns of Discipleship in the New Testament* (Grand Rapids, MI: Eerdmans, 1996), 50.

31. Longenecker, "Taking up the Cross Daily," 50.

not just about an individual's response to these questions. Christian life is never about a believer alone but always includes the believer's life with other believers within community.

The importance of both the community and the believer in spiritual formation is apparent in the construction of Acts. Using a narrative style, Luke first introduces readers to a deeper understanding of what it is to know life in Christ in community and then focuses specifically on the cost of discipleship as he traces the journey of Paul to Jerusalem and then to Rome. As we shall see, by focusing first on the stories of the life of the believers together and then dedicating the latter chapters to the travels of Paul, Luke draws the reader's attention to the inextricable link between the community of faith and the life of the believer. Moreover, the focus on Paul's travels aims to set out the demands of discipleship.

The narrative is never solely about the characters in the story. Certainly Acts is not just about Paul! Rather, it is about God and the work of God through the power of God's Spirit. However, as the reader follows the stories about the early communities of faith (with particular characters highlighted) and about Paul, it is clear that for Luke, responding to the call to be a disciple of Jesus must ultimately be the response of total surrender to God through relationship with the Risen Lord. Once a hand has been put to the plough, there can be no looking back (Luke 9:62).

Reading Acts for Spiritual Formation

The phrase "spiritual formation" has been very much in vogue over recent years. Since the 1980s, seminaries and divinity schools have required students to take classes relating to spiritual formation. Some churches in North America now employ a "minister of spiritual formation" (rather than using the term "minister of education"), and a vast amount of literature has been written on the subject. The need for Christians to be formed in the likeness of Christ has always been fundamental to Christian discipleship. From the earliest disciples of Jesus to the Christians in the modern day, there have been those who have wanted to learn more about the spiritual life. In the Gospel of Luke, there is a story about one person who came to Jesus and raised the fundamental question, "What must I do"?

> "Teacher," he said, "what must I do to inherit eternal life?" He said to
> him, "What is written in the law? What do you read there?" He answered,
> "You shall love the Lord your God with all your heart, and with all your

soul, and with all your strength, and with all your mind; and your neigh-
bour as yourself." And he said to him, "You have given the right answer;
do this, and you will live." (Luke 10: 25-28)

The answer to the question "What must I do?" was not about "doing"
but about "being" or perhaps "becoming" a person who loves and desires
God and also loves and desires the best for others. In effect, followers of
Jesus are to seek to love as God loves without qualification. For those who
truly love as God loves, there is to be no barrier of creed, color, nationality,
gender, orientation, or status.

Since from a New Testament point of view the focus of discipleship
is not on "what must I do?" but "who must I be or become?" it is not
surprising that down through the ages Christian formation has focused on
what it means to be "formed in the image and likeness of Christ." Early
followers of Jesus recognized that the "lure of the world" was ever before
them and began to question the attitudes that they should have toward
empire and culture. By the third century, some women and men fled to
the desert in order to focus on God alone.[32] These Desert Mothers and
Fathers, as they came to be known, claimed that they needed to withdraw
from the world in order to confront the things in their lives that challenged
their commitment before God. Because of an emphasis on withdrawal
and solitude, this movement has become known as *anchoritic* (meaning to
withdraw) monasticism. Their approach to Christian spirituality emphasized practicing spiritual disciplines. They also identified what later became
commonly known as the seven deadly sins: pride, greed, lust, envy, glut-
tony, anger, and sloth or *acedia* (defined as a type of apathy or the absence
or lack of care).[33] Against these "sins," cardinal virtues such as prudence,
temperance, fortitude, and justice were named. For Christians the "desires
of the flesh" are not to be gratified. Rather one is to live by the Spirit and
produce the fruit of the Spirit: love, joy, peace, patience, kindness, generosity, faithfulness, gentleness, and self-control (Gal 5:22-23).

However one might describe the sins or virtues, the point to be
made here is that early on, Christians realized that formation of character

---

32. See Louis Bouyer, *A History of Christian Spirituality: The Spirituality of the New Testament and the Father*, vol. 1 (Kent: Burns and Oates, 1968), 303ff.

33. St. Anthony (c. 251–356) is considered to be one of the greatest examples of the
anchoritic tradition. *The Life of St Anthony*, written by Athanasius in the fourth century,
emphasized the exemplary character of Anthony. Evagrius Ponticus (c. 345–399) a
fourth-century monk and theologian, wrote *Praktikos*, a guide to the ascetic life.

required great struggle. Indeed, those who fled to the desert likened it to fighting with demons and devils! Recognizing the need for the support and encouragement that comes as believers share in life together, some of those who had fled to the desert and lived alone in hermitages eventually joined with others to form what is now called *cenobitic* (meaning "common life") monasticism. Naturally, the emphasis on living and sharing together in communal life was not new. There are examples in Judaism of communities living together. The Essenes (meaning "pious," "holy"), for example, were a sect of Judaism that formed after certain strict Jews left Jerusalem in protest of the way the temple was being run. In the second century BC, they formed communities in the desert in order to get away from what they thought to be the corruption of Jerusalem and the worldliness of the temple. They wanted to strictly observe the law of Moses.[34]

For the followers of Christ, the emphasis was on sharing together in order to help one another become more like Jesus. They wanted to express genuine discipleship that was unsullied by what they considered to be the cares and entanglements of the world. Many of the early books and manuals written about the spiritual life continue to be read today: for example, *The Life of St Anthony* written by Athanasius, *The Sayings of the Desert Fathers and Mothers*, and Augustine's *Confessions*, as well as many others that are now considered classic works of Christian devotion.

In looking at the various manuals and guides for prayer and devotion, as well as books on discipleship and the spiritual life, that have been written across the ages, it is apparent that growing in the likeness of Christ has always been both a desire and a challenge. Confronted by a dominant culture of power and an institutional church accommodating to culture, time and time again writers, poets, pastors, novelists, mystics, hymnists, etc. have called for believers to rediscover a vision of life in and for Christ. It is not possible in this short introduction to spiritual formation to name all the books and treatises that are now considered to be classic writings of Christian devotion. An abbreviated list might include works such as *The Imitation of Christ*, attributed to Thomas À Kempis; *Revelations of Divine Love* by Julian of Norwich; *The Interior Castle* by St. Teresa of Avila; and *Dark Night of the Soul* by St. John of the Cross. Protestant reformers such as John Calvin, Ulrich Zwingli, Martin Luther, and Balthasar Hubmaier all wrote about prayer and discipleship and on life together in community,

---

34. J. G. Davies, *The Early Christian Church: A History of the First Five Centuries* (Grand Rapids, MI: Baker Book House, 1965), 5.

as well as on personal devotion. Seventeenth-century examples include the Moravians in Germany or the Puritans in Britain, some of whom then later made their way to settle in what was then the New World. This was the age of spiritual writings such *Pilgrim's Progress* by John Bunyan; *A Serious Call to a Devout and Holy Life* by William Law; *Pia Desideria* (Pious Desires) by Philipp Jakob Spener, and *Holy Living, Holy Dying* by Jeremy Taylor. Examples of nineteenth- and twentieth-century spiritual writers include Térèse of Lisieux, Teilhard de Chardin, Thomas Merton, Simone Weil, Douglas Steere, Thomas Kelly, Henri Nouwen, Dorothy Day, Evelyn Underhill, Baron Friedrich von Hügel, and Dietrich Bonhoeffer, as well as the works of countless others who reflected on Christian faith and asked the formative Christian questions: Who am I called to be? What is an authentic life in God and for God? What does it mean to be a true follower of Jesus Christ?

While down the centuries, there have been many fine works on the spiritual life, the starting place for spiritual formation is always an engagement with Scripture. A conversational approach to Scripture allows us to enter into the word rather than simply asking, "What must I do?" or "What is required?" This means that Scripture is not approached for information or simply to acquire knowledge. Rather, we approach the text from a devotional perspective with a desire to respond to a loving God who desires to be in relationship with us.

Francis Watson has emphasized that reading Scripture cannot be a "one way process in which readers impose meanings on the text that merely express their own prior convictions and ideological prejudices."[35] Rather Watson claims, "The act of reading entails interaction between text and reader, analogous to a conversation between two people."[36] In other words, reading Scripture is not simply a way to try to discover what God requires or what rules we are to obey, which is an approach that many people have mistakenly accepted. Rather, the word is one of the means by which we may commune with God. We are drawn into the presence of God. Marjorie Thompson has described spiritual reading in this way:

> The manner of spiritual reading is like drinking in the words of a love letter or pondering the meaning of a poem. It is not like skittering over the surface of a popular magazine or plowing through a computer manual. We are seeking not merely information but formation. Information is

---

35. Francis Watson, *Paul and the Hermeneutics of Faith*, 2nd ed. (New York: Bloomsbury, 2014/2016), xi.

36. Watson, *Paul and the Hermeneutics of Faith*, xi.

basically utilitarian; it is a means to some other end. We glean facts to strengthen our arguments; we garner knowledge to make our conversation convincing; we seek help with problem solving, ideas for programming, evidence for cases and illustrations for teaching. The same information may be used for a variety of purposes . . . . Formation, on the contrary, is generally understood as an end in itself. It has to do with the dynamics of change in the human heart, change that reshapes us into the kind of beings God intends for us to be.[37]

This type of ancient approach to praying the Scripture was expressed early on as *lectio divina* (literally divine reading). This practice has influenced both Protestant and Catholic approaches to the reading of Scripture. The sixteenth-century Protestant reformer Martin Luther claimed that there are three rules for reading Scripture: "prayer, meditation, and struggle (*tentatio*)."[38] For him, as for the other reformers, the Bible was not simply to be read and believed but to be read, meditated on, and taken to heart. Among the Puritans in seventeenth-century England there was, again, a call for greater attention to Scripture. The Puritans felt it was important to meditate on the word because there was a close association between the Spirit of God and the written word. Indeed they claimed, "the Spirit speaks in, by, or through the Word."[39]

When thinking about how to approach Acts with a focus on spiritual formation, the emphasis on both moving beyond a mere reading of the text and openness to the guidance of the Spirit to speak "in, by, or through the Word" is vital. This declared intent to struggle with the word in order to meet Christ in the text may sound outside the bounds of academic enquiry. However, arguably, this approach is not only essential in studying Acts as Scripture but also accords more closely with the original intent of Luke, the storyteller. For Acts was not intended to be a book simply for scholarly debate, but it was, and is, a work for those who want to be formed in the likeness of Christ. It is thus applicable for those who willingly open themselves to what the Spirit may say in the word because—more than

---

37. Marjorie J. Thompson, *Soul Feast: An Invitation to the Christian Spiritual Life* (Louisville, KY: Westminster/John Knox, 1995), 18.

38. In Esther Chung-Kim and Todd R. Hains, *Reformation Commentary on Scripture, New Testament, VI, Acts* (Downers Grove, IL: Intervarsity, 2014), xxxiv.

39. Geoffrey F. Nuttall, *The Holy Spirit in Puritan Faith and Experience* (Oxford: Basil Blackwell, 1946), 33.

anything—they yearn to discover what this God of love desires and to surrender their will to all that God wills.

Lest this all sounds too individualistic, it should be heeded that throughout Acts, Luke seeks to draw our attention to both the life of the community and the life of the believer. In the first part of the book, there is a great emphasis on the community and the development of life together. After telling the story of the ascension of Jesus, and then describing in chapter 2 the gift of the Spirit outpoured on the believers on the day of Pentecost, the story moves to the development and growth of the church. Here we are told of the joys of sharing together, but also we are reminded of the struggles of life together. As the story unfolds, the reader is called to reflect on various questions that arise about life in Christ and life in community: What does it mean to be in communion with Christ and one another? What happens when the desires of self-interest dominate? What are the causes of division in Christian community? These questions, as well as many others, will emerge as we engage with the text and reflect on spiritual formation within Christian community.

There are also questions that emerge for personal discipleship—especially when we reach the latter part of Acts and follow the journey of Paul and his companions. Here the reader's attention is drawn to the cost of discipleship. How are we to stand firm in faith when facing severe opposition? How do we deal with loss? How do we discern the way forward when it feels as though we have been abandoned? Can we depend on God and others? What does accommodation to culture mean? How do we deal with confronting violence? How do we pray? Can we really experience joy in the midst of pain?

Writing of the themes of discipleship in Luke-Acts, Richard Cassidy has suggested that there are stories relating to simplicity, concern for the sick and poor, affirmation of less-regarded groups, opposition to injustice, rejection of violence, prayer, and service and humility.[40] These, as well as other topics related to spiritual formation, will be noted in the commentary that follows. However, two particular themes seem to figure prominently for Luke and need further attention here. These are the concepts of waiting and remembering.

---

40. Richard Cassidy, *Society and Politics in the Acts of the Apostles* (Eugene, OR: Wipf and Stock, 1987), 2–10.

Waiting

Twentieth-century writer Henri Nouwen (1932–1996) claimed that a friend once wrote to him saying, "learning to weep, learning to keep vigil, learning to wait for the dawn. Perhaps this is what it means to be human."[41] Most of us would agree. From an early age, human beings develop (often with a growing sense of impatience) an awareness of what it means to wait.

Given the restlessness of our human condition, it is perhaps not surprising that the earliest patterns of Christian worship (which still shape liturgical Christian worship today) have waiting times woven into them.[42] Likewise, the structure of the Christian calendar has inbuilt an emphasis on periods of patient waiting. Liturgies for the seasons of Advent, Christmas Eve, Lent, and Holy Week often include prayers and readings that remind us of God's patience and our impatience. For example, a prayer for the Sunday before Easter day in *The Book of Common Prayer* reflects a desire to learn from the humility and patience of Jesus as he made his way toward Jerusalem and the cross:

> Almighty and everlasting God, who, of thy tender love towards mankind, hast sent thy Son, our Saviour Jesus Christ, to take upon him our flesh, and to suffer death upon the cross, that all mankind should follow the example of his great humility; Mercifully grant, that we may both follow the example of his patience, and also be made partakers of his resurrection; through the same Jesus Christ our Lord. Amen.[43]

While the overarching story in Acts is "action packed" with a great deal of emphasis on travel and movement, there is also a repeated stress on waiting moments. At the beginning of Acts, the followers of Jesus are portrayed standing in the presence of the Risen Lord. They are anxious and wondering what the future will hold. They are told not to leave Jerusalem but to wait on the promise of the Father. When they ask if this is the time the kingdom will be restored—the time when all that God desires will be realized—they are reminded that they are not in control of what God is doing. They must wait and see. Wait and pray. Wait and be open to God.

---

41. Henri J. M. Nouwen, *Reaching Out* (London: Collins, 1976), 36.

42. Joanne Robinson, *Waiting in the Christian Traditions: Balancing Ideology and Utopia* (London: Lexington Books, 2006), 68.

43. Collect for "The Sunday next before Easter," in *The Book of Common Prayer*, 1662.

After the coming of the Holy Spirit at Pentecost, as promised, the followers of Jesus receive power to be witnesses. Under the guidance of the Spirit, they go out to proclaim the good news to both Jews and Gentiles. Interpreters of Acts have rightly placed a great deal of emphasis on the movement of the followers of Jesus as they went out to be "witnesses in Jerusalem, in all Judea and Samaria, and to the ends of the earth" (1:8). Yet, through the stories in Acts, we experience many waiting moments: women and men gathered in prayer and in worship as well as in sickness, by the bedside of a friend, in grief, in prison, in despair, and in loneliness.

Learning to wait, as we are reminded often in Acts, is a vital part of spiritual formation and is especially important for those desiring to live as followers of Jesus. Toward the end of Acts, there is a great deal of activity in the story as Paul, following in the way of Jesus, goes to Jerusalem and then, finally, goes to Rome. Yet, while we will see that there is emphasis on both the movement of God as Holy Spirit and the literal movement of the "Followers of the Way" all through Acts, there is also an emphasis on waiting. In Rome, Paul is waiting to see the emperor but more importantly waiting to see what God will do even as he continues "proclaiming the kingdom of God and teaching about the Lord Jesus Christ with all boldness and without hindrance" (28:31).

As we enter into the stories that are told in Acts, it becomes evident that the waiting moments are not what might be described as "empty waiting"; rather it is "active."[44] Believers were waiting on, and with, and in, the power of the Holy Spirit. They were watching and waiting to see what God was doing or would do. It becomes evident that for Luke these "waiting moments" were opportunities for spiritual formation: moments when those reading the text are confronted by the realization that life is not under our control.

In reading Acts, the different experiences of waiting are noteworthy. Some are unforeseen waiting moments that are brought about by circumstances when the believers are under threat. Yet other waiting moments, such as times of worship in the synagogue and meetings for prayer and breaking bread together, are planned. Times like these in worship, when the discipline of waiting is practiced, no doubt help to prepare the believer to be open and aware of the guidance of the Spirit in more anxious or unexpected times of waiting.

---

44. Henri Nouwen, "A Spirituality of Waiting: Being Alert to God's Presence in Our Lives," in *Weavings, A Journal of the Christian Spiritual Life* 2/1 (Jan/Feb 1987): 7–17. See also W. H. Vanstone, *The Stature of Waiting* (London: Darton, Longman and Todd, 1982).

As we reflect on waiting moments in Acts, we recognize that we are at heart an impatient people. In a culture that stresses the "instant" now, we have grown accustomed to having quick replies and immediate attention. Yet, as we follow the story in Acts, we are beckoned to surrender, perhaps yet again, to the one in whom "we live and move and have our being" (Acts 17:28). This is the one who is above all and in all and through all, and the one whom we realize has been waiting on us.

Remembering Jesus

For many people, looking back is painful, especially when recalling the past brings to mind only thoughts of past failures, hurt, heartache, disappointment, pain, or loss. Yet remembering is a key theme in the Judeo-Christian tradition. In the Old Testament, we find a persistent call to remember the past—to remember how God led the people of old out of captivity and to believe that God continues to care for people now. This emphasis on memory, however, is not simply "natural recollection" of a single event.[45] Rather it is linked to a way of perceiving an event in the past that, taken as a whole, then informs action.[46] This way of using memory has long been part of the Jewish cultic practices. For example, to remember the exodus is not simply to recall the story of the people being led out of captivity. It is to experience entering into the story and participating in it. Brevard Childs described it in this way: "The act of remembering serves to actualize the past for a generation removed in time from those former events in order that they themselves can have an intimate encounter with the great acts of redemption. Remembrance equals participation."[47] Likewise, for the early Christians, memory was not simply recalling an event. Rather, as Nils Dahl notes, "To remember in the New Testament signifies almost always to recall something or to think about it in such a way that it is expressed in speech or is formative for attitude and action."[48]

In reading Acts, there is a persistent call to the followers of Jesus to remember. Chapter 1 begins with Luke reminding the reader of what has already been said in the Gospel account. Then he tells the story of the

---

45. See discussion in Bruce T. Morrill, *Anamnesis as Dangerous Memory: Political and Liturgical Theology in Dialogue* (Collegeville, MN: Liturgical Press, 2000), 155.

46. Morrill, *Anamnesis as Dangerous Memory*, 176.

47. Brevard Childs, *Memory and Tradition in Israel* (London: SCM Press, 1967), 56.

48. Nils Alstrup Dahl, *Jesus in the Memory of the Early Church* (Minneapolis: Augsburg, 1976), 13, as cited in B. Morrill, *Anamnesis as Dangerous Memory*, 148.

ascension of Jesus. At times scholars have puzzled over why Luke mentions the ascension here since he has already given an account in the Gospel of Luke (Luke 24:50-53). Some have speculated on the reasons for the variations in the accounts. Given the fact that stories are sometimes told with more or less detail, and with a difference of emphasis, it seems likely that Luke was using this story as an aid to memory. Significantly, Luke is not simply reminding the reader of what he has already said about Jesus. To remember here is not recalling an event. Nor was Luke suggesting that the reader should just think about the stories of Jesus' encounter with others. Rather, here as in the Gospel narrative, memory is linked to a present and personal encounter with the living Christ. The story of the ascension reemphasizes the Christian belief that Christ is alive. While he is no longer moving and walking on earth—he has ascended—he is alive, and his Spirit will form the followers of Jesus into a new community whose members will be active witnesses to others.

For the reader, remembering this story is a call to reenact the event; to stand with the risen Christ and hear the call to gather, to wait, and to pray. In entering into the story, we also experience the vulnerability and insecurity of the followers of Jesus. What does it mean to wait on the Spirit? Like the early group of followers, how are we to discern God's will and way? What does the future hold? The act of remembering by entering into the story is a crucial element of spiritual formation.

As we shall see in Acts, Luke uses different means to draw our attention to reminders of the past. It may be simply the mention of a number such as forty that triggers memories of the stories of the desert experience of Moses or Jesus' time of testing. Likewise, there are the repeated speeches where Peter recalls the life, death, and resurrection of Christ. The story of the martyrdom of Stephen is, in essence, a call to remember again the death of Christ and the cost of following him. Paul's conversion story, which is told three times in slightly different ways, is among other things a reminder of the radical way in which God brings about change and transformation through personal encounter with a living Lord. The emphasis on encounter with the living Lord is at the heart of spiritual formation.

Above all, in seeking to read Acts for spiritual formation, it is important to underscore that engaging the text and entering into the story is not ever simply to provide a means for thinking about a text. Rather, the sole purpose must be to meet the living Christ. In a discussion of "Memory and Communion," Richard Kidd put it this way:

All great spiritual movements live "from" and "in" the memory of their founders and founding events. Israel remembers Moses and the crossing of a particular sea, as the event recorded in Exodus 14:21-31 is recalled throughout Israel's history as a peculiarly formative moment. Christians remember Jesus and a specific death outside the walls of Jerusalem, and it has often been noted that each of the three Synoptic Gospels uses around half of its respective texts to explore the final stages and death of its leading character. Indeed, Christians highlight "memory" and "remembering" in their most distinctive community ritual, the Lord's Supper (or Communion meal), calling each other to "remembrance." . . . The crucial point is that memory—far from being a merely mechanical device to replay newsreel from the distant past, somewhat akin to a high-quality digital recording—has the potential to occasion something enormously dynamic and vital, in which all kinds of "coming alive" begin to happen.[49]

As was noted in our discussion on waiting, so too these words remind us that, in the past, remembering was built into the structure of worship. Reflecting on the way that memory serves faith and enables us to encounter the living Christ in worship, Alexander Schmemann wrote,

> The essence of our faith and the new life granted in it consists in *Christ's memory*, realized in us through our *memory of Christ*. From the very first day of Christianity, to believe in Christ meant to *remember* him and keep him always in mind. It is not simply to "know" about him and his doctrine, but to *know* him—living and abiding among those who love him. From the very beginning the faith of Christians was memory and remembrance, but memory restored to its life-creating essence.[50]

Schmemann, an Orthodox Christian, was speaking primarily about meeting Christ in worship and especially in the sacrament of the Lord's Supper. This remembering is not to recall a historical event but to experience a present reality.

Christians consider celebrating the Lord's Supper or the Eucharist to be one of the most important times in worship when we meet the risen Christ. However, the emphasis on remembering in worship is not only at a service

---

49. Richard Kidd, "Memory and Communion," in *Baptists and the Communion of Saints: A Theology of Covenanted Disciples*, ed. Paul S. Fiddes, Brian Haymes, and Richard Kidd (Waco, TX: Baylor University Press, 2014), 33–34.

50. Alexander Schmemann, *The Eucharist* (Crestwood, NY: St Vladimir's Seminary Press, 2003), 128–29. For more on memory and worship see also A. Schmemann, *For the Life of the World: Sacraments and Orthodoxy* (rev.; Crestwood. NY: St Vladimir's Seminary, 1973).

of Communion where there is a definite call to "do this in remembrance of"; we may argue that the living presence of Christ may be known also in other elements of worship, such as in hymnody. While many people think that hymns should be relegated to the past and new worship songs should take their place, it should be noted that hymns are an important aid to remembering in worship. This may be so because, as J. R. Watson points out, they speak to the "whole person, spiritual, emotional, physical, the feeling and thinking human being."[51] Hymns are also firmly rooted in Scripture and intended to be both didactic and worshipful. Unlike many of the contemporary songs now used in worship, hymns were written in order to teach Christian faith and doctrine and were constructed so that the gospel story unfolds verse by verse. Many hymns were written in the eighteenth century by ministers as a memorable way of summing up their sermons. Some of these hymns continue to be cherished and sung in worship. As they tell the story of the birth, death and resurrection of Christ, they enable us to remember, and in remembering to meet and to commune with the living Christ.

Highlighting the importance of memory in the process of spiritual formation is not to suggest that communion with the living Lord in any way depends on our memory alone. The gift of God's relationship with us—as Luke often points out in Acts—is God's gift to all who will receive it through the unhindered power of God as Holy Spirit. Yet, while we do not control the Spirit of God, it is evident that certain spiritual practices, such as hymn singing or repeating the Lord's Prayer, may still be an aid to remembering and meeting Christ, even when physically our memory is failing. For example, those who have visited friends or family members with dementia may have experienced the joy of saying the Lord's Prayer or singing hymns with those who could no longer carry on a conversation. In singing the hymns, it may be argued that they did not need to depend on the simple recall of memory to know the words of a hymn or song. If the words have been sung so many times before in the context of worship, and taken to heart, it is possible to move beyond the words to the immediacy of the experience and thus to commune with God and others through hymn singing.

On one occasion, while I was serving as pastor of a church, I visited a member of my church who had severe dementia and had been taken into

---

51. J. R. Watson, *The English Hymn, A Critical and Theological Study* (Oxford: OUP, 1999), 4.

hospital. She was moved into a bed in a single room on a side ward. When I came into the room, she pulled the sheet over her face and covered her head. I sat in a chair by the bed, greeted her, and asked if she would like for me to read some Scripture. There was no response, and the bed covers remained firmly over her head. I read Scripture to her and then prayed. Still, there was no reaction from her. I sat quietly by the bed for a while longer, and then, because I could not think of anything else to do, I began to sing very quietly: "What a friend we have in Jesus." Slowly the sheet began to come down until she was looking at me. When I finished singing she simply said, "Yes." The moment was a gift to us both: a moment of communion. While she would not have been able to repeat the gospel story to me, it seems that the words of the familiar hymn provided the means for us to meet together and to meet with the living Christ.

In Acts, as we shall see, there is a persistent call to remember. As we enter into each story and wait on the Lord to speak through Scripture, we also must give careful attention to the memories that are called forth. Some may be good memories of times when we first encountered the living Lord. We may also be reminded of times when we were impatient, selfish, or self-serving. Like the Christians before us, we are well aware of the reality of sin. Yet, as we reflect on and enter into the stories in Acts, we have the opportunity not only to meet the risen Lord but also to discover afresh what it means to be formed in the likeness of Christ.

Draw Your Own Conclusions

1. How would you describe an "authentic" Christian life?

2. What difference does it make to Christian formation if we ask the question, "What am I to be or become with God's help?" rather than asking, "What must I do?" or "What does God require?" Do the questions evoke different pictures of God?

3. What changes might occur in the life of the church if more attention was given to waiting and remembering?

4. How might worship be shaped to focus more on the sense of encounter through remembering?

5. How do we move beyond the culture's perception of waiting as "wasted time"?

Acts 1

Spiritual Guides and Guidance, 1:1-5

Part two of Luke's narrative, the account that we know as the Acts of the Apostles, begins exactly as the Gospel account does, with an address to Theophilus. Over the years there has been speculation over the identity of Theophilus. Was he a friend or someone known in the churches? Since the name Theophilus means "God lover" or "dear to God," it has been suggested that Luke used the name symbolically in order to address a wider group rather than a single individual. Those who reject this view suggest that since he personally addresses Theophilus, this indicates that he was writing to an individual.[1] Whether Luke was writing to one man specifically or using the name as a rhetorical device, perhaps we can agree with the sixteenth-century Reformation preacher Johann Spangenberg (1484–1550), who wrote,

> Whether the evangelist Luke had a good friend by this name or whether he understood by this little word Theophilus—which translated means "God's friend"—every lover and friend of God should not worry us. This is certain, that Luke in this book intended to instruct not just one person but every lover and friend of God in the highest things that are beneficial and necessary for salvation.[2]

---

1. I. Howard Marshall, *Acts: Tyndale New Testament Commentaries* (Grand Rapids, MI: William B. Eerdmans, 1980, 1983), 55. David Garland suggests that "Theophilus likely was a prominent Christian, and he may have financed the production and dissemination of the two works" (*Acts, Teach the Text Commentary Series* [Grand Rapids, MI: Baker Publishing, 2017], 14).

2. Johann Spangenberg, "Brief Exegesis of Acts 1:1" (Der Apostel Geschichte, 2r), in *Reformation Commentary on Scripture, New Testament VI, Acts*, ed. Esther Chung-Kim and Todd R. Hains (Downers Grove, IL: IVP Academic, 2014), 4.

Spangenberg's emphasis on instruction is important. In the Gospel of Luke, Luke's stated aim was to write "an orderly account . . . so that you may know the truth concerning the things about which you have been instructed" (Luke 1:1-4). In Acts, Luke begins with the story of the ascension of Jesus and then describes in narrative form the life and witness of some of the early followers of Jesus. By using stories in order to teach, Luke applied one of the oldest forms of guidance. Indeed, Jesus himself used stories or parables as a way of teaching his disciples.

Reflecting on the importance of story, we are reminded by the Old Testament scholar Walter Brueggemann that in the Jewish tradition, when a child asks a question, the teacher, priest, or parent will answer with a story.[3] For the people of God, Brueggemann says, story is our "primal and most characteristic mode of knowledge."[4] Stories are layered communication; they often have a multifaceted approach that communicates more than one message at the same time. Moreover, the stories may evoke a response that appeals to more than one dimension of a person's life and character.

In addition to using the ancient method of storytelling, Luke also adopted one of the oldest approaches to spiritual formation: the role of an apprentice student under the leadership of a master or teacher. The idea of spiritual guidance being given by an older, wiser person is not a distinctively Christian practice, and it was not unusual in the Græco-Roman world.[5] Likewise, in Judaism it is understood that those who are more advanced in the life of faith will serve as teachers. Jesus himself was referred to as a teacher (Luke 11:45; 12:13; 18:18). By assuming the role of guide, Luke was not suggesting that he was taking the place of Jesus, as Master and Lord. The duty of a spiritual guide in Christian faith is not to create disciples in the image of the guide but to encourage others as they seek to listen to what God might be saying to them.[6] From the very beginning of this narrative, Luke is keen to emphasize that faith in Christ is not to be equated with simply learning about Jesus. He wants the readers to experience for themselves a relationship with the living Lord.

---

3. Walter Brueggemann, *The Creative Word, Canon as a Model for Biblical Education* (2nd ed.; Minneapolis: Fortress Press, 2015), 24.

4. Brueggemann, *The Creative Word*, 31.

5. For a discussion of spiritual direction, see Kenneth Leech, *Soul Friend: A Study of Spirituality* (London: Sheldon Press, 1977), 38ff.

6. For a good introduction to spiritual guidance, see W. Paul Jones, *The Art of Spiritual Direction: Giving and Receiving Spiritual Guidance* (Nashville: Upper Room Books, 2002).

Acts 1 begins with the author's reminder that in the first book (the Gospel According to Luke), he has already written "about all that Jesus did and taught from the beginning until the day when he was taken up to heaven" (vv. 1-2). Luke then narrates what happened after Easter Day. He is not simply recording some past event of history; rather he is emphasizing that Jesus, who died and was raised from the dead, is alive! "The risen Lord," as Luke puts it, "presented himself alive to them [the Apostles] by many convincing proofs, appearing to them during forty days and speaking about the kingdom of God" (v. 3). "While staying with them, he ordered them not to leave Jerusalem, but to wait there for the promise of the Father" (v. 4).[7]

"Waiting," a key theme in spiritual formation, is emphasized throughout Acts.[8] As is often the case with many people today, it seems that the early followers found waiting to be difficult. Yet, as Luke knew well, the ability to wait is essential for spiritual development. As with physical growth, so spiritual formation never occurs in an instant. It takes time. Just as trees and plants do not spring forth fully grown and babies do not arrive in the world as adults, so it is in our spiritual lives. Hence, Luke begins this narrative account of the growth and development of the early Christian community by emphasizing the need for believers to wait on God. He tells the disciples not to rush back to whatever they were doing but to return to Jerusalem and wait.

If, as many scholars now claim, Luke was a Jew, his emphasis on waiting in the holy city is important. For some scholars, Jerusalem was central to Luke's understanding of Christian faith.[9] Others have suggested that in Acts there is a "geographical movement away from Jerusalem" and that at times it appears that Luke was seeking to "demote" Jerusalem.[10] Reflecting on the instructions to the disciples that they were to wait in Jerusalem for "the promise of the Father" (v. 4), it does not seem that Luke was seeking

---

7. Talbert pointed out that references to forty days are frequently found in Jewish writings, e.g., Genesis 7:17; Exodus 24:18; 34:28; 1 Kings 19:8. He suggested that this may emphasize that they were fully instructed and point to a definite end to post-resurrection appearances (Talbert, *Reading Acts*, 5–6).

8. See the discussion on waiting in the introduction.

9. See, for instance, Hans Conzelmann, *The Theology of St. Luke* (New York: Harper, 1961), 70.

10. Mikeal Parsons, "The Place of Jerusalem on the Lukan Landscape: An Exercise in Symbolic Cartography," in *Literary Studies in Luke-Acts: Essays in Honor of Joseph B. Tyson*, ed. Richard P. Thompson and Thomas E. Phillips (Macon, GA: Mercer University Press, 1998), 159.

to undermine the importance of Jerusalem. Rather, it may be, as Mikeal Parsons has pointed out, that in the Gospel of Luke Jerusalem represented the end of Jesus' journey, and at the beginning of Acts, Jerusalem is the starting place for the mission of the church.[11]

Aligning Our Longings, 1:6-8

Even as Luke wrote Acts, the Jewish people had already been waiting a very long time for the Messiah who would restore the kingdom of Israel. So it is not surprising that Luke addresses the question that confronted those who followed Jesus: Since Jesus is the Messiah, why must they continue waiting for the establishment of the kingdom? They are restless and impatient, and they want action. In the Gospel account, Luke spoke of the kingdom being present and "among" them (Luke 17:21) and promised that the kingdom of God was near when they observed certain signs (21:31). Rather than seeing the kingdom primarily as God's rule or way in their lives and in the life of the world, many of the followers of Jesus believed that "the kingly rule of God is certainly present in the person of the King-Messiah; but it would be fully manifested only at the end of time."[12]

It has been suggested that at the time Luke wrote Acts, some of the followers of Jesus no longer believed that his return was imminent. Given the message found in Acts of the proclamation of the gospel to "the ends of the earth" or to all people, it may be that Luke saw the return of Christ as delayed rather than imminent.[13] Hence, in the account of the ascension in Acts 1, the two messengers question whether the disciples of Jesus need to "stand looking up toward heaven" (v. 11). It was not for the followers of Jesus to know how God's purposes would be worked out. Rather they were to return to Jerusalem and wait to receive power when the Holy Spirit came upon them and they would be "witnesses in Jerusalem, in all Judea and Samaria, and to the ends of the earth" (v. 8). Before rushing out to witness, the overarching message is that the followers of Jesus must wait.

It is not difficult to imagine the frustration of the early disciples. Today we know how difficult waiting moments can be, especially with regard to seeking God's will and purposes. We want evidence that we are doing what

---

11. Parsons, "The Place of Jerusalem," 167.

12. Eric J. Sharpe, "Kingdom of God," in *A New Dictionary of Christian Theology*, ed. Alan Richardson and John Bowden (London: SCM Press, 1983), 317.

13. See Robert F. O' Toole, S.J., *The Unity of Luke's Theology: An Analysis of Luke-Acts* (Eugene, OR: Wipf and Stock, 2016), 77–78, 151, 159.

God wants us to do. The difficulty is that the kingdom of God is never obvious. Moreover, our understanding of God's will or what we believe to be "kingdom values" often does not accord with God's way and will. The twentieth-century pastor Harry Emerson Fosdick (1878–1969) warned of the dangers of missing the "kingdom's goal" in the third verse of his hymn, "God of Grace and God of Glory":

Heal your children's warring madness,
bend our pride to your control;
shame our wanton, selfish gladness,
rich in things and poor in soul.
Grant us wisdom, grant us courage
lest we miss your kingdom's goal.[14]

Throughout the centuries, at times Christians have confused the institutional structures of the church with a visible kingdom. Sometimes people measure what they consider to be signs of "kingdom growth" by the number of people attending the church or the number of services or meetings held at a church. Yet the kingdom of God is never to be equated with outward signs of human achievement. A church may be able to demonstrate that they are financially sound, have multiple worship services on a Sunday and during the week, maintain an active program for people of all age groups, and still not focus on the kingdom of God. The kingdom is not to be equated with a place, a position, prestige, or achievement.

To see the church or any other institution as the kingdom is to miss the point. Rather, as James K. A. Smith has suggested, perhaps the kingdom is to be understood as wanting what God wants or "aligning our loves and longings with his . . . to hunger and thirst after God and crave a world where he is all in all."[15] Luke would have agreed. Acts was not written, as is sometimes suggested, as a blueprint for the growth and development of the church. Luke was trying to encourage people "to align their loves" in order to be faithful followers of Jesus Christ.

---

14. Harry Emerson Fosdick, "God of Grace and God of Glory," in *Baptist Praise and Worship* (Oxford: OUP,1991), 877. Fosdick served for many years as pastor of the Riverside Church in New York City. A popular author and regular contributor to radio, he was an advocate for social change and spoke out against racism and injustice. See Robert Moats Miller, *Harry Emerson Fosdick: Preacher, Pastor, Prophet* (Oxford: Oxford University Press, 1985).

15. James K. A. Smith, *You Are What You Love* (Grand Rapids, MI: Brazos Press, 2016), 2.

So what does the kingdom look like? How are we to know when the kingdom will be restored? According to Luke's account, this is what the followers of Jesus wanted to know just before Jesus ascended into heaven. Jesus said, "It is not for you to know the times or periods that the Father has set by his own authority. . . . But you will receive power when the Holy Spirit has come upon you" (vv. 7-8). Then, when the messengers appeared to the disciples after the ascension, the disciples were asked why they were "looking up toward heaven" (v. 11). The risen Lord had told them to wait in Jerusalem for the "promise of the Father." They were not told to go and try to create the kingdom in their own strength. Rather they were told to go and wait on the Spirit. While there is often much emphasis in the church on getting things done, it is instructive to reflect on the importance of waiting on God and recognizing our dependence on God's power at work.

Members of the Benedictine order, founded by Benedict of Nursia (c. 480–543), incorporate waiting into daily life as they live by the motto *ora et labora*: pray and work.[16] In the *The Rule of St. Benedict*, there is a reminder that "the divine presence is everywhere" though especially known when at worship. Hence, Benedict urged, "Let us consider, then, how we ought to behave in the presence of God and his angels, and let us stand to sing the psalms in such a way that our minds are in harmony with our voices."[17] With this in mind, the Benedictine tradition in worship is to meditate on the Psalms antiphonally. Slowly the words are sung or said, and then there is a moment of silence before the response is given. It seems that waiting on God, and in God's presence, is to be ingrained in worship as well as our lives.

Critics might suggest that nothing would ever get done if we all lived our lives at this pace. Surely, they claim, there is a need to take advantage of the moment. Many of us have been taught from an early age to take matters into hand, push forward, and work hard for what we suppose are the kingdom's goals. Yet there is a place for spending time to "be" and "become." There is a need to think about what we really long for and desire and what matters most to us. Certainly, Luke says that the risen Lord's instruction to his followers was to wait in Jerusalem for the promise of the Father, the gift of the Holy Spirit.

---

16. According to their rule, monks are expected to devote time to prayer, to sleep, and to manual work, sacred reading, and/or works of charity each day. See *The Rule of St Benedict*, ed. Timothy Fry, O.S.B. (New York: Vintage Spiritual Classics, 1998).

17. *The Rule of St Benedict*, 28.

Waiting, 1:9-11

Waiting on God may not be easy, but it is not without hope and purpose. The followers of Jesus were promised that they would receive power when the Holy Spirit came upon them, and they would be "witnesses in Jerusalem, in all Judea and Samaria, and to the ends of the earth" (v. 8). When Jesus had said this, according to Luke, he was "lifted up, and a cloud took him out of their sight" (v. 9). Over the years, the significance of the story of the ascension of Jesus has been debated, especially since this account is much longer than the account given at the end of the Gospel (Luke 24:50-53). If we are honest, the ascension stories with the emphasis on the risen Lord being "lifted up" and "carried up" into heaven are difficult for many modern readers to understand. In one sense, the language highlights the "otherness" of the experience and suggests that it was a unique encounter for the early disciples. While artists have sometimes portrayed scenes of Jesus taking off into space like a rocket, the language is intended to point to something for which there is no language. Our experience is earthbound and our language is limited, but the picture language here is intended to point to the important Christian teaching that Christ was crucified and rose from the dead and then returned to the Father. He lives, and everyone may experience his presence for himself or herself. Perhaps we are not to try to analyze or "understand" the story but, in meditating on it, to be reminded, in the words of Dean Inge (1860–1964): "Faith lifts us out of the time series, in which the past has ceased to be and the future is not yet, and exalts us into the eternal world, in which the future is as real as the present."[18]

Listening, 1:12-14

The followers of Jesus "returned to Jerusalem from the mount called Olivet" and gathered in a room and prayed (v. 12). Luke lists the names of the men who gathered and says that "certain women, including Mary the mother of Jesus, as well as his brothers" had gathered, too (v. 14). There are differing views about Luke's inclusion of women in both the Gospel account and in Acts. It has been suggested that the treatment of women in Luke-Acts seeks

---

18. W. R. Inge, *Personal Religion and the Life of Devotion* (London: Longmans, Green and Co., 1924), 41–42. The book was dedicated to his only child, a daughter, Margaret Paula, who died during Holy Week 1923. William Ralph Inge was an English author, Anglican priest, professor of divinity at Cambridge University, and Dean of St Paul's Cathedral from 1911 to 1934.

to play down their leadership roles and to portray them in passive roles by depicting the "ministry of the table" as subordinate to "the ministry of the word."[19] However, given Luke's desire to teach and encourage the followers of Jesus, it seems likely that he was portraying the witness of women as an example of those who were truly following in the way of Jesus.[20] It has been argued that in the early house churches there was a great emphasis on "discipleship of equals," which was only later replaced by patriarchal organization in the second century.[21] While Luke has been criticized for seemingly portraying women in ways that would have been culturally acceptable in the imperial world, this portrayal may simply reflect his desire to see the expansion of Christian faith that extended to all people and "to the ends of the earth."[22]

The picture of women and men, together, gathered for prayer and worship will be replicated by Luke in other places in Acts. For Luke, it seems that disciples gathering to wait on God in prayer is arguably more important than scenes of exalted worship. While there is a place for public exhortation by proclamation of the word, equally important in Luke's view is the small gathering of those who join together to pray and to listen for the voice of God.

Those who have been nurtured in an "active" or "word-based" faith tradition may find this emphasis on prayer, silence, and waiting on God to be uncomfortable. Parker Palmer claims that when he first came into contact with Quaker worship, which values silent waiting in community for God to speak, he felt angry. Having been brought up in a liturgical tradition that valued the reading and formal proclamation of the word, he

---

19. See, for example, Elisabeth Schüssler Fiorenza, *In Memory of Her* (New York: Crossroads, 1983), 161.

20. See for instance, Constance F. Parvey, "Theology and Leadership of Women in the New Testament," in *Religion and Sexism*, ed. Rosemary Radford Reuther (New York: Simon and Schuster, 1974), 139–46; Mary Rose d'Angelo, "Women in Luke-Acts: A Redactional View," *Journal of Biblical Literature* 109/3 (Autumn 1990): 441–61.

21. Schüssler Fiorenza, *In Memory of Her*, 285–315.

22. The discussion about Luke's view of the role of women is wide-ranging. See, for instance, Ben Witherington III, *Women and the Genesis of Christianity* (Cambridge: CUP, 1990), especially chapter 13, "Women and the Third Evangelist," 201ff. Also see Bonnie Thurston, *Women in the New Testament* (New York: Crossroads, 1998); Robert J. Karris, "Women and Discipleship in Luke," in *The Catholic Biblical Quarterly* 56/1 (January 1994), 1–20; and Ivoni Richter Reimer, *Women in the Acts of the Apostles* (Minneapolis: Fortress Press, 1995).

claimed, "My faith had been formed and sustained by words."[23] Initially, when he was gathering with others in the silence, he did not feel that he could hear God speaking. Palmer wrote, "In the silence I could find no personal grounding for the theological words and ideas that had become the foundation of my faith. I had a headful of notions about religious reality, but little direct experience of the reality itself."[24] Later, Palmer realized that while there is a place for expressing ideas within a religious tradition, times of quiet contemplation are equally important. However, he first had to come to the realization that "God is no object," and that came about as he learned to listen for God's voice in the silence.[25]

The emphasis on listening in prayer is a reminder that God is not hidden from us. Joachim Jeremias notes that the notion of God's silence originated in Judaism and was linked to the idea that before God spoke in creation, God was silent. God's silence has sometimes been viewed negatively in Judaism. Silence was often linked with darkness, war, and punishment.[26] On the other hand, there were those who equated God's silence with "inexpressible majesty," and in the Hellenistic world silence was even viewed as a symbol of the highest deity.[27] Jeremias claimed that the message of the Christian church was that "God is no longer silent" or, perhaps more accurately, is no longer to be perceived as hidden and silent.[28] In the life, death, and resurrection of Jesus, God spoke clearly. Through the gift of the Holy Spirit at Pentecost, the believers would discover that there was no barrier to communion with God in prayer except their own inability to listen as well as to speak.

Praying, 1:15-26

The followers of Jesus met for prayer and waited on God to show them the way forward. Perhaps some had their own ideas about Jesus and the way the kingdom would be realized, but no one seemed sure about the future. How were they to continue to be followers of Jesus? As they gathered together

---

23. Parker J. Palmer, *To Know as We Are Known: A Spirituality of Education* (San Francisco: Harper and Row, 1986), 118.

24. Palmer, *To Know*, 119.

25. Palmer, *To Know*, 120.

26. Diarmaid MacCulloch, *Silence, A Christian History* (London: Penguin, 2014), 13.

27. Joachim Jeremias, *The Central Message of the New Testament* (London: SCM, 1965), 89.

28. Jeremias, *The Central Message*, 90.

and prayed, it appears that they came to a decision: it was time to select someone to take the place of Judas, who had betrayed Jesus.

The mention of Judas here is not intended to call for any character analysis or judgment. However, his betrayal was surely a reminder of the need for faithful disciples. Judas did not stand firm in his confession of faith but betrayed Jesus with a kiss (Luke 22:48). The brief mention

> The communion of the soul with the Divine necessarily has a reciprocal character; there must be moments of pure receptivity, moments of conscious self-expression. He [She] who would pray must at one time speak, at another listen. He [She] who would praise must at one time cry aloud, at another contemplate in peaceful adoration. Passivity must alternate with activity, but the passivity must be that of restful reception, not that of inattention. When attention ceases, worship ceases with it.
> —B. H. Streeter, "Worship," in *Concerning Prayer* (London: Macmillan, 1918), 266.

of Judas's actions at the beginning of Acts is a poignant reminder of the expectation of faithfulness and the terrible consequences on the lives of those who turn away. Moreover, Judas's failure is held in sharp contrast to the sacrifice made by Stephen in Acts 7.

Notably, Luke's description of Judas's fate does not seem to agree with the account in the Gospel according to Matthew, which claims that Judas confessed his guilt to priests and then went out and hanged himself (Matt 27:3-10).[29] Luke's emphasis on Judas's betrayal and death seems to emphasize punishment for sin. The point of the story is not to stand in judgment over Judas but simply to explain the decision that since there are only eleven apostles, another person should be appointed to take his place.[30] The emphasis on a group of twelve points to the assumption in the Gospel and in Acts that twelve are needed because they symbolize the twelve tribes of Israel. For Luke, the twelve disciples may have been a reminder that in the life and ministry of Jesus, God was fulfilling a promise to reconstitute

---

29. M. Wilcox, "The Judas-Tradition in Acts I.15-26," *New Testament Studies* 19/4 (1973): 438-52.

30. There is a third story found in Papias, "Interpretations of the Sayings of the Lord," which claimed that Judas died from swelling to such a size that he could not get through where a wagon would normally pass. See Charles H. Talbert, *Reading Acts* (Macon, GA: Smyth & Helwys, 2005), 14.

Israel.[31] Moreover, the person to be appointed as an apostle, in Luke's view, should have been with Jesus during his public ministry.[32]

Luke offers scriptural support for the appointment by drawing on Psalm 69:25. It has been suggested that the words of the psalmist offered a "prophecy" of what might happen to anyone who has betrayed a godly person.[33] Two people, Joseph (called Barsabbas) and Matthias, were put forward as candidates to replace Judas. The appointment, however, was not to be dependent on human choice. Rather, what was crucial was that the community of believers gathered to pray and in praying they were seeking to be open to God. The symbolism of casting lots was simply an indication that what mattered most to them was that God's will was done. There is no suggestion that this was intended to set a pattern for the selection of leaders in the future. Both prayer and the casting of lots were ways of underscoring that Matthias was not simply the group's choice. In the whole drama of Acts, the appointment of the twelfth apostle is one more step toward being prepared for the church's mission.

Draw Your Own Conclusions

1. Today, many congregations have adopted a "business model" with an "executive board" determining the outcomes when making decisions about the life of the church. What difference might it make if the congregation focused on trying to align their longings with God's longings?

2. What is the root of your impatience with life? with God? with the church?

3. Do you find silence personally to be uncomfortable? If so, why?

---

31. Garland, *Acts*, 23.

32. For a discussion of the way apostleship is viewed in Acts see Talbert, *Reading Acts*, 15–21.

33. Marshall, *Acts*, 65.

Acts 2

The Reality of Fellowship with God, 2:1-13

Pentecost was the name Greek-speaking Jews gave to the wheat harvest festival that is celebrated fifty days after Passover. It is also associated with the day the law was given to Israel at Sinai.[1] Yet, while this may have been a day associated with the myriad ways that God had provided for the people of Israel in the past, there is no indication that the followers of Jesus were then expecting God to act in a miraculous way. Rather, they were simply waiting together and praying as they had been instructed to do when, as Luke describes it, they were surprised by God:

> And suddenly from heaven there came a sound like the rush of a violent wind, and it filled the entire house where they were sitting. Divided tongues, as of fire, appeared among them, and a tongue rested on each of them. All of them were filled with the Holy Spirit and began to speak in other languages, as the Spirit gave them ability. (vv. 2-4)

These verses from Acts have been the topic of many sermons and Bible studies with widely differing interpretations. The description of the "divided tongues, as of fire" and utterances of new speech suggests that Luke may have associated this event with the experience at Sinai (Exodus 19). Just as God had established the old covenant with the people of Israel, so God was establishing a new covenant.[2] Other parallels between this story and stories from the Old Testament may be drawn. For instance, by describing the

---

1. In the Old Testament it is often referred to as the festival of weeks or festival of harvest; see Exodus 23:16; Leviticus 23:15-21; Deuteronomy 16:9-12. Second-century Judaism associated Pentecost with the gift of the law at Sinai (Garland, *Acts*, 25; Marshall, *Acts*, 68).

2. Talbert, *Reading Acts*, 27.

experience of the disciples as a theophany, or "an intrusion of the heavenly world into human affairs" in which multiple languages were spoken, Luke offers a firm reminder of similar experiences in the Old Testament.[3] Yet, however the narrative is interpreted, a central emphasis of the story is on the fact that the disciples were not expecting or seeking this experience; rather what transpired reflected the activity of God—an outpouring of the Holy Spirit.

Many years ago, a friend wrote a letter to me in which she described an experience that she had in worship. She enclosed a leaflet that explained what a person must do in order to have this experience. The implication of the letter was that unless I had an identical experience to hers, I was somehow lacking in my understanding of the work of

> Spiritual life is not mental life. It is not thought alone. Nor is it, of course, a life of sensation, a life of feeling—"feeling" and experiencing the things of the spirit, and the things of God. Nor does the spiritual life exclude thought and feeling. It needs both.
> —Thomas Merton, *Thoughts in Solitude* (Tunbridge Wells: Burns and Oates, 1958), 29

God as Holy Spirit! While I imagine she sent the letter and leaflet with my best interests at heart, I think she made the same mistake many people make when reading this story from Acts. When reflecting on Luke's account of the coming of the Holy Spirit among the early followers of Jesus, often it is assumed that everyone must have the same, or at least a very similar, experience! Yet the picture language Luke used to describe the experience (the "rush of a violent wind" and "divided tongues, as of fire") is a way of emphasizing that this event was God's work. This unique experience was not something that the believers had expected or brought on themselves. They gathered and waited and prayed as they were told to do, but they had no idea how God would pour out the Holy Spirit on them. Luke does not suggest that the same experience of the Holy Spirit, which he dramatically described, is to be sought after by all Christians. Nor does he suggest that the reader needs to measure or evaluate his or her spiritual experience with the experience of others. Rather, all Christians are to be open to the work of God as Holy Spirit, who is not bound by our notions. We are each unique and our relationship with God is unique.

---

3. The symbolism is similar to that used in other Old Testament theophanies, e.g., 2 Sam 22:16; Job 37:10; Ezek 13:13. See Marshall, *Acts*, 68. Charles Talbert has noted that the emphasis on xenolalia (speaking in real languages that have not been acquired by natural means) may be found in other places in Judaism of the period (Talbert, *Reading Acts*, 24–26).

An experience of God as Holy Spirit is not learned behavior. The story of the people at Pentecost cannot be orchestrated by the sheer effort of a group gathered in worship. However, the power of the Holy Spirit may be seen at work in the lives of people in the world. God may not speak to us through the sound of a violent wind or in a way that feels like a fiery experience. Rather it may be in a still, small voice in the middle of the night, in a very strong thought that comes out of nowhere, in the words of a hymn, or by the song of a bird. We all have different personalities and different temperaments. There are thousands of ways that the Spirit speaks to and through us, but this is all God's work.

A Baptist theologian of the twentieth century, H. Wheeler Robinson (1872–1945), spoke of meeting God in this way:

> Fellowship with God is a reality, but it is a "spiritual" reality; though we may see no visions and dream no dreams of Him, His presence is not the less real. The discovery of God is not, then, the discovery of something in a corner of our experience. It is the discovery of Someone Whose presence gathers the whole of our experience into the comprehensiveness of His being, and gives it a new unity. We know that presence by the newness of life, the increased vitality and power, the new relation to men [and women], the new sense that all things are now possible.[4]

This seems to be a good summary of the way we experience the presence and power of the Holy Spirit in our lives. Essentially God changes everything and enables us to see that nothing is impossible for God. Perhaps the true miracle on the day of Pentecost was not speaking in unknown languages but the picture of a people who had surrendered to God. Philosopher and theologian Howard Thurman (1899–1981) claimed that the work of the Spirit is not linked to any special gift that we may grasp for ourselves but is discovered in surrender:

> In Christianity there is ever the central, inescapable demand of surrender. . . . The ability to do this, to say, "Yes", is not the result of any special talent, gift, or endowment. It is not the product of any particular status due to birth, social definition, race or national origin. It is not a power one can exercise only if given the right by one's fellows. It is not contingent upon wealth or poverty, sickness or health, creed or absence of creed.

---

4. H. Wheeler Robinson, *The Christian Experience of the Holy Spirit* (London: Nisbet and Co., 1928), 204.

No, the demand is direct and simple: Surrender your inner consent to God—this is your sovereign right—this is your birthright privilege. And a [person] can do it directly and in [their] own name. For this [they] needs no special sponsorship. He [She] yields [*their*] heart to God and in so doing experiences for the first time a sense of coming home and of being at home.[5]

The story of the coming of the Holy Spirit on the believers at Pentecost is a reminder that God as Holy Spirit does break into our experience, as has been the case through the long history of God's people. Luke was keen to point out to the early believers that while Jesus had gone up to heaven, by his Spirit they could still experience his presence. They were instructed to gather, to wait, and to pray. But they were not instructed to keep looking for an experience of God that would somehow enable them to validate their experience or to compare and contrast it with others. Nor is the gift of the presence of God with us always associated with a moment of great celebration.

Describing the day of Pentecost as the "birthday of the church," some churches have treated the day as a time for a party. The gift of the Spirit is, indeed, something to celebrate with great rejoicing. Yet history reminds us that listening to God as Holy Spirit is not without cost. Often the moments when we are most vulnerable, when we experience trouble, sickness, pain, grief, or despair, are the very times when we feel most distinctly aware of the presence of the Spirit. As shall become evident in later chapters of Acts, the early Christians realized that following the guidance of the Spirit often led to great hardship but to deep joy, too.

> Come, Holy Spirit, Lord God,
> fill with the goodness of your grace
> the heart, will, and mind of Your believers.
> Enkindle Your burning Love within them.
> O Lord, through the radiance of Your Light
> You have assembled in the Faith
> People of all the world's tongues;
> May that be sung, Lord, to Your praise.
> Alleluia, alleluia!
>
> —Cantata for Pentecost, *Wer mich liebet, der wird mein Wort halten*, BWV 59, by J. S. Bach in Alfred Dürr, *The Cantatas of J. S. Bach*, trans. Richard D. P. Jones (Oxford: Oxford University Press, 2005), 349–50.

---

5. Howard Thurman, *Disciplines of the Spirit* (New York: Harper and Row Publishers, 1963), 19–20.

Speaking the Truth, 2:14-36

Having emphasized the need for the believers to wait together and to listen, Luke now turns to speech as he introduces a discourse from Peter. Over the years, scholars have discussed the nature of the "speech material" found in Acts. While Luke puts emphasis on the fact that Peter was an eyewitness to the ministry of Jesus, it would seem improbable that these represent anything close to verbatim accounts, and in any case they are very brief.[6] Significantly, the speeches here, as with those of Paul later in Acts, may reflect in abbreviated form a summary of the type of sermons preached by the Apostles. Hence, the content of this speech offers the reader a good idea of how the early Christians understood and proclaimed the message of Jesus rather than a word-for-word account of an actual speech.[7] Moreover, Luke makes use of speeches in different ways. Here, according to Charles Talbert, Luke may be offering further explanation of the Pentecost event he has just described or an "illustration of what the fulfillment of Jesus' promise" in Acts 1:8 ("you will be my witnesses") means. It may also serve as a "front piece" or a "catalyst for what is about to happen," in this case the conversion of the Jews.[8] Having emphasized the importance of followers of Jesus knowing how and when to listen, Peter's speech also serves as a reminder that, especially when the character and integrity of the followers of Jesus is questioned, believers must always be prepared to speak, too.

Ironically, Peter's speech begins as a response to the "speech of the crowd" that accuses the followers of being "filled with new wine" (v. 13). Then he calls for the people to listen to what he has to say and immediately makes a connection with his Jewish audience by pointing to the prophecy of Joel, and so he declares the fulfillment of God's promise through the prophet: "I will pour out my Spirit upon all flesh" (v. 17). Having established that what happened was all the work of God, the speech then proceeds to explain the life, death, and resurrection of Jesus.

In the twentieth century, C. H. Dodd suggested that in this text we find a pattern for preaching the message of the kingdom of God. The pattern Dodd sets out may be summarized in this way:

---

6. Allison A. Trites, "Two witness motifs in Acts 1: 8 and the Book of Acts," in *Themelios* 7 (1970): 18. For a more detailed study of witness in Acts see A. A. Trites, *The New Testament Concept of Witness* (Cambridge: Cambridge University Press, 1977/2004).

7. Talbert, *Reading Acts*, 28–31.

8. Talbert, *Reading Acts*, 30.

(1) The age of fulfillment, or the coming of the kingdom of God has dawned.

(2) The coming of the kingdom takes place throughout the ministry, death, and resurrection of Jesus.

(3) By virtue of the resurrection, Jesus is exalted at the right hand of God as the messianic head of the new Israel.

(4) The Holy Spirit in the church is a sign of Christ's present power and glory.

(5) The messianic age will reach its consummation in the return of Christ.

(6) Forgiveness, salvation, and the Holy Spirit come with repentance.[9]

While Dodd's summary highlights some important themes, it should not be forgotten that Peter's speech is the speech of a Jew to a group of Jews. As William Willimon has noted,

> For Luke the Scriptures of the Jews are the primary context within which Jesus' life is comprehended. The Old Testament is not "Christianized " in this process, rather it is allowed to speak its own word about the coming salvation. Nowhere does Luke speak of the "founding" of the church or of the formation of some "new Israel." There is only one Israel—the faithful people who respond faithfully to the promises of God.[10]

Feeling Where the Words Come From, 2:37-41

Luke emphasizes that the message Peter gave to the people was strong and forthright. They were "cut to the heart" by it, and they then said to Peter and to the other apostles, "Brothers, what should we do?" (v. 37). The phrase "cut to the heart" is Luke's way of emphasizing that they had not simply listened to the message but had inwardly digested it. They had listened not just with their ears but also with their hearts, and they knew a response was required. This type of listening is often referred to in Scripture, and it is recognized as a key feature of the Christian spiritual life.

In his book *On Listening to Another*, Douglas Steere, an American Quaker, began with a story taken from the journal of the eighteenth-century

---

9. C. H. Dodd, *The Apostolic Preaching and Its Developments* (London: Hodder and Stoughton, 1936), 37ff.

10. Willimon, *Acts*, 36.

social reformer John Woolman (1720–1772). The story is about a meeting that took place in a Native American village along the upper Susquehanna River in Pennsylvania. Woolman rose to speak, but as he began, the interpreter who was supposed to translate Woolman's words into the indigenous language was asked to sit down. After the meeting, the Native American chief, Papunchang, explained through the interpreter that while he did not understand the English language, he wanted to hear what Woolman had to say without an interpreter. He claimed, "I love to feel where the words come from."[11]

This ability to listen behind and beyond spoken words is an important part of engaging with the Christian story. A true listener, according to Steere, has at least four characteristics: vulnerability, acceptance, expectancy, and constancy. Vulnerability relates to the way a listener may be open to being changed by what is heard. Acceptance reflects that the listener is not quick to form an opinion about the person or the story being told. Finally, to genuinely hear another requires that a person listen with expectancy and constancy. This means that there is an awareness of the possibility and potential in the other person that is realized in telling the story and therefore a willingness on the part of the listener not to rush to assume understanding of what is being said.[12] Those who truly listen, however, may realize that what they have heard requires a response. The word has cut them to the heart, and they therefore want to respond.

"What should we do?" they asked. Peter responded by saying, "Repent, and be baptized every one of you in the name of Jesus Christ so that your sins may be forgiven; and you will receive the gift of the Holy Spirit" (v. 38). On the basis of this text, it has sometimes been argued that baptism is always linked to the reception of the Holy Spirit. Yet it does not appear that Luke is trying to make a link in this way. Later in Acts, as we shall see, some Samaritans are baptized without receiving the Holy Spirit (8:16)! Arguably, Luke's focus here is not on baptism or on the Holy Spirit but rather on repentance. He is emphasizing that if a person has heard the word and responded, there is a desire to repent—quite literally, to turn around.

Repentance is sometimes viewed in a negative way. On one occasion when I was speaking with a group of theological students about repentance and faith, they said to me that they felt that words like "sin" and

---

11. Douglas V. Steere, *On Listening to Another* (San Francisco: Harper and Row, 1955), vii.

12. For a discussion on spirituality and listening, see K. E. Smith, *SCM Core Text: Christian Spirituality* (London: SCM Press, 2007), 44–45.

"repentance" were now outdated and old-fashioned. In their view, these were "negative" words and should never be used today, especially when reaching out to people with the gospel. Eugene Peterson must have had similar conversations, for in his book *The Contemplative Pastor*, he argued that the word "sinner" is a theological designation and not a moralistic judgment. He claimed,

> The word *sinner* is a theological designation. It is essential to insist on this. It is *not* a moralistic judgment. It is not a word that places humans somewhere along a continuum ranging from angel to ape, assessing them as relatively "good" or "bad." It designates humans in relation to God and sees them separated from God. *Sinner* means something is awry between humans and God. In that state people may be wicked, unhappy, anxious, and poor. Or, they may be virtuous, happy, and affluent. Those items are not part of the judgment. The theological fact is that humans are not close to God and are not serving God. To see a person as a sinner, then, is not to see him or her as hypocritical, disgusting, or evil. Most sinners are very nice people. To call a man a sinner is not a blast at his manners or his morals. It is a theological belief that the thing that matters most to him is forgiveness and grace.[13]

Peterson may be right, though I have often reflected on the conversation with my students. While I, too, still believe that it is valid to use words like "sin" and "repentance" when talking about a life of faith, I have mused over other ways that we might speak of the call to "turn around" and begin a new life in relationship with Christ.

The poet Kathleen Norris was brought up in the Christian faith but moved away from it. Later in life, when she began to make her way back to church, she claimed that the vocabulary of the Christian faith "seemed dead" to her.[14] In her book *Amazing Grace, A Vocabulary of Faith*, she has compiled what she describes as a "lexicon of faith" in which she reflects on the meaning of words so often used in church. In her discussion of repentance, she tells of her experience of being the artist-in-residence at a school, and she says one young child wrote a poem titled "The Monster who was sorry." The poem began by admitting that when his father yelled at him, the boy's response was to throw his sister down the stairs and then wreck his

---

13. Eugene H. Peterson, *The Contemplative Pastor: Returning to the Art of Spiritual Direction* (Grand Rapids, MI: Eerdmans, 1988), 118–19.

14. Kathleen Norris, *Amazing Grace: A Vocabulary of Faith* (New York: Riverhead Books, 1998), 5.

room and then wreck the whole town. The poem concluded, "Then I sit in my messy house and say to myself, 'I shouldn't have done all that.'" Norris concludes, "my 'messy house' says it all"; it is a metaphor for sin. Perhaps what is needed is to be willing to clean it up and make a place that God might dwell.[15] Luke would agree. We are sinners all.

Life Together Day by Day, 2:42-47

After the believers responded to the call to repent, Luke offered a summary statement, which claims that then the newly baptized believers "devoted themselves to the apostles' teaching and fellowship, to the breaking of bread and the prayers" (v. 42). Furthermore, Luke claimed, "All who believed were together and had all things in common; they would sell their possessions and goods and distribute the proceeds to all, as any had need" (vv. 44-45). These verses, depicting life shared together in unity, have often been put forward as the ideal for the church. Often, stress is placed on the meaning of breaking bread together, and it is questioned whether the reference was to sharing the Lord's Supper. Yet, while this may be a point of interest in their common life together, early commentators seem to have focused on a different Lukan theme, namely, detachment from wealth.[16] John Chrysostom (c. 347–407), for example, claimed that Peter was emphasizing the "regulation of life" that reflected a kind of "single-ness of heart." For, he wrote, "no gladness can exist where there is no simplicity."[17] He was speaking of the simplicity of life that finds its focus not on possessions but on relationship with God and others.

However one understands these verses, it is obvious that for Luke, the work of the Spirit is not only to bring individuals to faith but also to create a bond of unity between believers together—unity expressed in sharing life, including table fellowship, worship, and caring for the needs of one another. Yet the establishment of genuine fellowship or oneness among people takes time. The phrase "day by day" used by Luke seems to indicate as much. It is a reminder that community does not happen in a minute but in life

---

15. Norris, *Amazing Grace*, 70.

16. Craig Keener claims that for Luke, possessions are "worthless when compared to the kingdom" (*Introduction and 1:1–2:47*, vol. 1 of *Acts: An Exegetical Commentary* [Grand Rapids, MI: Baker Academic, 2012], 1023).

17. John Chrysostom, "Homilies on the Acts of the Apostles," in *Ancient Christian Commentary on Scripture, New Testament V, Acts*, ed. Francis Martin, 37, as cited in P. Schaff et al., *A Select Library of the Nicene and Post-Nicene Fathers of the Christian Church* (Buffalo, NY: Christian Literature, 1887–1894; repr., Peabody, MA: Hendrickson, 1994), 11:45–46.

together day by day. The picture given to us by Luke is of people gathering together because they are focusing on God and what God has done and is doing all around them. The community is gathered by God and gathers for the purpose of worshipping God. In the gathering, as believers seek to listen carefully to one another, sometimes they are surprised by God.

In the theological college where I served, it was our practice for many years to gather as a community at the end of the afternoon in the chapel for prayer. In truth, it was never the most inspiring part of my day. Often, I was quite tired and struggled to stay awake in the quiet. I went day by day because it was part of my commitment to God and to the community where I was serving. Often, as soon as prayers were over I left straightaway to go back to my office to work. On one particular day, however, I did not get up and rush away as soon as the prayers were over. Rather I sat quietly and then fell into conversation with one of the students sitting beside me. We mused together about calling and about discerning God's will. Suddenly, we realized that the chapel was getting quite dark. Several hours had passed as we sat and pondered the ways of God. It is hard to describe now, but as I went back to my office, I felt somehow lighter and filled with joy. Later, I reflected on that experience and marveled that having gathered for worship with others (and without any great expectation) at the end of a long but ordinary day, I was surprised by the extraordinary presence of God as Holy Spirit.

Luke says that "great awe" came over them! This awe and wonder was not of their own making. Rather, as it is for us at times, it was the result of God's surprising presence among them. This picture of God's people gathering together seems a far cry from the institutional "business" model of the church, which emphasizes budgets and plans for church growth, practiced in many congregations today. Luke simply says that they had "glad and generous hearts" and "day by day the Lord added to their number those who were being saved" (vv. 46-47).

Draw Your Own Conclusions

1. Reflect on Luke's summary statements about the nature of Christian community. What does it mean to be a community that is called together by God?

2. How might the idea of being called together by God differ from simply attending a church that we like or that suits our needs?

3. In our fast-paced world, we may claim that we have little time to gather together. What challenge does this text bring to the way we live our lives and share together in Christian fellowship?

Acts 3

The Attentive Gaze, 3:1-10

There are differing opinions about the attitude of the early Christians toward temple worship. There are those who feel that, for the most part, the followers of Jesus developed their own approach to worship and that the idea of the church eventually replaced the idea of temple worship. Others have claimed that the early followers of Jesus did not completely reject temple worship and that, in Acts, Luke tries to hold on to the central place of temple worship. Indeed, perhaps Luke even viewed worship in the temple as necessary if the message of Jesus was, as the followers of Jesus claimed, for both Jews and Gentiles.[1]

This is not to suggest that the followers of Jesus maintained attendance at the synagogue and temple just for evangelistic purposes, though speaking in each of these contexts obviously was seen as an opportunity for sharing faith in Jesus. Rather, it may be assumed that the disciples who had been with Jesus still cherished the Jewish heritage. The very fact that it is noted that they went to the temple at the "hour of prayer" indicates that they continued to incorporate the Jewish spiritual practice of set times of prayer into their daily lives.[2]

By the third century, Christians were writing treatises that offered suggestions for ordering prayer. Origen (c. 185–255), for instance, wrote a

---

1. Eyal Regev, *The Temple in Early Christianity: Experiencing the Sacred* (New Haven: Yale University Press, 2019), 155.

2. The ninth hour of prayer was 3 p.m., the hour of the incense offering (Exod 29:39-41; Num 28:4). Keener notes that from an early period people offered prayer during the incense offering. (At some point, prayer in the synagogue settled on three times a day and Christians followed that pattern; Did. 8:3.) See Craig Keener, *3:1–14:28*, vol. 2 of *Acts: An Exegetical Commentary* (Grand Rapids, MI: Baker Academic, 2013), 1044–45.

work titled "On Prayer" in which he suggested that prayer should include certain elements, especially thanksgiving and intercession. Moreover, much of the well-known work *The Confessions* by Augustine (354–430) of Hippo was written as a meditation or extended prayer. These and many other works suggest that prayer as fellowship or communion has always been central to Christian spirituality.

The discipline of regular times of prayer, individually and in some communities corporately, is still an essential part of Christian devotion. However, there is great diversity among Christians in their approaches to prayer. Some Christian writers draw a distinction between mental and vocal prayer. Vocal prayer, as the name suggests, is when people give voice to their prayers. Sometimes this is done extemporaneously, though in many Christian traditions the words used in prayer may be part of a formal liturgy.

Mental prayer is viewed as more meditative and does not necessarily depend on any form of words.[3] Mental prayer may also be described as reflective and affective. In a discussion on the approaches to prayer, Miles Lowell Yates described what he called reflective mental prayer as "simply thinking before God, trying to get hold of more of God's truth or to see more deeply into it."[4] By contrast he described affective mental prayer as "offering our affections rather than our reflections to God."[5] Moreover, he suggested that this approach to prayer is the most "intimately personalized relationship we can have with God," and it is "not concerned primarily with logic as such, but with love."[6] He wrote this:

> In meditation or reflective mental prayer, the understanding is primarily at work, the intelligence or the reasoning faculty is dominant. But in affective prayer, we are not concerned with logic as such, but with love. It is not getting light on the things of God; it is not *getting* at all, at least by any purpose; it is pure *giving*. Such prayer is mental in the sense that we must *think* what we are doing, with a good deal of concentration; but the mind is not exploring and expanding ideas, but lifting itself in various ways straight up to God.[7]

3. Miles Lowell Yates, *God in Us: The Theory and Practice of Christian Devotion*, ed. W. Norman Pittenger and William H. Ralston Jr. (London: SPCK, 1960), 130.

4. Yates, *God in Us*, 135.

5. Yates, *God in Us*, 147.

6. Yates, *God in Us*, 146.

7. Yates, *God in Us*, 146.

Yates goes on to describe some of the ancient ways of approaching this type of prayer, but perhaps the most important point is that in both types of prayer, mental and vocal, the first requirement is commitment to a regular time and practice of prayer.

The early followers of Jesus seem to have emphasized the importance of a regular time of prayer. As they entered the temple via the temple gate,[8] they saw a man who had been brought to the temple gate daily so he could beg. It is not difficult to imagine the vulnerability of the man. Keener points out that the "dominant ethos toward the poor was disdain."[9] Beggars were often unwashed, with sores and lice. The man was not simply unclean, and considered unclean in terms of entry into the temple, but he was vulnerable, dependent, seemingly always lying at the feet of someone.

The apostles did not have money, but they offered the man what they had. Luke claims that Peter and John stopped and looked intently at the man. They focused on his need and called him to fix his attention on them. He did so, probably expecting that they would give him money. They said to him that they had no "silver or gold," but what they had they would give to him. "In the name of Jesus Christ of Nazareth," they commanded him to stand up and walk. Then, taking him by the hand, they brought him to his feet. Luke says that "his feet and ankles were made strong," and "he entered the temple with them, walking and leaping and praising God" (vv. 7-8).

Emphasis is placed on the fact that his healing was in the name of Jesus, which may point to the authority that was given to the followers of Jesus. Marshall suggests that the story notes that the followers of Jesus did what Jesus had done before them, "thus continuity between the ministry of Jesus and the witness of the church is expressed."[10] From the man's point of view, he received far more than physical healing. He was given the words of life and a hand that helped him to his feet beyond simply the ability to stand and walk.

It is significant that Luke stresses that the encounter with the man took place because the apostles took notice of him on their way into the temple. Luke claims that the man called to them and asked for alms. They did not pass him by. Rather, Luke says, "Peter looked intently at him, as did John" (v. 4). They saw him. They gazed on him. He knew he had been heard.

---

8. The exact location of the gate has been debated. It is suggested that it was the East Gate or Nicanor Gate (I Howard Marshall, *Acts*, 87; C. Williams, *Black's Commentary on Acts*, 74).

9. Keener, *Acts: An Exegetical Commentary*, 2:1062.

10. Marshall, *Acts*, 86.

Many years ago, I read a book by Christopher Nolan about a young man who, after a difficult birth, was severely physically challenged with cerebral palsy and quadriplegia. The book, titled *Under the Eye of the Clock* (which was largely autobiographical), told how a young boy called Joseph was confined to a wheelchair and unable to speak. Thus, he was ignored by many people and for the most part treated, as Nolan put it, as a "crippled, speechless boy."[11] Speaking of a few of his teachers who seemed able to see beyond his disability, Nolan claimed that in them Joseph saw the face of God. Poignantly, he wrote,

> Such were Joseph's teachers and such was their imagination that the mute boy became constantly amazed at the almost telepathic degree of certainty with which they read his facial expressions, eye movements and body language. Many a good laugh was had by teacher and pupil as they deciphered his code. It was at moments such as these that Joseph recognized the face of God in human form. It glimmered in their kindness to him, it glowed in their keenness, indeed, it caressed in their gaze.[12]

Often when reading this story about the man by the temple gate, attention is focused on the miraculous healing. Twice, Luke mentions the man walking and leaping and praising God (vv. 8-9). Clearly, the joyous celebration of the man who had not been allowed in the temple but was suddenly walking and leaping and praising God cannot be ignored. Yet equally important is the fact that Peter and John stopped and looked intently at the man. They saw him and listened to him.

A friend of mine told me of an experience he had while volunteering in a shelter for homeless young people. He went to the shelter once a week in order to be available to talk to the young people who came there. He had no specific role but was there to be a "presence" and to try to listen to them and offer encouragement. One day, he said he was talking to a young man who asked my friend if he could give him some money. "No, I don't have any money I can give you," he said, "but I can give you something far more valuable, I can give you my time. If you want to talk, I am glad to listen." My friend said that the young person looked quite shocked but then spent some time talking to him.

---

11. Christopher Nolan, *Under the Eye of the Clock* (London: Orion Publishing/ Weidenfeld & Nicolson, 1987), 4.

12. Nolan, *Under the Eye of the Clock*, 11.

Seeing and hearing are often at the heart of the stories in Acts. This does not mean that Christians should never offer physical and material help. However, before simply handing out money, it is always good to first stop and listen to try to determine what the real need might be. Douglas Steere once said, "To listen another's soul into a condition of disclosure and discovery may be almost the greatest service that any human being performs for another."[13]

The Temptation to Take the Credit, 3:11-26

The next scene in Luke's narrative presents a reminder of one of the greatest temptations to the early followers of Jesus and to Christians today. That is to take credit for what is obviously the work of God. Picture the scene: while the man clung to Peter and John, "all the people ran together to them in the Portico called Solomon's Portico, utterly astonished" (v. 11). It would have been easy for Peter and John to take credit for the man's healing and, at least for a few minutes, to bask in the praise. Instead they pointed to Christ. As John Cassian, writing in the fourth century, rightly put it,

> Those men who received power from God never used that power as if it were their own but referred the power to him from whom they received it . . . and so both the apostles and all the servants of God never did anything in their own name but in the name and invocation of Christ.[14]

Peter and John were not calling people to follow them. They were not trying to establish a new movement. They were calling the people to a relationship with the living God, as the healing took place in the name of Jesus Christ. This is the activity of God: "Jesus remains active and works through the agents he has chosen and commissioned."[15] In an age when life is often dominated by personality cults and celebrity leaders, even in the church, people sometimes focus on the preacher/leader rather than the Savior.

Peter and John were not drawn to seek praise for themselves or stand in the limelight. When Peter addressed the crowd, he refused to take credit for the healing and instead put stress on the authority of God. Peter and John

13. Steere, On Listening to Another, 14.

14. John Cassian, "On the Incarnation of the Lord Against Nestorius," in Ancient Christian Commentary on Scripture, New Testament V, Acts, ed. Martin, 40, as cited in Schaff et al., eds., A Select Library of the Nicene and Post-Nicene Fathers of the Christian Church 2, 11:614.

15. Keener, Acts: An Exegetical Commentary, 2:1042.

did not have any power of their own. The healing was done in the name of the Lord Jesus, but not because it was a magical formula or a power that operated apart from the person it represented. As Peterson suggested, the name is "a dynamic, personal symbol of Jesus' continuing presence and power on earth."[16] To use the name is not only to remember the Lord but to know his presence with them.

> God, at his most vitally active and most incarnate, is not remote from us, wholly apart from the sphere of the tangible; on the contrary, at every moment he awaits us in the activity, the work to be done, which every moment brings. He is, in a sense, at the point of my pen, my pick, my paintbrush, my needle—and my heart and thought.
> —Pierre Teilhard de Chardin, *Hymn of the Universe* (New York: Harper and Row, 1965), 76–77.

Peter went on to point out that the man had been healed by the power of the very same Jesus whom the people had denied and rejected. He then reminded them of the claims of Old Testament prophets, and of Moses, that "the Lord your God will raise up for you from your own people a prophet like me" (v. 22). The appeal referring to the Old Testament prophets and to Moses was an attempt to emphasize the continuity of the Christian faith with the Jewish tradition. The description of Jesus' rejection, death, and exaltation in the speech mirrors the portrait of a servant in Isaiah 53.[17] The emphasis here is on the fact that this was not a "new religion" but the fulfillment of God's intention for Israel.[18]

Finally, Peter called the people to repent, which may signal the primary purpose of the speech. They were reminded of how wrong it was to reject the one whom God sent as Messiah. While they may have acted in ignorance, they had the truth now and they had no excuse. They must repent. The purpose of the speech was not to highlight a miracle but to indicate that true followers of Christ are always seeking to point to Christ and to call people to repentance.[19] All who hear the name of Jesus and respond in repentance may find freedom and new life. The call was extended not simply to the man at the temple gate but to all who would respond. This story is a reminder that Jesus came to proclaim "release to the captives

---

16. Peterson, *The Acts of the Apostles*, 176.

17. Peterson, *The Acts of the Apostles*, 174.

18. Peterson, *The Acts of the Apostles*, 174.

19. Keener, *Acts: An Exegetical Commentary*, 2:1076.

and recovering sight to the blind, to let the oppressed go free" (Luke 4:18-19). Peter and John were followers of Jesus, doing his work on earth.

Draw Your Own Conclusions

1. Have you had the experience of someone genuinely listening to you? How did it affect you? Have you had the opposite experience when you felt that you were not heard? How did you feel?

2. How would you describe the difference between prayer that is not based on logic but on love?

3. We live in a culture where people want "to give and receive credit." How might the church set an example of a different way of being?

4. What does it meant to live to glorify God alone?

Acts 4

God's Healing Power, 4:1-12

As the story continues, the apostles were confronted by the captain of the temple,[1] priests, and Sadducees who came to Peter and John "much annoyed" because they were teaching the people and proclaiming that in Jesus there was the resurrection of the dead (vv. 1-2). Why the annoyance? What was the problem? First, the officials considered the temple area to be their domain. Second, the Sadducees did not believe that on the last day there would be a general resurrection of the dead, and they did not want this notion of the resurrection promoted among the people. Finally, it appears that many of these religious leaders felt threatened when they heard that people were responding to the proclamation of Peter and John. It was reported that "many of those who heard the word believed; and they numbered about five thousand" (v. 4). The temple leaders wanted to put a stop to these men, so they arrested Peter and John and put them in prison overnight.

The next day Peter and John were brought before the "rulers, elders, and scribes assembled in Jerusalem, with Annas the high priest, Caiaphas, John, and Alexander, and all who were part of the high-priestly family" (vv. 5-6). Luke's attention to the actual names, together with the seeming importance of those who gathered highlight the fact that the teaching of Jesus was strenuously opposed. By drawing a sharp contrast between people who seemed to have power and the power of the Spirit at work, Luke emphasizes again that God was at work bringing down the powerful and lifting up the lowly (Luke 1:52).

---

1. The captain of the temple was the highest-ranking priest after the high priest (Peterson, *The Acts of the Apostles*, 187).

As Peter and John stood in the midst of the throng, they were asked, "By what power or by what name did you do this?" (v. 7). According to Luke, Peter, "filled with the Holy Spirit," then offered another speech. Once again, as he spoke, Peter refused to draw attention to himself but announced, "let it be known to all of you, and to all the people of Israel, that this man is standing before you in good health by the name of Jesus Christ of Nazareth, whom you crucified, whom God raised from the dead" (v. 10). Instead of focusing on "how the healing happened," Peter's message puts stress on "what it meant."[2] Peter was not offering defense of his actions; he was proclaiming the action of God. Moreover, he was not going to be deterred from proclaiming the truth about Jesus to the religious leaders and "to all the people of Israel" (v. 10).

Citing Psalm 118:22 to the religious leaders, Peter claimed that "the stone that was rejected by you, the builders; it has become the cornerstone." The cornerstone was essential and not seen as ceremonial or merely commemorative, but it was the keystone.[3] Luke means that the leaders missed what God was doing. They had not listened and responded. God was seeking to restore Israel and they had turned away from what God was trying to do. "There is salvation in no one else, for there is no other name under heaven given among mortals by which we must be saved" (v. 12). Peter's bold proclamation incited anger among the assembled leaders and deserves some attention here. Talbert has suggested that it should be noted first that Luke is a Messianic Jew speaking to Jewish leaders at a time when many Jewish groups (Essenes, Pharisees, Sadducees, Messianists, and others) were claiming that they were the rightful "heir to the Scriptures of Israel and the promises made by God to ancient Israel."[4] Moreover, in a culture that promoted magic and "polytheistic paganism," Luke wanted to assert that only by the grace of the Lord Jesus are people saved.[5] As Talbert put it,

> Acts does not consider all religious positions as equal. Some, like magic, receive only condemnation; others, like popular paganism, receive only correction; still others, like the god-fearers and nonmessianic Jews, are offered completion as well as correction. Acts, however, does not consider

---

2. Talbert, *Reading Acts*, 57.

3. Beverly Roberts Gaventa, *Acts: Abingdon New Testament Commentaries* (Nashville: Abingdon, 2003), 93.

4. Talbert, *Reading Acts*, 42.

5. Talbert, *Reading Acts*, 42.

any of the other religious options as equal to the Messianists' stance. Conversion (repentance/faith/baptism) is necessary in every case, even in the case of nonmessianic Judaism (cf. 2:38; 15:7-11). Acts 4:12 is a specific instance of such a demand for nonmessianic Jews.[6]

The Danger of Pride and Vainglory, 4:13-22

The leaders of the temple were shocked and annoyed at the boldness of these "uneducated and ordinary" followers of Jesus. Yet, when they saw the man who had been healed standing beside Peter and John, they could only look on in amazement. They realized that they had nothing to say in opposition. So the religious leaders sent everyone away in order to discuss among themselves what to do with Peter and John. It is ironic in many ways that the very people who believed they had power were afraid of those who had no obvious power, except the power that they claimed came from God working through them.[7] While the religious leaders acknowledged that a "sign has been done through them," they did not want Peter and John to continue at work. They were furious that these common Galilean men spoke so boldly but were also wary of the crowds who had been praising God for the work they saw through these men. Lacking in understanding, they decided to try to silence Peter and John, failing to realize the futility of the endeavor.

Peter and John were called back and ordered "not to speak or teach at all in the name of Jesus" (v. 18). They responded, "Whether it is right in God's sight to listen to you rather than to God, you must judge; for we cannot keep from speaking about what we have seen and heard" (vv. 19-20). "Finding no way of punishing them because of the people, for all of them praised God for what had happened" (v. 21), the leaders simply threatened Peter and John again and released them.

The entire drama underscores that the followers of Jesus were emboldened by the power they received from God as Holy Spirit. The name they proclaimed was not some talisman.[8] They were not working in their own strength. The healing of the man was a sign of what God can do through those who both act in obedience to God and are alert to God's continuing presence at work in the world. Once again, the contrast between Peter and John and the religious leaders could not be more stark. The religious leaders

---

6. Talbert, *Reading Acts*, 43.

7. Peterson, *The Acts of the Apostles*, 193–94.

8. Peterson, *The Acts of the Apostles*, 176.

sought to protect the stones of tradition while ignoring the living stone who is the corner. In their obsession with maintaining control, status, and influence among the people, they missed the opportunity for relationship with the living God. They ignored what God sought to do in their midst. Yet the risen Christ, still today, continues to minister through his followers who have received power through the Holy Spirit.

As he tells the story of this confrontation with the religious leaders, Luke seems to emphasize that any "sign" exhibited by the disciples was not to be credited to them as an achievement. The healing of the man and their ability to stand against the authorities who wanted to silence them were reflections of the power and guidance of the Holy Spirit and the power of Jesus' name. As we ponder the story, however, we can imagine how easy it would have been for Peter and John to accept credit for themselves. As they reflected on the amazement of the crowd, as they observed the joy and delight of the healed man as he danced into the temple, and even as they witnessed the consternation of the religious leaders, they could have taken the opportunity to bask in the adulation of the people; they could have taken pride in what had been achieved, but they did not.

Noting the danger of "vainglory" to those seeking to follow in the way of Christ, Evagrius (c. 345–399), a fourth-century theologian, claimed,

> For vainglory has a frightful power to cover over and cast virtues into the shade. Ever searching out praise from men, it banishes faith. Our Lord has put it very well: "How can you believe when you get your praise from other men and are not interested in the praise that God alone gives?" The Good must be pursued for its own sake, not for some other cause.[9]

Following close on the heels of vainglory, according to Evagrius, was the chief sin among all sins: pride. Evagrius, like many other early Christian writers, warned that pride was nothing less than an act of taking credit for things that are of God. Furthermore, Evagrius believed that pride led to the most "damaging fall of the soul" because it causes a person to "deny that God is his [her] helper and to consider that he himself [she herself] is the cause of virtuous actions."[10]

As we pause to ponder this episode in Acts, let us for a moment imagine ourselves in a portrait gallery gazing on a picture of Peter and John listening

---

9. Evagrius Ponticus, *The Praktikos and Chapters on Prayer*, trans. John Eudes Bamberger (Abbey of Gethsemane in Trappist, KY: Cistercian Publications, 1972), 13.

10. Evagrius, *The Praktikos and Chapters on Prayer*, 20.

to the plaudits of the crowds. While they know that God alone brings healing and hope, we may reflect on the obvious temptation they faced to bask in praise. In our imaginary gallery of paintings, let us now shift our attention to another picture. This is a more modern scene of a minister of a church who delights in claiming the number of baptisms that have been held during her or his ministry there. Or we may imagine another scene of church leaders standing proudly before new buildings, boasting about the success of mission trips, or applauding the numbers of people attending the church services. The opportunities for vainglory in the service of God are endless.

It is not difficult to imagine that when Peter and John were called before the high priest, they might have been tempted to take credit for the healing of the man. Indeed, how easy it would have been for them to defend their actions by pointing to themselves. They might have suggested that their ability to meet the man's need and their "success" in delivering his healing was dependent on their own good habits, their willingness to listen carefully to God, their deep prayer life, or some other attribute. Instead, they simply pointed to Jesus. It is a simple matter to highlight but a necessary one, and one that emerges time and again Acts. The glory must always be given to the Lord. Just as they made it clear to the healed man that they were not acting in their own power, so they claimed before the high priest that the healing of the man had taken place in the name of Jesus.

Praying for Boldness, 4:23-31

Peter and John stood firm in their witness, and even when the officials released them, they did not seek to run away or hide. Instead, they returned to their friends and held a prayer meeting. The prayer, as Talbert has noted, has certain parallels with Isaiah 37:16-20, and it is used to assert the believers' total dependence on the power of God.[11] The believers are seeking to do God's will. They are acknowledging God's plan and confessing that they are in God's hands. They ask for one thing only: greater boldness. Luke underscores that genuine power is given by God alone, claiming "the place in which they were gathered together was shaken; and they were all filled with the Holy Spirit and spoke the word of God with boldness" (v. 31).

The emphasis on bold witness through the power of the Spirit is made repeatedly in Acts. This was not simply enthusiasm for the task or a desire

---

11. Talbert, *Reading Acts*, 46.

for church growth. Their boldness is presented as obedience to God. They have been charged to be witnesses in Judea, Samaria, and to the ends of the earth. In order to do that, they need more than human strength. They must offer themselves in great trust and obedience to God as Holy Spirit to lead them. Nothing they accomplish can be accredited to their own bravery, valiant advance, or ingenuity. Rather, boldness is the sign of their submission to the Holy Spirit. To be filled with the Spirit means readiness for humble obedience and costly service.

Many years ago, I attended a meeting of a wider association of churches that was hosted by a small church on a rough housing estate in Wales. Both the minister of the church and the only deacon were elderly women. From the perspective of an outsider, it appeared to be an impossible situation. The

> O God, we pray for thy church, which is set today amid the perplexities of a changing order, and face to face with a great new task. We remember with love the nurture she gave to our spiritual life in its infancy, the tasks she set for our growing strength, the influence of the devoted hearts she gathers, the steadfast power for good she has exerted. When we compare her with all other institutions, we rejoice, for there is none like her. But when we judge her by the mind of her Master, we bow in pity and contrition. Oh, baptize her afresh in the life-giving spirit of Jesus! Grant her a new birth, though it be with the travail of repentance and humiliation. Bestow upon her a more imperious responsiveness to duty, a swifter compassion with suffering, and an utter loyalty to the will of God. Put upon her lips the ancient gospel of her Lord. Help her to proclaim boldly the coming of the kingdom of God and the doom of all that resist it. Fill her with the prophets' scorn of tyranny, and with a Christ-like tenderness for the heavy-laden and down-trodden. Give her faith to espouse the cause of the people, and in their hands that grope after freedom and light to recognize the bleeding hands of Christ. Bid her cease from seeking her own life, lest she lose it. Make her valiant to give up her life to humanity, that like her crucified Lord she may mount by the path of the cross to a higher glory.
> —Walter Rauschenbusch, "Prayer for the Church," in *Walter Rauschenbusch: Selected Writings*, Sources of American Spirituality, ed. Winthrop S. Hudson (New York: Paulist Press, 1984), 232.

small building was regularly attacked by local, rowdy youths who threw stones to break windows, and the ruffians had covered the outside walls with graffiti. Yet, in the meeting, these two women stood up and without any fear described how they were witnessing to the love of God in that community. They asked those who had gathered to please keep them in their daily prayers. They were clearly witnesses to Christ who were emboldened and empowered by the Spirit, but they claimed no special credit or spiritual maturity.

If You Ever Need Anything . . . , 4:32-37

The picture of the church presented in Luke's summary statement at the end of chapter 4 has long been long upheld as the ideal for Christians far and wide to emulate. As in chapter 2 (2:43-47), Luke emphasizes the unity of the community. The text in chapter 4 claims, "the whole group of those who believed were of one heart and soul, and no one claimed private ownership of any possessions, but everything they owned was held in common" (v. 32). However, it has been suggested that this does not necessarily mean that they all owned property together as a community. Rather, it may mean that those who owned property did not "claim it as such" but thought of it as property shared with those in need.[12] The main emphasis of the text is that "there was not a needy person among them" (v. 34).

The spirit of this text is captured in a story told by Fred Craddock about his time as a student pastor serving in a small mission in the Appalachian Mountains. Apparently, it was the practice of the church to have a baptismal service on Easter Day. Since this church practiced baptism by immersion, it was the tradition to hold baptismal services at a nearby lake at sundown on Easter evening. Craddock described how the small congregation gathered by the lake, built a fire, cooked supper, and sang hymns around the campfire. When the time for the baptismal service came, using hanging blankets the people set up little changing booths so that after the candidates were baptized they could change clothes and then gather by the fire. Each of them in turn went into the water and then, after changing, took their place with the group by the fire. Finally, Craddock said, last of all, he came out of the water, changed clothes behind the blanket, and then took his place standing by the fire. He described what happened next:

> Once we were all around the fire, this was the ritual of that tradition. Glenn Hickey, always Glenn, introduced the new people, gave their names, and where they lived, and their work. Then the rest of us formed a circle around them, while they stayed warm by the fire. The ritual was

---

12. Gaventa, *Acts*, 100.

that every person in the circle then gave her or his name, and said this, "My name is . . . if you ever need somebody to do washing and ironing . . ." "My name is . . . if you ever need anybody to chop wood . . ." "My name is . . . if you ever need anybody to baby-sit . . ." "My name is . . . if you ever need anybody to repair your house . . ." "My name is . . . if you ever need anybody to sit with the sick . . ." "My name is . . . if you ever need a car to go to town . . ." and around the circle.[13]

Then, Craddock said, they ate together and had a square dance. Following that, at a time which they knew but he said he didn't know, Percy Miller, with his thumbs in his bibbed overalls, would stand up and say "time to go" and everybody would leave. Craddock said that on the first occasion when he attended the baptismal event, he lingered behind. Percy Millersaw him standing there and said to him, "Craddock, folks don't ever get any closer than this." Craddock concluded his story by saying this: "In that little community, they have a name for that. I've heard it in other communities too. In that community, their name for that is 'church.' They call that 'church.'"[14]

The picture in Acts of people sharing together is at the very least a scene of complete openness—to God and to others. A certain generosity of spirit is in evidence, and it serves as a reminder that Christian faith is about "hand, head, and heart." Being part of a church is not just about supporting the church financially. Nor is it simply about attending, as one might regularly attend a club. Rather it is about being bound to others in the love of Christ: a love that says to others "if you ever need anything . . . just let me know." As if to underscore this idea, Luke introduces us to "a Levite, a native of Cyprus, Joseph, to whom the disciples gave the name Barnabas (which means "son of encouragement")." According to Luke, Barnabas "sold a field that belonged to him, then brought the money, and laid it at the apostles' feet" (vv. 37). Thus, Acts 4 ends on a high note. In the midst of adversity, the people have prayed for boldness, and they have joined together in expressing openness to God and to one another. In the next chapter, however, we are reminded that the closeness they have achieved and the bond they have discovered are not easy to maintain.

---

13. In Mike Graves and Richard F. Ward, *Craddock Stories* (St. Louis: Chalice Press, 2001), 151–52.

14. In Graves and Ward, *Craddock Stories*, 152.

Draw Your Own Conclusions

1. Both the believers and the Jewish leaders acted boldly. How would you describe the difference between their actions or perhaps in their motives?

2. How is it possible to describe boldness as a sign of submission to God?

3. What might hinder a church today from being of "one heart and soul"?

4. Have you ever been part of a church when you knew the place where you gathered was "shaken" as you ventured to respond to God together with a "yes"?

Acts 5

The Danger of the Divided Self, 5:1-11

In chapter 4, Luke presents a picture of camaraderie and contentment among the Christians who were "one in heart and soul." They were sharing together in a spirit of generosity and boldly as they witnessed to their faith in the risen Lord. Joseph, whom the apostles named Barnabas ("the son of encouragement"), is pictured as a symbol of true discipleship as he sold a field and laid the money at the apostles' feet (v. 37).[1]

In Acts 5, what follows this picture of love, generosity, and oneness among the early believers is a scene of greed and deception. The sharp contrast between the generosity of Barnabas and the selfish desires of Ananias and Sapphira is unmistakable. Like Barnabas, Ananias and Sapphira professed to be followers of Jesus. In both instances, property is sold and money is "laid at the feet" of the apostles. Luke's repetition of the phrase "laid it at the apostles' feet" highlights the contrast between the two gifts. Barnabas laid down all of the proceeds from his sale. Ananias, with his wife's knowledge, laid down only part of the money (vv. 1-2).

The story underscores what has already been identified by Luke's Gospel account as one of the great challenges to discipleship: wealth. In the Gospel stories, Jesus speaks about the danger of thinking life is about possessions. Emphasis is placed on life as God's gift that should be lived in dependence on God (Luke 12:13-34; 14:33; 18:18-30; 19). The Gospel stories make it plain that God is a generous God, and God's people are to be generous people. Possessions provide false security. Those who welcome Jesus into

---

1. Garland draws attention to the contrast with Judas, who bought a field (1:8). Luke may also be drawing parallels between Barnabas the Levite and another Levite who walked by a man in need in the Gospel story (Luke 10:32) (Garland, *Acts*, 51).

their homes and lives are to be eager to share with others. Clinging to possessions will lead to division with others as well as to a divided self.

While the language about the rich and poor is not as prominent in Acts as in the Gospel of Luke, still, as Hays has pointed out, the ethical teachings of Acts are in keeping with the Gospel directives.[2] Namely, God's people should acknowledge that all things come from God, who is the generous "Giver," and believers are to live toward others and toward God with open hands and open hearts. The story of Ananias and Sapphira raises a number of questions: What does it mean to live in a way that reflects the generosity of God? How is wealth to be shared and distributed? What are our responsibilities toward others both within the community of faith and in the world at large? What does stewardship of our resources entail? What difference might it make to discipleship if the church rejected a "business model" and instead focused on the unity that results from being of "one heart and soul"?

Any discussion of money within the church in a Western context is likely to cause some discomfort. Suggest that spiritual growth may be stunted by attention to money and possessions, and the cry goes up: God is not opposed to people having money! God has blessed us with possessions! There is no need to rehearse once again the many reasons we might give for clinging to wealth. Whatever the reasons we may wish to give (what we have is a product of our hard work, we have been "blessed," we are using our money wisely and saving for the next generation, etc.), there is no escaping the overwhelming power of money that is often the cause of great division in families, among friends, with neighbors, and within in a church fellowship or even in a wider group of congregations.[3]

While it is easy to see some of the problems raised when money rather than relationship becomes a predominant concern, this story presents other challenges to a spiritual life. One might suggest that the main problem with Ananias and Sapphira was not a love of money but their willingness to "lie to the Holy Spirit" (v. 3). Reflecting on this story, many Christian writers down the centuries have commented on the characters of Ananias and Sapphira. Fourth-century writer Gregory of Nyssa (c. 335–395) suggested that when a person is "dragged down" to avarice, the Holy Spirit no longer

---

2. Christopher M. Hays, *Luke's Wealth Ethics, A Study in Their Coherence and Character* (Tübingen: Mohr Siebeck, 2010), 190.

3. See for instance the "collection" that Luke does not mention but the Apostle Paul refers to in 1 Cor 16:1-4; 2 Cor 8:1-15.

controls that person.[4] In effect, the person is no longer living for God. Those who live in this way are no longer whole. They lack authenticity and in effect have become a "divided self." Whenever we shift to being divided in ourselves, we tend toward being divided from God, too.

Those who have struggled with the dilemma of being torn between loving God and loving something else will recognize the dilemma of the "divided self." In his classic autobiographical work *The Confessions*, St. Augustine described a sort of restlessness of the heart that he knew would not be eased until it found its rest in God. He also described the inner conflict he experienced as being bound by his "own iron will," and he confessed,

> A new will, which had begun within me, to wish freely to worship you and find joy in you, O God, the sole sure delight, was not yet able to overcome that prior will, grown strong with age. Thus did my two wills, the one old, the other new, the first carnal, and the second spiritual, contend with one another, and by their conflict they laid waste my soul.[5]

The description of struggling with the sense of a divided self is a common theme among Christian writers. In the twentieth century, the founder of the Catholic Worker movement, Dorothy Day (1897–1980), described being torn by her desire to be for God and the desire to cling to her old life and relationships. She knew a measure of happiness and peace in her own life, but she described the peace she had found as being "curiously enough, divided against itself," and it was during this time that she began to pray more.[6] She knew that life would change drastically when she openly declared her faith, and as she put it, she was all for "putting off the hard day."[7] Ultimately, she made the choice and then adopted a life of simplicity in which, led by the Spirit, she sought to care for the poor and the oppressed.

Yet another well-known figure of an earlier era who spoke of a certain restlessness before finding peace with God was St. Francis of Assisi (c. 1181–1226). Born into a wealthy family, as a young man Francis turned his back on wealth in order to live a life that he felt was imitating the way of Christ. He adopted a life of poverty and devoted himself to preaching and

---

4. Gregory of Nyssa, "On Not Three Gods," in *Ancient Christian Commentary*, ed. Francis Martin, 60, as cited in Schaff, *A Select Library of Nicene and Post-Nicene Fathers*, 25:333.

5. Augustine, *The Confessions* (Garden City, NY: Image Books, 1960), 189.

6. Dorothy Day, *The Long Loneliness* (San Francisco: Harper Collins, 1952/1997), 116.

7. Day, *The Long Loneliness*, 138.

to calling others to a life for, and with, God. Later, he founded a religious community known as the Franciscan Order. Such was his devotion to God, and his desire to walk in the way of Christ even to the point of suffering, that stories were told about the appearance of stigmata on his hands and feet. These stories highlight the emphasis on the fact that those who follow Christ must be willing to let go of anything that would hinder them from focusing on God alone. The stories also reflect the fact that life in Christ is never free from suffering.

The emphasis on suffering love is seen not only in the stories about the life of St. Francis but also in the writings of his friend Clare (c. 1193/4–1253) who, with Francis, founded the religious order The Poor Sisters or Poor Clares. While St. Francis is a well-known figure in history, only in recent years has Clare's work been studied. Like Francis, Clare grew up in Assisi where she became very aware that the culture not only allowed but even encouraged the exploitation of the weak and poor by the rich. St. Francis and Clare believed that if they were to be able to proclaim the good news to the poor and the oppressed, they had to be close to the poor.[8] She and a group of women who had joined her in dedicating their lives to God and caring for the poor moved to San Damiano, a place that was outside the walls of Assisi. Here they formed a community that tried to reflect their desire to follow "the poor Christ."[9] Like Augustine and many other Christian writers, Clare highlighted the fact that human beings are born with a very deep desire, longing, or restlessness. In one her letters, she described the desire as a basic need for "heavenly nourishment," that is, for relationship with God. She continued,

> Whether we are conscious of it or not, throughout our lives we are seeking to fill the abyss of this fundamental desire. We can keep the yearning at a distance. We can judge it, choose it, endure it, reject it, question it, or accept it. . . . However, because this yearning is essential and ineradicable, it can offer an opportunity for us or a perilous risk.[10]

Ultimately, Clare maintained that the only answer to this longing or desire—which in essence reflects God's desire for us—is to follow in the way of the "poor Christ." That is, to follow in the generous way of the one

---

8. Clare Marie Ledoux, *Clare of Assisi: Her Spirituality Revealed in her Letters*, trans. Colette Joly Dees (Cincinnati: St Anthony Messenger Press, 1996), 14.

9. Ledoux, *Clare of Assisi*, 14.

10. Ledoux, *Clare of Assisi*, 35.

who, "though he was rich, yet for your sakes he became poor, so that by his poverty you might become rich" (2 Cor 8:9).

The decision to follow in the way of Jesus, as these and many other stories of Christians through the ages show, requires unreserved commitment to God. From Luke's perspective it may seem that the man who was healed in the previous chapter had no earthly goods and was given no money by Peter and John. Rather, he was given healing in the name of Jesus. Those who seemingly have everything money can buy will not find the healing needed from a broken and divided self by clinging to material goods. What is needed is the wholeness that comes by "letting go" and being guided by the Spirit.

Any discussion on the need to "let go" or to "lose life in order to find life" inevitably leads to questions about the freedom that comes with a life of simplicity. It is easy to speak of letting go of possessions and aiming always to simply have enough and no more. Yet how much is enough? How do we know when something has not only captured our attention but our hearts and minds as well? The great difficulty in trying to answer these questions is that captivity to possessions is often only a symptom of a greater captivity to culture. Even if we think we are free of bondage to possessions, we may still be held captive to culture. This was demonstrated vividly to me when, in a discussion about Christian discipleship, one person claimed that he was not bound to possessions. In his view, simplicity was about being surrendered to God and living a holy life, but it was not about what we wear, purchase, or strive after. The problem with this understanding is that according to the teachings of Jesus found in the Gospels, there is no way to lead a holy life without complete surrender of everything to God. As the nineteenth-century pastor and Social Gospel leader Washington Gladden (1836–1913) put it, to claim that commitment to Christ has nothing to do with possessions is to "ignore the life of Christ and to admit that the church has often very dimly understood its Lord, and very imperfectly represented him."[11]

In reflecting on the story of Ananias and Sapphira, it seems that they had but "dimly understood" the way of Christ as they not only withheld money from the community but also lied about it. In doing so, they

---

11. Washington Gladden, "The Church and the Social Crisis," in Report made to the National Council of the Congregational Church, Thirteenth Triennial Session, October 8–17, 1907 (Boston: Office of the Secretary, 1907), 11. Gladden (1836–1913) was pastor of the United Church of Christ in Columbus, Ohio, and along with Walter Rauschenbusch (1861–1918) he spoke out for social change in America.

demonstrated that they each were living as a "divided self," and the implication is that they acted against the community and so against the Lord, too. Their sin was not just a personal failing; their actions had repercussions on the whole church (v. 11). Luke claims that they received swift punishment from God for their wrongdoing. When Ananias and Sapphira were both struck down, Luke says, "Great fear seized the whole church." This reaction is understandable. The story of Ananias and Sapphira is a firm reminder that commitment to God is not something to be entered into lightly. "Letting go" and not clinging to anything but God alone is not only a challenge but also an imperative. Moreover, the very thought of the gravity of the call to abandonment should make us tremble before God as well.

Whoever Has God Lacks Nothing, 5:12-16

Following the story of Ananias and Sapphira, Luke says, "many signs and wonders were done among the people through the apostles" (v. 12). As the reputation of the disciples began to spread, "great numbers of both men and women" were "added to the Lord" (v. 14). Hearing of the healing, people brought sick friends and family members to the streets so that Peter's shadow might fall over them.

Those who have sat by the bedside of a desperately ill loved one or faced ill health themselves can imagine the sense of desperation the people felt as they brought their loved ones to be healed. Yet Luke makes it clear that Peter and the other disciples had no special powers; his shadow had no efficacy as such. Rather, as Luke puts it, the many "signs and wonders" were done among the people through the apostles. "Through" is the operative word here.[12] Luke is again pointing to the work of the Spirit through Peter and the others. These scenes are presented as evidence of God's work in and through the community as a whole.

While at times these stories have provoked debate about the "signs and wonders" and those who might have the gift of healing today, it is significant that here Luke gives little attention to the words or actions of the apostles.[13] Rather than the healing being seen as a direct result of the actions of the apostles, the healings are noted as something that happened simply as they walked along. Moreover, as was noted in the story of the person who was healed in chapter 3, there is no sense that Peter and John sought to draw

---

12. Gaventa, *Acts*, 104.

13. Garland, *Acts*, 58.

attention to themselves or desired any kudos from the community. Any healing that took place was simply the work of God through them. They had no control over who was healed, but they were willing for God to work through them. They realized that now, through the power of the Spirit, they were to be the hands and feet of Christ. In the oft-quoted words attributed to the sixteenth-century spiritual writer Teresa of Avila (1515–1582),

> Christ has no body now on earth but yours; no hands but yours; no feet but yours. Yours are the eyes through which the compassion of Christ must look out on the world. Yours are the feet with which He is to go about doing good. Yours are the hands with which He is to bless His people.[14]

Throughout history there has sometimes been a tendency to forget that the Spirit works through people of all faiths and of no faith. Fine preachers of the gospel are at times particularly vulnerable to the temptation to bask in the adulation offered by members of a congregation for their oratory. Alarmingly, worship in churches can quickly change from the praise of God to applause for those leading or contributing to worship. It may happen almost unwittingly as the "band" is placed center stage, the lights lowered, and the applause encouraged by those who, following a cultural model, are treated as celebrities performing at a concert. Yet the emphasis in this text is not on the apostles but on the presence of God at work through them. Luke pictures them not as those who have sought or achieved celebrity status by accepting the applause of others but as humble instruments. Indeed, they seem almost unaware that people are being healed.

> Dearest Lord, teach me to be generous;
> Teach me to serve thee as thou deservest;
> To give and not to count the cost,
> To fight and not to heed the wounds,
> To toil and not to seek for rest,
> To labor and not to seek reward,
> Save that of knowing that I do thy will.
> Amen.
>
> —Ignatius of Loyola (1491–1556)

Or, rather, they are only aware that God is at work. This is the genuine sign of a life open to God and ready to be used by God.

---

14. Teresa was a Spanish Carmelite and mystical writer. Her writings include *The Interior Castle*, *The Way of Perfection*, and *The Life*. See also Rowan Williams, *Teresa of Avila* (London: Geoffrey Chapman, 1991).

Obeying God Rather than Human Authority, 5:17-42

The final scene in Acts 5 tells the story of the arrest and persecution of the apostles as they continued to go to the temple to tell others the good news about Jesus Christ. By telling this story, Luke may have been trying to encourage his own community to stand firm in their faith.[15] Yet, as Keener suggests, it is also true that the power of God will always "invite" persecution.[16] Hearing of the excitement of the crowds over the teachings and works of the apostles, the high priest arrested Peter and John and had them imprisoned. It is noteworthy that they were imprisoned not simply because of what they preached but, as Luke claims, because the officials were "filled with jealousy" (v. 17). The irony of this statement should not be missed. When compared to the temple rulers, the apostles were "nobodies." Yet the temple rulers were threatened by them. As Spangenberg put it in the sixteenth century, "The temple rulers knew well that the apostles were fishermen, tax collectors, and uneducated people, and they were being humiliated by them. This they could not bear; they were after all the heads and pillars of Judaism."[17]

Jealousy is often a thorn in human relationships. It can dig deep into a person and cause such resentment and bitterness to the point that she or he is no longer able to take pleasure in the good that may happen in another person's life. Thomas Aquinas, writing in the thirteenth century, lamented that envy was directly opposed to love and was caused by "sorrow over another's good."[18] In the case of the apostles, as the crowds began to follow them and, as Luke put it, "held them in high esteem," the leaders of the temple were threatened by the way these common men had gained popularity with the populace. The high priest and the Sadducees decided to take action and tried to publicly shame the apostles by having them arrested and imprisoned. During the night, Luke says that an angel of the Lord, a messenger of God, came and opened the prison door and told them

---

15. Gaventa, *Acts*, 104.

16. Keener, *Acts: An Exegetical Commentary*, 2:1205.

17. Johann Spangenberg, "Brief Exegesis of Acts 5:17," *Der Apostel Geschichte, 45r-v* as cited in *Reformation Commentary*, ed. Chung-Kim and Hains, 66.

18. Thomas Aquinas, "Of Envy," Question 36, "Treatise on Virtues," in *Summa Theologica*, 1947, https://www.sacred-texts.com/chr/aquinas/summa/sum291.htm.

to "go, stand in the temple and tell the people the whole message about this life" (v. 21).

As the story continues, at daybreak they went and stood in the temple and proclaimed the story of Jesus. When the temple police went to collect Peter and John from prison to bring them before the temple officials, they found the "doors securely locked and the guards standing at the doors," but the prisoners were not there (v. 23). When the captain and the chief priests heard this, they were perplexed and wondered what might be going on. Then they were told that Peter and John were in the temple teaching the people. The temple police were sent to bring them to the council. They were then questioned as to why they were teaching after they had been given "strict orders not to teach in this name" (v. 28), to which Peter and John replied, "We must obey God rather than any human authority" (v. 29).[19]

Escape stories are part of an ancient literary tradition. However, the idea of escape is not the emphasis of this story. Rather the emphasis is on a willingness to witness and to be obedient to God. Once again we find the apostles giving a simple testimony to the authorities:

> The God of our ancestors raised up Jesus, whom you had killed by hanging him on a tree. God exalted him at his right hand as Leader and Saviour that he might give repentance to Israel and forgiveness of sins. And we are witnesses to these things, and so is the Holy Spirit whom God has given to those who obey him. (vv. 30-32)

Peter and John claimed that the Jewish leaders were wrong and needed to repent of their disobedience. The apostles' witness was met by outrage, and the temple leaders wanted to kill them. However, at this point, a Pharisee named Gamaliel stood and pointed to the fact that there had been other movements led by men who claimed to be "somebody," but they had eventually failed. On that basis, he suggested that they should leave these men alone. "If this plan or this undertaking is of human origin, it will fail; but if it is of God, you will not be able to overthrow them—in that case you may even be found fighting against God!" (vv. 38-39). Luke records that the leaders were convinced by this argument, but then he also narrates

---

19. The emphasis on obeying God rather than people echoes a phrase often quoted in the Greek world pointing to the fact that Socrates tried to claim that he would obey God. See Keener, *Acts: An Exegetical Commentary*, 2:1217–18; Talbert, *Reading Acts*, 54.

that they had the disciples flogged again, ordering them not to continue speaking of Jesus.

Although they were threatened and also given a severe beating, Luke presents a joyous scene as the apostles left the council: "They rejoiced that they were considered worthy to suffer dishonor for the sake of the name" (v. 41). "And every day in the temple and at home they did not cease to teach and proclaim Jesus as the Messiah" (v. 42). The triumphant ending of this story speaks for itself. Luke recounted this story in such detail not to point to the escape of the apostles or to suggest that the threats and flogging had no effect on them. Rather, he was emphasizing the cost of trusting and obeying in God while also underscoring that the gospel is God's and cannot be stopped by human powers.[20] According to Luke, the joy of knowing Christ (even under duress through persecution) far outweighs the joy of the world.

Drawing Your Own Conclusions

1. What does it mean to say that suffering is inevitable for the disciples of Jesus?

2. How might obedience to God put us in conflict with obedience to human authority?

3. Where does envy sometimes creep into church life or discipleship?

4. Why do we need to guard against the temptation to indulge in celebrity culture?

5. What does it mean to say from the heart "Soli Deo gloria" ("For the glory of God alone")?

---

20. Gaventa, *Acts*, 110.

Acts 6

Serving Others, 6:1-7

As the number of believers increased and the community became more diverse, inevitably at times there were differences of opinion among the believers. Luke describes an occasion when Hellenists (Jews who only spoke Greek) began to complain that their widows were being neglected in the daily distribution of food to the poor. The Hellenists may have felt that the finances were not being handled properly.[1] Money was a recurring theme for Luke. In the Gospel, Luke emphasized Jesus' concern for the poor. Moreover, disciples of Jesus were to consider the needs of others and share their resources with one another.

The differences between the Hebrews and the Hellenists does not seem to have been as important to them as their belief in Jesus and their unity in him. Since they had come together because of their focus on Christ, they did not allow a difference of opinion on organization to divide them. Hence, when the twelve apostles were approached with complaints, they did not become defensive. Rather they realized that they needed to share certain responsibilities within community. They called together the whole community to suggest delegating the administrative duties and that seven men should be appointed to "wait on tables" while the apostles continued to devote themselves to prayer and "to serving the word." There is no suggestion that they thought their responsibility of devoting themselves to the word was more important than serving tables. Rather it was simply that they did not want to fail to do the primary tasks they were called to

---

1. Raymond E. Brown, *Once and Coming Spirit at Pentecost: Liturgical Readings Between Easter and Pentecost Taken from the Acts of the Apostles* (Collegeville, MN: The Liturgical Press, 1994), 43ff.

do. They realized that they needed to appoint others to share in the tasks of service.

Following the Jewish custom of boards of seven men for particular duties, the apostles suggested that the community should select seven honorable men of good standing, "full of the Spirit and of wisdom, whom we may appoint to this task" (v. 3).[2] This pleased the whole community, and they chose Stephen, Philip, Prochorus, Nicanor, Timon, Parmenas, and Nicolaus, a proselyte of Antioch. While the names of the men are listed, with Stephen at the head of the list, it does not appear that Luke is trying to emphasize any one in particular. Moreover, while this is sometimes seen as the establishment of the first deacons, the position of these Hellenists was not the same as the role of deacons as described in the New Testament pastoral letters. Nor should the laying on of hands be thought of as a formal ordination; rather it is a commissioning for a task.[3] While at times in the history of the church there has been a tendency to place a value on one role in the community over another, Luke's stress here is not on status or authority. Each person had a part to play in the life of the community. In the church, one person's contribution, however small or seemingly insignificant, should not be valued less than the contribution of another.

On one occasion, my husband and I were in London, and we went into St. Paul's Church in Covent Gardens. Sometimes known as the "actors' church" because of its long association with the theatre community in the West End, the walls of the church are covered with memorials remembering some of the great actors who attended services there. As we walked round the church, I was familiar with many of the names on the memorials: Charlie Chaplin, Noel Coward, Gracie Fields, Vivien Leigh, Ivor Novello, and many others. Among all the star-studded names, however, there was one plaque that simply read,

Tony Sympson
1906–1987
"inspired player of small parts"

I didn't recognize the name of the actor, but later I discovered that while Tony Sympson never had a starring role in any production, he had acted in many small roles in films and on television. Since that day I have often

---

2. Marshall, *Acts*, 126.

3. Witherington, *Acts*, 251.

thought about the description of him as an "inspired player of small parts." In many ways, this description could also be applied to those who are part of a community of faith. Every person is to be valued, and every contribution is important to the life of a Christian community.

Having appointed seven men to wait on tables among the Hellenists, Luke claims that the number of disciples among the Hebrews increased, and, indeed, "a great many of the priests became obedient to the faith" (v. 7). This suggests that the growth in the number of followers of Jesus was among both Jews and Gentiles. Noting this growth, it has been suggested that chapters 6 to 8, or perhaps 6 to 9, may be seen as a turning point for Luke as he points to the transition between the Jerusalem church and the beginning of the Gentile mission.[4] It is noteworthy that here the followers of Jesus are referred to as disciples for the first time in Acts.[5] Most importantly, they were all followers of Christ. All were called to serve under the power of God as Holy Spirit and to show by their words and deeds that they were reflecting the life of Christ in their own lives. Commitment to Christ meant a willingness to serve, and as the next scene shows it might even require believers to give up their own lives for the cause of Christ.

The Shining Face of Truth, 6:8-15

One of those selected to serve the tables was Stephen, whom Luke described as a person who was "full of faith and the Holy Spirit" (v. 5) as well as "full of grace and power," doing "great wonders and signs among the people" (v. 8). The Jews in Jerusalem were divided socially and culturally and had formed their own synagogues along those lines. However, they were all united in their desire to protect temple worship and adherence to the Jewish law, and they believed that the teaching of Stephen posed a threat to both. Some of the Hellenist Jews who belonged to the synagogue of the Freedmen[6] stood up and argued with Stephen. They were no match for him, so they decided to try to make up lies about him and claimed that he had spoken against Moses and the Law (Exod 34:29-35). They drummed up false witnesses against him and stirred up the crowd as well as the elders and

---

4. Keener, *Acts: An Exegetical Commentary*, 2:1247–49.

5. Garland, *Acts*, 64.

6. Freedmen were Roman prisoners (or the descendants of prisoners) who had later been granted freedom. Moreover, since only ten men were needed to form the nucleus of a synagogue, it is probable that different nationalities formed their own synagogues in Jerusalem (Marshall, *Acts*, 129).

scribes. "This man," they said, "never stops saying things against this holy place and the law" (v. 13). When he was brought before the council, they "all looked intently" at him, for "his face was like the face of an angel" (v. 15). It is ironic that Luke says Stephen's face was shining like that of Moses when his face reflected the glory of God, even as he was accused of opposing Moses.[7]

Over the years, Stephen has been upheld as a model disciple, and it has been suggested that the reference to his face "shining" was intended to convey a sign of holiness or sanctity or inno- cence. Chrysostom pointed to his shining face as "his grace," which meant that he stood apart from others. He wrote,

> Lord, make me an instrument of your peace;
> Where there is hatred, let me sow love;
> Where there is injury, pardon;
> Where there is doubt, faith;
> Where there is despair, hope;
> Where there is darkness, light;
> And where there is sadness, joy.
> O Divine Master,
> Grant that I may not so much seek
> To be consoled, as to console;
> To be understood, as to understand;
> To be loved, as to love;
> For it is in giving that we receive,
> It is in pardoning that we are pardoned,
> And it is in dying that we are born to Eternal Life.
> Amen.
>
> —St. Francis of Assisi (1181/2–1226)

"For indeed there are faces full of spiritual grace, lovely to behold for those who desire them and commanding respect from enemies who hate them."[8]

Stephen has been revered in the Christian church as a holy person and a martyr. Yet, for Luke, the emphasis on Stephen's shining face being a grace or a gift draws attention to the fact that holiness of life is not a possession to be acquired. Rather his shining face was a reflection of his inward life. In other words, his outward appearance reflected his inner life, a life of commitment and obedience to God.

At one time or another, many of us have met a person who seemed to shine with God's life and love. Even now, I recall quite distinctly the day that, as a young child, I overheard two women speaking glowingly about a woman in our church. They exclaimed that she was kind, caring, sensitive,

---

7. Keener, *Acts: An Exegetical Commentary*, 2:1326–27.

8. Chrysostom, "Homilies on Acts," cited in Martin, ed., *Ancient Christian Commentary on Scripture, New Testament V, Acts*, 73.

and loving. They thought her face seemed to shine with the love of God. From Luke's point of view, this would have been evidence that the Spirit of God was at work in a person's life. He described Stephen as "full of faith and the Holy Spirit" and therefore shining with the light of God's presence.

Drawing Your Own Conclusions

1. Is there truth to the suggestion that we will always face opposition if we are seeking to be true to Christ?

2. Why has the church sometimes overlooked the contribution of those who are not in the limelight?

3. How would you describe the outward signs of a holy life?

Acts 7

A Spiritual Life Is More Than . . . , 7:1-53

Once, while preaching on the feast of St. Stephen, the sixteenth-century reformer Martin Luther declared that in many ways, the story speaks for itself: "It gives us in Stephen an example of faith in Christ."[1] Viewing Stephen as "an example" of faithfulness is the view held by preachers and commentators before and after Luther. To take the stance of an observer, however, suggests that the reader is viewing the scene by standing to one side or "looking on" from a distance. Yet Scripture bids us to shift our position. Instead of gazing at Stephen, as we reflect on this story perhaps we should imagine that we are standing by him, and the members of the council are looking "intently" at us (6:15).

From this vantage point, we may feel that this is an impossible situation. They have set up false witnesses and stirred up the crowd. Yet with Stephen we stand before the accusers and listen as the high priest asks if the lies being told about Stephen are true. "Are these things so?" How do we defend him and ourselves against scheming accusers and their false statements? We are nervous, frustrated, and very afraid. We stand quietly by him. Surely now Stephen will attack the lies and mount a robust defense of his actions. His face, which appears like "the face of angel," will surely turn thunderous with rage!

But Stephen doesn't respond in anger. Rather, he retells the ancient story of how the glory of God was revealed to the Jewish people and how, instead of accepting those whom God sent to lead them, they rejected

---

1. Martin Luther, "Epistle on the Feast of Saint Stephen," Weihnachtenpostil (1522) in Chung-Kim and Hains, eds., *Reformation Commentary on Scripture, New Testament VI, Acts,* 85.

them and disobeyed God's laws.[2] Beginning with God's call to Abraham (7:2-18), the speech moves on to Joseph, who was rejected by his jealous brothers but rescued by God. Stephen then offers a longer survey of the history of the people of Israel. He points out that God called Moses to lead the people out of captivity, but the people rejected Moses (7:25, 39-43). Finally, the speech points to the way the Jews built a tabernacle, described here as a "tent of testimony" in the wilderness, and then worshipped in the temple built by Solomon (v. 44). Their mistake was to begin to think that God dwells in "houses made with human hands" (v. 48).

Having surveyed the history of rejection and betrayal of God's messengers, Stephen's speech returns to the present. Boldly, he says that he has not rejected God. Rather, echoing the words of the prophets of old, he states that by not accepting the message of the good news of Jesus Christ, the people are "stiff-necked people, uncircumcised in heart and ears" who are "forever opposing the Holy Spirit, just as your ancestors used to do" (v. 51).

Notably, unlike the speeches of Peter, Stephen's speech seems to focus more on the history of the people of Israel than on the story of Jesus Christ.[3] Yet, while there is only one direct reference to Jesus (7:52), a "Christological theme" emerges in verse 37 when the audience is reminded that God promised to "raise up a prophet for you from your own people."[4] The emphasis of this speech, however, is to make a direct correlation between the attitudes of their ancestors and their own attitudes. Like those before them, they have rejected the true worship of God.

As we continue to stand with Stephen, we fear the worst. The council is enraged. What is he doing? Why not try to placate them? By all means, speak the truth, but do so in a safe way; surely that is the best tactic when faced with an angry mob. The strong language referring to the "uncircumcised in heart and ears" (v. 51) is taken from the book of Deuteronomy (10:16) where the people are called to repentance and reminded that the requirement of God is to "fear the LORD your God, to walk in all his ways, to love him, to serve the LORD your God with all your heart and with all your soul, and to keep the commandments of the LORD your God" (Deut

---

2. Marshall, *Acts*, 131.

3. It has been suggested that the speech indicates that "neither Stephen nor his speech were Christian (but, rather Hellenistic Jewish)." Yet Marshall argues that "a Christian outlook pervades the speech as a whole" (Marshall, *Acts*, 134). For further discussion, see J. C. O'Neill, *The Theology of Acts in its Historical Setting* (London: S.P.C.K., 1961), 89–94.

4. Garland claims that Stephen is interpreting this as a reference to Jesus (*Acts*, 71).

10:12-13).[5] Stephen accuses them of not loving God above all else. While Stephen's face may be like the face of an angel, at the end of the speech he declares to the people, "You are the ones that received the law as ordained by angels, and yet you have not kept it" (v. 53).

The accusers of Stephen are incensed. The tables have been turned. His accusers are accused with the very Scripture that they claim to defend and obey. They have rejected the word of God and confused worship in a building with worship of the true living God. They have emphasized temple worship and their interpretation of the law, and in doing so they have turned away from the one true living God, who is not confined by systems whether structural, organizational, or institutional.

The speech is a stark reminder that life in and for God is never a matter of conforming to particular religious rules or regulations. While the "law was given through Moses; grace and truth came through Jesus Christ" (John 1:17). As the speech of Stephen makes plain, merely keeping the letter of the law and ritually observing the Sabbath can never replace relationship with the living God. Reflecting on the scene is discomforting to us, for it offers a stark reminder that the spiritual life is always more than anything we might do, perform, or admire. It is more than attending church services. It is more than dutifully saying prayers or reading the Bible. It is more than attending religious meetings or engaging in activities. It is more than simply saying, "I am Christian" or "I have been brought up as a Christian."

In other words, the spiritual life is far more than mere conformity to the patterns and practices of worship with which we have grown comfortable. Just because we have "always" done something or believed something does not mean that it is a true expression of walking in all God's ways. What does it mean to love God above all? How do we serve the Lord our God with all our heart and with all our soul? How do we love our neighbor as ourselves? Luke will return to this theme again in the next chapter as the gospel moves out to Samaria and beyond.

Discernment of God's Way, 7:54–8:1

Mob violence is not a surprise to us. It was a part of the ancient world, and it still exists today. So the council's reaction to Stephen's speech does not shock us. Yet, as we continue to stand alongside him, we recognize that the

---

5. Stubbornness of heart and stiff-necked is the way the disobedience of the people was described in other places in the Old Testament, e.g., Exod 32:9; 33:3, 5; Lev 26:41; Isa 63:10.

contrast between Stephen and the council could not be greater. Stephen is calm, focused, and filled with the Spirit. He looks up into heaven and declares to the crowd, "Look! I see the heavens opened and the Son of Man standing at the right hand of God!" (v. 56). The members of the council "covered their ears" (v. 57).

The picture of people refusing to listen is an uncomfortable one. Were these people not willing to have their own beliefs challenged? Had they stopped trying to discern the will of God? Did these religious leaders assume that they already knew all there was to know about God and God's ways? Did they question anything that might undermine their certainties and self-assurances?

Standing alongside Stephen as he makes his speech, we sense that discernment of God's way requires a radical openness and a willingness to listen. But the council members are in no mood to hear more. "With a loud shout all rushed together against him" (v. 57). We shrink away as we watch them drag Stephen out of town and begin to stone him. It is an appalling sight. Yet, undeterred by the hatred of those set against him, Stephen—even as he is being stoned to death—offers himself into God's hands and prays, "Lord Jesus, receive my Spirit." He also prays for their forgiveness: "Lord, do not hold this sin against them" (vv. 59-60).

> Grant, O Lord, that in all our sufferings here upon earth, for the testimony of thy truth, we may steadfastly look up to heaven, and by faith behold the glory that shall be revealed; and, being filled with the Holy Ghost, may learn to love and bless our persecutors by the example of thy first Martyr Saint Stephen, who prayed for his murderers to thee, O blessed Jesus, who standest at the right hand of God to succour all those that suffer for thee, our only Mediator and Advocate. Amen.
> —Collect for St. Stephen's Day, 26 December, from the *Book of Common Prayer* (1549).

The parallels with Luke's account of the death of Jesus and Stephen's death are striking. Both commit their spirit to God, and both pray that their enemies should be forgiven. Thus, Stephen is portrayed as a faithful follower who was willing to imitate Christ even to the point of losing his life.[6] This is the picture of a disciple who realized, as the twentieth-century martyr Dietrich Bonhoeffer put it, that "when Christ calls a man [person],

---

6. Garland points out that there are also parallels with the Markan account of Jesus' trial and death (*Acts*, 79).

he bids him [her] come and die."[7] Bonhoeffer makes it clear that he is not simply speaking of a physical loss of life, though that might happen. Rather, he is talking about ~~dying to the old self~~ or to the things that we attach ourselves to in our search to discover meaning in life.

The whole idea of "dying to self" raises many questions. As Roberta Bondi has rightly pointed out, at times in the past, the emphasis on "dying to self" in some church traditions has led to a denial of one's true, "God-given self" as if that self were worthless. This is not what Christian faith teaches. Rather, the emphasis of Christian discipleship is on giving up the "false self" that, as Bondi explains, is "constructed out of our position in life, ~~our families, our work, our possessions, our desires and fantasies, and other people's desires, fantasies, and approval or disapproval.~~"[8] Moreover, the way of Christ is not just enduring suffering, but it is enduring suffering that we experience for the sake of Christ. Bonhoeffer put it this way:

> To endure the cross is not a tragedy; it is the suffering, which is the fruit of an exclusive allegiance to Jesus Christ. When it comes, it is not an accident, but a necessity. It is not the sort of suffering which is inseparable from this mortal life, but the suffering which is an essential part of the specifically Christian life. It is not suffering *per se* but suffering-and-re-jection, and not rejection for any cause or conviction of our own, but rejection for the sake of Christ. If our Christianity has ceased to be serious about discipleship, if we have watered down the gospel into emotional uplift which makes no costly demands and which fails to distinguish between natural and Christian existence, then we cannot help regarding the cross as an ordinary everyday calamity, as one of the trials and tribu-lations of life. We have then forgotten that the cross means rejection and shame as well as suffering.[9]

Luke depicts Stephen's suffering as suffering for the sake of Christ, as he faced rejection and death because he "bore the name." Significantly, however, attention is not just given to physical suffering and death but also to the way he followed Jesus by reflecting genuine submission to God and desiring to forgive those who were persecuting him.

---

7. Dietrich Bonhoeffer, *The Cost of Discipleship* (London: SCM Press, 1959), 79.

8. Roberta C. Bondi, "Forgiveness, Judgmentalism, and the Sense of Self," in Andrew Weaver and Monica Furlong, eds., *Reflections on Forgiveness and Spiritual Growth* (Nashville: Abingdon Press, 2000), 31.

9. Bonhoeffer, *The Cost of Discipleship*, 78.

The story of Stephen as the first Christian martyr has been told many times. In the tradition of some churches, a special day is set aside to commemorate his life and witness. Great emphasis is placed on his willingness to be rejected and suffer for the sake of Christ, even to the point of death. Yet, while the call to "die" may not require physical suffering and death, a follower of Jesus must daily seek to die to the false self and stand ready to face rejection and suffering for the sake of Christ. Discernment of God's way requires a willingness to embrace Christian faith that is not simply an "emotional uplift" but is a costly and demanding commitment.

Draw Your Own Conclusions ~~Saul~~.

1. What does it mean to die to a "false self"?

2. Why do you think many people substitute church attendance with a "spiritual life"?

3. How would you describe the cost of discipleship?

Acts 8

Joy in God's Presence, 8:2-8

The stoning of Stephen not only reminds the reader of the cost of discipleship but has also been regarded as a turning point in the story of Acts because it introduces us to Saul, a chief persecutor of the church. Luke claims that Saul approved of the stoning of Stephen, a very public torment that seemed to unleash a severe backlash of persecution against the church in Jerusalem. The maltreatment was so severe that "all except the apostles were scattered throughout the countryside of Judea and Samaria" (v. 1). As "devout men buried Stephen and made loud lamentation over him," Saul was himself "ravaging the church by entering house after house; dragging off both men and women, he committed them to prison" (v. 3). Many fled from Jerusalem, though, "those who were scattered went from place to place, proclaiming the word," and thus they continued to witness to their faith in Jesus Christ (v. 4).

Philip (one the seven who had been set apart to serve) went to Samaria and preached to crowds who gathered to hear him. According to the historian Josephus, this was often the place to which people fled if they were driven out of Jerusalem.[1] Although there was great animosity between the two groups, Samaritans and Jews had a common heritage. The Samaritans were descendants of those who had intermarried with the mixed population that settled in Israel after the Assyrians conquered the northern kingdom (2 Kings 17:24-41).[2] But when Philip went to proclaim the good news, he found that crowds "with one accord listened eagerly" (v. 6) as he proclaimed the Messiah to them. As a result, there were a number of outward signs of

---

1. Talbert, *Reading Acts*, 69.

2. Talbert, *Reading Acts*, 69.

healing (similar to those experienced by the apostles) that served to validate his mission.[3] While Luke mentions that some people were set free from unclean spirits and other cures, notably he also states that there was great joy in that city (v. 8).

Luke uses the word "joy" (or "rejoicing") on a number of occasions in Acts to refer to the response of the people. This joy is not to be confused with happiness or well-being, and it certainly is not related to success. On some occasions when Luke uses the word it is during, or immediately after, difficult circumstances. In Acts 5, for instance, having been flogged, the apostles "rejoiced that they were considered worthy to suffer dishonor for the sake of the name" (5:41). As the people discovered, joy is not a possession. It cannot be bought or sold. It cannot be achieved or given as a reward. Rather, joy is an inner gladness or delight that comes from experiencing the presence of God as Holy Spirit. Here, the joy of the people was a reflection of the fact that God was present and at work through the preaching of Philip.

The Process of Change, 8:9-25

Among those who heard Philip preach was a man named Simon who had been a magician in the city. Because he practiced sorcery, he was considered to be wise and many people thought he was someone great. They revered him and even equated his power with the power of a god. Along with other men and women, Simon listened to Philip and was so convinced by his teaching that, along with others, he was baptized. He then stayed with Philip and "was amazed when he saw the signs and great miracles that took place" (v. 13). This power was clearly greater than any power he had ever seen.

When the apostles in Jerusalem heard that people had accepted Philip's message about the word of God, they sent Peter and John to lay hands on them so they could receive the Holy Spirit. For, as Luke explains, they had only been baptized in the name of the Lord Jesus, and apparently, "the Spirit had not come upon any of them" (v. 16). This seems an extraordinary statement! How is it to be understood? It has been suggested that perhaps the Spirit did not come to the Samaritans until after Peter and John came in order that the Samaritans could be viewed as fully incorporated into the

---

3. Garland, *Acts*, 83.

community of Jerusalem Christians who received the Spirit at Pentecost.[4] If it is assumed that Jerusalem continued to have an important place in Luke's narrative, and that it was somehow important for the Samaritans to be united with the believers in Jerusalem, this might be plausible. Yet, while continuity with Jerusalem may have been important to Luke, it seems more likely that Luke was once again indicating that the Spirit of God is not predictable and does not always work in a recognizable pattern.[5] Nor is the Spirit under the authority of the church or any individual.

Peter and John laid hands on those who had been baptized and prayed for them, and those people then received the Holy Spirit. When Simon saw that the Spirit was given through the laying on of hands, he offered money to Peter and John, saying, "Give me also this power so that anyone on whom I lay my hands may receive the Holy Spirit" (v. 19). Peter rebuked him sharply, saying,

> "May your silver perish with you, because you thought you could obtain God's gift with money! You have no part or share in this, for your heart is not right before God. Repent therefore of this wickedness of yours, and pray to the Lord that, if possible, the intent of your heart may be forgiven you. For I see that you are in the gall of bitterness and the chains of wickedness." Simon answered, "Pray for me to the Lord, that nothing of what you have said may happen to me." (vv.20-24)

Down through the ages, the idea of buying or selling church offices (leadership positions in the church) and power became known as "simony," as Simon has been castigated for his ill-timed request. It has even been suggested that Simon did not really believe but simply acted a part and pretended to believe in order to be baptized and perhaps stay in favor with the crowd drawn by Philip's teaching. However, there is no reason to believe that Simon was insincere in his faith or his desire to be baptized. Rather, it may be argued that just as the story reminds us that the coming of the Spirit is solely under the control of God, so conversion and the formation of the spiritual life is the work of God alone.

While it is difficult to evaluate the genuine nature any of religious experience, James D. G. Dunn suggested that Luke's treatment of religious experience in the early church is "inevitably lopsided" and that his

---

4. This view was suggested by G. W. H. Lampe, *The Seal of the Spirit* (London: 1967), 70–72 as cited in Marshall, *Acts*, 157.

5. See discussion about the significance of Jerusalem in Acts 1.

treatment of the Spirit (as of religious experience generally) can only be described as "fairly crude." Likewise, Dunn warned against placing too much emphasis on a particular kind of manifestation.[6] There is not one pattern for conversion. Equally there is not one pattern for receiving the Holy Spirit. As Talbert claimed, "God is free; experience varies."[7] This is an important point. All too often in the history of the church, people have set up standards by which to judge if a person's experience was genuine. However, as the numerous stories of how God has worked among people down through the ages indicate, there are as many ways to encounter God as there are people. In Acts it seems that the response to the message proclaimed by Peter and John was repentance and a confession of faith in the Lordship of Christ and baptism. However, there was no set procedure for receiving the Holy Spirit.

Peter and John claimed that Simon's difficulty was that his heart was not right before God (v. 21). This is another way of saying that he needed to examine his inner motivation. Was he embracing Christian faith in order to gain by it? Talbert has pointed out that "magician was a term of defamation in antiquity," and magicians were viewed as those who were simply seeking to make money.[8] As Talbert has put it, "according to Mediterranean belief, magicians looked for customers, not converts."[9] Did this man think that by embracing Christian faith he would acquire more power, benefit economically, or enhance his own status as he drew attention to himself? The desire for power or personal gain has always been a motivating factor for human beings. The church is not and never will be exempt from those who seek status or desire financial gain. However, these issues have no place in a genuine Christian response. While it is possible to argue that Simon's mistake in offering money for power to heal meant that he was not a believer, his actions may also serve as a reminder that spiritual growth, like conversion, is a process.

There are many stories of those who described coming to Christ over a period of time and, indeed, confirmed through their own experience that conversion is a lifelong process. In his book *Surprised by Joy*, C. S. Lewis described his movement toward God as a long process. He longed for "Joy," as he put it, but struggled to believe in God. He was, in his own mind, a

---

6. James D. G. Dunn, *Jesus and the Spirit* (London: SCM Press, 1975), 190–92.

7. Talbert, *Reading Acts*, 73.

8. Talbert, *Reading Acts*, 70.

9. Talbert, *Reading Acts*, 71.

convinced atheist. Then one day as a student in Oxford, as he was riding in a bus up a hill, he claimed that he realized he had a free choice.

> The odd thing was that before God closed in on me, I was in fact offered what now appears a moment of wholly free choice. In a sense. I was going up Headington Hill on the top of a bus. Without words and (I think) almost without images, a fact about myself was somehow presented to me. I became aware that I was holding something at bay, or shutting something out. Or, if you like, I was wearing some stiff clothing, like corsets, or even a suit of armour, as if I were a lobster. I felt myself being, there and then, given a free choice. I could open the door or keep it shut; I could unbuckle the armour or keep it on.[10]

Lewis claimed that he made the choice to open, to unbuckle, to loosen the rein. Yet this was only the first step in his movement toward Joy. Lewis said that when he was on the bus, he unbuckled the armour and the snowman started to melt, but he realized that more was needed. In time, he realized that the demand was simply "All." He described a scene in his room in Oxford in 1929 when "I gave in, and admitted that God was God, and knelt and prayed: perhaps, that night, the most dejected and reluctant convert in all England."[11]

Lewis was not the first to describe a process of moving toward God or his reluctance to finally give in to God. Nor is he alone in speaking of how it was in stages that he came to belief in God and confess faith in Christ. It is possible to think of growth in faith as a constant process. One is never fully mature in Christ, but always we are growing and becoming.

Reflecting on the story of Simon, we may see him as a person who was desperate to be "somebody" in the eyes of others and therefore willing to offer money to obtain the attention and status he craved. It is also possible that he may have wanted to enhance his income by possessing what he probably viewed as "a new power." On the other hand, he may have been a person who had just embarked on a journey of faith. It would seem that he did not yet understand that the Holy Spirit is not under the control of women and men. When he made his untimely request to Peter, he was harshly rebuked and then called to repentance. His response was to ask for prayer. Tellingly, Ambrose (c. 340–397), the fourth-century Bishop of Milan, noted that Peter condemned Simon's action "and yet did not exclude

---

10. C. S. Lewis, *Surprised by Joy* (London: Collins, 1955/1982), 179.

11. Lewis, *Surprised by Joy*, 182.

him from the hope of forgiveness, for he called him to repentance."[12] It is another reminder that repentance, too, is not a "one-time" event but is best seen as part of continual process for those who seek to be formed into the likeness of Christ. This turning from the "false self" is an ongoing endeavor.

Simon's mistake in offering money for the power he saw at work through Peter and John was not simply thinking he could purchase the power of the Holy Spirit. The real difficulty with his request was his desire for glory. Simon had enjoyed the favor of the people. Perhaps he liked being "somebody" and wanted to continue gathering crowds and being the center of attention. What he did not realize is that human self-worth is not measurable and certainly can't be bought or sold. Human worth is not dependent on the judgment or approval of other people. Everyone is of worth, and everyone has a place in the life of God.

Open Hearts and Hands, 8:26-40

Peter and John returned to Jerusalem, even while proclaiming the good news to many villages of the Samaritans. Philip, on the other hand, was told by a messenger of God that he must go toward the south to the road from Jerusalem to Gaza. Luke offers a reminder that "this is a wilderness road" (v. 26). Having heard the message, without any hesitation Philip got up and went.

The emphasis on receiving and immediately responding to what seems an unreasonable or unusual command is found in other places (Acts 5:20; 10:13; 20:22-23; 21:4-14). Here Luke seems to use the story to point out that the Spirit of God blows where it will, and, when prompted, people must be ready to respond to God's command without delay.

When Philip goes to the wilderness road, he discovers an Ethiopian eunuch. Given that he was from what today would be Sudan, he would have had a darker complexion than Philip.[13] He rode in a chariot that set him apart as a person who had risen to a high rank in the court of Candace. Since he was coming from Jerusalem and reading a scroll, it has been suggested that he was a God-fearer. Yet, having been castrated and thus made "sexless," he may have been considered ineligible for temple worship.

---

12. Ambrose, "Concerning Repentance 2.4.23," in *Ancient Christian Commentary on Scripture, New Testament V, Acts*, ed. Martin, 94.

13. Talbert, *Reading Acts*, 55.

He would have been considered an outcast.[14] As the story unfolds, though, it becomes clear that the gospel really is open to everyone. No one is to be excluded.

Seeing that the man was reading from the scroll, Isaiah 53:7-8 (in the ancient world he would have been reading aloud as he went along), Philip asked if he understood what he was reading. "How can I unless someone explains it to me?" the eunuch asks. This question signals a crucial part of the story, especially if it represents the story of Jesus being proclaimed more

> We are saints a-borning by your grace, O God.
> Without your help we will not become what we long to be.
> This day we pray that you will go on changing us by grace.
> Generate in us a still stronger desire not to be successful but to be faithful.
> Create in us a still greater strength to keep on despite discouragement.
> Fill us with dreams that renew us and others in an age of pessimism and despair.
> Heighten our longing to dare and to be daring.
> Stir within us the deep desire to commune ever more fully with you.
> Through Jesus Christ we pray. Amen.
> —E. Glenn Hinson, "Kindlers and Purifiers of Dreams," *Weavings* 11/3 (May/June 1996): 45.

widely to those who are not strictly Jews. Here Luke is indicating that not only is the gospel for all people, but it is necessary for those who have responded in faith to be ready to explain and interpret the faith to others. In other words, Christian faith is not a religion to practice alone. It is not about fulfilling the perceived demands of a religion; rather it is about relationship with God and with others, regardless of status or position in life. Moreover, there is no such thing as a genuinely purely private faith.

According to the story, the person Philip met in this deserted place realized his need for spiritual accompaniment. He needed someone else to help guide him.[15] Through the years, emphasis has been placed on the need both for guidance in understanding the Scriptures and for help to discover

---

14. Keener claims that Ethiopia here refers to all of Africa south of Egypt, especially ancient Cush and Nubia. He also notes that it is not clear if the eunuch was a proselyte or a God-fearer, though it seems more likely that he was the latter (*Acts: An Exegetical Commentary*, 2:1534–35). See also John B. Polhill, *Acts, The New American Commentary*, vol. 26 (Nashville: Broadman Press, 1991), 223–24.

15. Keener notes that for a member of the royal court to invite Philip to share his chariot was an honor and an act of humility by the eunuch (*Acts: An Exegetical Commentary*, 2:1585).

what it means to be a follower of Jesus Christ. In recent years there has been a renewed interest in the ancient practice of having a spiritual guide, or director, to help those who seek to grow in their understanding and practice of the Christian faith.[16] Some people associate spiritual guidance with the monastic life. However, the existence of many diaries and letters of counsel indicate that many others have practiced spiritual guidance, both formally and informally.

Finding a spiritual guide is sometimes problematic because it is important to have someone who is skilled at listening and able to help another person to discern the way of Christ. Evelyn Underhill, the well-known twentieth-century author who offered spiritual guidance to many through her books as well as through personal contact through retreats, meetings, or correspondence, took several years before she asked Baron Friedrich von Hügel to be her spiritual guide. To her this decision was life changing. Significantly, the fact that he was a Roman Catholic and she was an Anglican was not a barrier. Although he only served as her guide for four years before he died, she claimed later that "she owed him her whole spiritual life."[17]

Significantly, the existence of correspondence from spiritual masters like Baron Friedrich von Hügel enables Christians to benefit from the guidance of those we have never met. Douglas Steere, for example, an American Quaker, benefited greatly from the spiritual counsel of von Hügel. Drawing from von Hügel's writings, Steere wrote later of the four gifts that von Hügel had for Spiritual Direction. First, he had an ability to be "saturated with an awareness that God was at work," that God was "present and operative and laying siege to every soul before, during, and after" any time the spiritual director might have had contact with the person.[18] Second, Steere claimed that von Hügel knew himself to be needy. He spoke often of his need for religion and claimed in a letter to his niece that "I simply cannot get on without it. I must have it to moderate me, to water me down, to make me possible. I am so claimful, so self-occupied, so intense. I want everything my own way."[19] The third gift of a spiritual director was

---

16. See the discussion on guidance in Acts 1.

17. Margaret Cropper, *Evelyn Underhill* (New York: Harper, 1958), 68, as cited in Douglas Steere, ed., *Spiritual Counsel and Letters of Baron von Hügel* (New York: Harper and Row, 1964), 21.

18. Friedrich von Hügel, *Letters to a Niece*, ed. Gwendolyn Greene (London: Dent, 1928), xxv, as cited in in Steere, ed. *Spiritual Counsel and Letters of Baron von Hügel*, 10.

19. Steere, *Spiritual Counsel*, 11.

a profound reverence for the differences in souls. Finally, as Steere pointed out, von Hügel considered himself "expendable as a spiritual guide."[20]

The emphasis on spiritual guidance being for a limited period of time and the stress that the guide only contributes to what God is already doing seems applicable to this story of Philip and the Ethiopian. In this account, when they met on the road, the Ethiopian was already searching the Scriptures. In other words, here Luke emphasizes that God was already at work. Philip, according to Luke, was drawn to the place by God and joined the man in his chariot. He then explained the Scripture with an emphasis on Christ as the "suffering servant" in whom one may find life as a gift from God.[21]

Having discussed the Scriptures, when they came to water the official said, "Look, here is water! What is to prevent me from being baptized?" (v. 37). He commanded the chariot to stop, and both he and Philip went down into the water. When they came up out of the water, Luke says that the Spirit of the Lord snatched Philip away. This was again Luke's way of emphasizing that the focus was not on Philip. Neither the spiritual guidance nor the baptism was Philip's achievement. This was the work of God as Holy Spirit.[22] Philip then "found himself at Azotus" and began proclaiming the good news there (v. 40). Again, the attention is not on Philip but on the message that he is proclaiming, and he is wherever the Spirit of God prompts him to be.

It has been rightly said that this story begins as the story of someone else's journey, and then we realize that it is our own journey.[23] For this is the story of all those who, in hearing the word of God, recognize the need to repent and be baptized. While the story of the Ethiopian eunuch is far from our own time and experience, in a strange way we may also identify with a pilgrimage in the wilderness, hungering for deeper meaning to life. In a reflection on this text, John Mogabgab described it in this way:

> The spiritual journey draws us away from the comfortable and familiar places, perspectives, and people that have shaped our lives. Whether we leave behind the beauty, power, and privilege of a regal court, the security and collegial support of a particular career track, or the hearth like assurance of long-held beliefs, the path of pilgrimage is marked by increasing

---

20. Steere, *Spiritual Counsel*, 12.

21. Talbert, *Reading Acts*, 77–78.

22. Talbert, *Reading Acts*, 90.

23. Richard I. Pervo, *Luke's Story of Paul* (Minneapolis: Fortress Press, 1990), 33.

vulnerability. The protective layers of habit that have insulated us from our yearning slowly fall away. Ironically, however, sometimes the most obvious places to go for the wholeness we seek turn out to be wrong destinations. The eunuch may have discovered this at the Temple in Jerusalem, with its limited access to Gentiles. We meet the same irony in churches suspicious of spiritual questions, clergy untutored in spiritual guidance, friends or family fearful of the challenges our growth places before them.[24]

In addition to calling us to reflect on the ways and means of conversion, and the need for continual spiritual nurture and growth, this story also signals that the gospel is being taken step by step to the ends of the earth (Acts 1:8). Philip is still close to Judea and has not gone to the ends of the earth. So perhaps the story is also a reminder that the ends of the earth sometimes come to us.[25] Mission is on our doorstep, and spiritual growth can be associated with the wilderness at hand.

For years my parents invited international students who attended the agricultural college in our town to come to our house on Christmas Day. As children, we often resented what seemed to us to be an invasion of strangers in our home on what we thought should be a special family day. I see now that my parents, indeed, believed that "the ends of the earth" were in our town, and as Christians our responsibility was not only to "go" but to say "come" as we extended hospitality to them. I suppose my parents were also trying to teach us that part of being "Followers of the Way" meant that we were alert to God's call to meet people who might be in a wilderness place far away from home. It is not always necessary to climb into a chariot with someone; perhaps we need only open the door or dare to cross the road.

This multi-layered story from Acts is rich in meaning, and there is no "right way" of interpreting or understanding it. Rather, by the very nature of the story, the reader is challenged, in imagination, to have the courage to respond to the call of God even when it means leaving our own places of comfort or threatens the security we have established for ourselves and to which we often cling. In responding to the call of God either to give or to receive spiritual counsel, we will discover that we are led along many different wilderness roads. We must step forward with courage and hope,

---

24. John S. Mogabgab, "Along the Desert Road: Notes on Spiritual Reading," in E. Glenn Hinson, *Spirituality in Ecumenical Perspective* (Louisville, KY: Westminster/John Knox Press, 1993), 181.

25. Talbert, *Reading Acts*, 87.

knowing that God as Holy Spirit is always at work before us as well as in and through whatever we feel we are prompted to undertake for the sake of the gospel.

Drawing Your Own Conclusions

1. In what ways might we be drawn by God to take the seemingly unattractive or unprofitable route?

2. What aspect of Christian compassion or pastoral urgency does the image of Philip running in the desert present?

3. Why is it that the work of the Spirit is neither something we can presume or take for granted?

4. Why does increasing vulnerability always mark the pilgrimage of faith?

Acts 9

A Change of Mind and Heart, 9:1-19a

We have already seen that while he carefully notes signs of the work of the Holy Spirit eliciting and evolving faith, Luke is keen to emphasize that no two conversions are the same. While some people assume that a genuine conversion is equated with a radical and dramatic experience, this is not always the case. Moreover, for Luke, the Christian experience begins with repentance, a turning away from sin and turning toward God, but this is not a singular event. As already noted, conversion may best be described as an ongoing process. To put it another way, we are constantly turning toward God and growing in the likeness of Christ. Lest this sound as if conversion is merely an arbitrary, individual choice, it is evident that for Luke, this change is never something that we bring about for ourselves. It is always God's work. Faith is God's gift, and our response is obedience to God's call.

Since conversion is a change of mind and heart, we may note again that the idea of such change by "conversion" is embedded in many stories throughout Acts. (For instance, there is a kind of "conversion" of Peter, and later the apostles in Jerusalem, to accept Gentiles and the conversion to new faith of the Samaritans and the Ethiopian eunuch.) Charles Talbert has pointed out that there are many different kinds of conversion outlined in ancient literature and suggested that in looking at the pattern presented by the author, this narrative may be seen not only as (1) a conversion in which "Christ changes an opponent to an ally" but also as (2) a conquest in which Christ overpowers an enemy and as (3) a commissioning in which Christ chooses an emissary.[1] In many ways, all three patterns are woven together

---

1. Talbert, *Reading Acts*, 83.

in the overall experience of Saul, the persecutor of the church who became the Apostle Paul, servant of Jesus Christ.

The story of Saul unfolds as a great drama, and over the years it has often been put forward as a template for a true conversion experience. There is no evidence, however, that Luke intended to set down a pattern to be followed. Indeed, while attention is given to Saul's dramatic experience, in looking at this chapter alone we are confronted by two conversions.[2] The first is the obvious story of Saul who, on the Damascus road, is blinded by light and brought to his knees. He hears his name called out, which echoes some of the "call" narratives found in the Old Testament.[3] He responds, "Who are you, Lord?" The voice replies, "I am Jesus, whom you are persecuting. But get up and enter in the city, and you will be told what you are to do" (vv. 5-6). This is followed by the dramatic scene of Saul being led by the hand back into Damascus, where for three days he was without sight and neither ate nor drank. He was, indeed, brought to his knees.

While we tend to concentrate on the story of Saul, equally important in Acts 9 is the second conversion story of a disciple, Ananias, who lived in Damascus. Notably, in the narrative Ananias also hears the voice of the Lord speaking to him in a vision; and in the language of the Old Testament, when he hears his name called, he responds, "Here I am." He is hesitant, however, especially when he hears that he is to go to a street called Straight and, at the house of Judas, look for a man from Tarsus called Saul (v. 11). Ananias knows all about Saul and the trouble he has caused for the "saints in Jerusalem" (v. 13). Yet he is told by the Lord that this one who has been seen as an enemy will be "an instrument," and "I myself will show him how much he must suffer for the sake of my name" (vv. 15-16).

While Ananias is unsure and very afraid of Saul, in the end he responds in obedience to the word and goes to find Saul. Luke emphasizes that the decision to go to Saul was not Ananias's choice. Rather this is a picture of a disciple of Jesus who is submitting his will to the will of God, and in doing so he takes another step in his own conversion process. Moreover, the fact that he is guided by the Spirit and trusting in God is apparent in the way that he greets Saul as "Brother, Saul." His greeting is not only a witness to the way the Spirit of God breaks down barriers of fear, enmity, or suspicion

---

2. D. G. Peterson claims that there are three conversions in Acts 8-10: the Ethiopian, Saul, and Cornelius (*Acts*, 299). However, if conversion is a lifelong process, these experiences might be better described as a first step in the process of conversion.

3. Genesis 22:11; 31:11.

that may have previously existed; it also reflects the profound change of heart and mind that Ananias has experienced, too.

The Tables Are Turned, 9:19b-25

When Saul meets Ananias, the scales fall from his eyes, he is baptized, and he begins to preach in Damascus. Luke says that for several days, Saul was with the disciples in Damascus and proclaiming Jesus in the synagogues, saying, "He is the Son of God" (v. 20). After some time, there was a plot against him, and because they were watching the gates night and day, a plan was hatched that Saul would be lowered down in a basket through an opening in the outer city wall. While a serious point is being made about Saul's acceptance as a believer and his dependence on fellow disciples to help him escape, this is also a humorous scene. Moreover, it is another example of "those who have exalted themselves being humbled" (Luke 14:11; 18:14). This was the mighty Saul who had gone into people's homes ruthlessly searching for men and women who claimed the name of Jesus in order to arrest them. This was Saul who had approved of the stoning of Stephen. Now the tables have turned. Here Saul is portrayed as vulnerable and needing help to escape from those who want to kill him. Amazingly, he is helped by the very people he had persecuted as they slip him out of harm's way under the cover of darkness, in a basket of all things.

Encouragement and Comfort of the Holy Spirit, 9:26-31

Saul goes to Jerusalem, but the disciples there are fearful. His reputation has gone before him, and no one can quite believe that he has changed. They assume that this is a ruse to catch them out and arrest more believers. Barnabas, however, comes to Saul's aid as a spiritual friend. Barnabas, Luke says, took Saul and brought him to the apostles, described to them what had happened to Saul on the Damascus Road, and reported how Saul had spoken boldly in Damascus in the name of Jesus.

Again, Luke's emphasis on the support of other believers is to be noted. There is no such thing as a believer alone, but only in community with others. While later, Saul (or Paul as he will become known) becomes the prominent figure in Acts, here he is the one who is dependent on the companionship and acceptance of Barnabas, "the encourager." It is

Barnabas who, in befriending Paul, helps to validate his calling to others, thereby furthering the cause of proclaiming the gospel to the ends of the earth.

The emphasis on spiritual friendship is important in the history of Christian faith. Jesus, according to the Gospels, was not simply master and Lord to his disciples; he also called them friends. We can imagine that they often laughed together and shared moments of disappointment and grief. They worshipped and prayed together. It also seems apparent from the Gospels that Jesus was a friend to those outside the circle of the twelve. Opponents of Jesus claimed that he was "a friend of tax collectors and sinners" (Luke 7:34). They meant it as a slur, but it was a statement about the way the love of God breaks down all barriers.

Reflecting on the way we understand Jesus as friend, and through him the friendship we may have with others, theologian Jürgen Moltmann claimed that the titles the church has used for Jesus usually reflect

> One there is, above all others,
> well deserves the name of Friend;
> his is love beyond a brother's,
> costly, free, and knows no end.
> They who once his kindness prove
> find it everlasting love.
>
> Which of all our friends, to save us,
> could or would have shed his blood?
> But our Jesus died to have us
> reconciled in him to God.
> This was boundless love indeed;
> Jesus is a Friend in need.
>
> When he lived on earth abasèd,
> "Friend of sinners" was his name.
> Now above all glory raisèd,
> he rejoices in the same;
> still he calls them brethren, friends,
> and to all their wants attends.
>
> Could we bear from one another
> what he daily bears from us?
> Yet this glorious Friend and Brother
> loves us, though we treat him thus:
> though for good we render ill,
> he accounts us brethren still.
>
> O for grace our hearts to soften!
> Teach us, Lord, at length to love.
> We, alas! forget too often
> what a Friend we have above:
> but, when home our souls are brought,
> we will love you as we ought.
>   —John Newton (1725–1807), "One there is,
>   above all others," in *Baptist Praise and Worship*
>   (Oxford: Oxford University Press, 1991), 855.

"title of office," such as prophet, priest, or king. "But the fellowship which Jesus brings men [people], and the fellowship of people with one another to which he calls, would be described in one-sided terms if another 'title' were not added, a title to describe the inner relationship between the divine and the human fellowship: the name of friend."[4]

Over the years, many spiritual writers have written about God's friendship with us through Jesus and about our friendship with one another through the Spirit of God. Aelred of Rievaulx (c. 1110–1167), a twelfth-century Cistercian monk in Yorkshire, believed that friendship might flourish at different levels and to different degrees. However, a spiritual friendship is different from a relationship that draws people together just because they have certain things in common or similar likes or dislikes. He claimed that "the spiritual, which we call true friendship, is desired not with an eye to any worldly profit or for any extraneous reason, but for its own natural worth and for the emotion of the human heart, so that its fruit and reward is nothing but itself."[5] He was making the point that this friendship flourishes beyond the bond that all Christians may know in Christ. Hence, this kind of friendship, on a higher plane than simply commonality of belief, would exhibit four qualities: loyalty, right intention, discretion, and patience.[6]

In the Celtic tradition, a spiritual friend became known as an *anam ċara*, a soul friend.[7] In the early Celtic church, this was a person "who acted as teacher, companion or spiritual guide."[8] Such friendship, according to John O'Donohue, was an act of recognition and belonging," and within it you feel able to "share your innermost self, your mind and your heart."[9] The friendship is "creative and critical; it is willing to negotiate awkward and uneven territories of contradiction and woundedness."[10] John Cassian (c. 360–435) claimed that through such bonding there is a friendship "no

---

4. Jürgen Moltmann, *The Church in the Power of the Spirit* (London: SCM Press, 1977), 115.

5. Aelred of Rievaulx, *Spiritual Friendship*, ed. Marsha L. Dutton, trans. Lawrence C. Braceland, S.J. (Collegeville, MN: Liturgical Press, 2010), 64.

6. Stephanie Ford, *Kindred Souls: Connecting through Spiritual Friendship* (Nashville: Upper Room, 2006), 40–41.

7. John O'Donohue, *Anam Ċara* (London: Bantam Books, 1997), 35.

8. O'Donohue, *Anam Ċara*, 35.

9. O'Donohue, *Anam Ċara*, 35.

10. O'Donohue, *Anam Ċara*, 49.

interval or time or space can sever or destroy, and what even death itself cannot part."[11]

Today when people speak of having a spiritual friend, a spiritual guide, or a spiritual director, there is sometimes an emphasis on the person having been specially trained to listen to another. A spiritual guide is not the same as someone who is trained in counseling. However, we often think of a spiritual director functioning in a more formal role. Yet there are examples of spiritual friendship where the relationship is based on mutuality and where guidance emerges through dialogue and exchange. This does not mean that there is not a level of friendship with many others, but with some there is a bond that is somehow different. According to his good friend Eberhard Bethge, Dietrich Bonhoeffer distinguished between levels of friendship, indicating that some were spiritual friends, by speaking of friendship plural and singular. In the plural he meant friends who were companions, people whom he related to and on whom he could rely. However, a singular friendship seems to have been one with whom he had a particular relationship or bond in Christ. Bethge, who was certainly one of Bonhoeffer's "singular friends," received a letter written on Bonhoeffer's birthday in 1941, in which he described friendship to Bethge in this way:

> Our letters on the occasion of today are notably similar in their content. This is surely not a coincidence, and confirms that things really are the way it says in the letters. You wished me, among other things, good, stimulating friends. That is a good thing to wish, and today it is a great gift. But the human heart is created in such a way that it seeks and finds refuge in the singular rather than in the plural. That is the claim, the limit and the richness of genuine human relationship, to the extent that it touches on the area of individuality and to the extent that it rests essentially on loyalty. There are individual relationships without loyalty and loyalty without individual relationships. Both are to be found in the plural. But together (which is seldom enough!) they seek the singular, and happy is he who "succeeds in this great luck."[12]

Reflecting on the emerging friendship of Barnabas and Saul that is revealed in this story, it appears that it was Barnabas who reached out to

---

11. John Cassian, Conference 16, chapter 3, "How friendship is indissoluble," in *Conferences*, at *New Advent*, newadvent.org/fathers/350816.htm.

12. Eberhard Bethge, *Friendship and Resistance: Essays on Dietrich Bonhoeffer* (Grand Rapids, MI: Eerdmans, 1995), 87–88.

Saul and affirmed the validity of Saul's testimony to a newfound faith in Christ. In later chapters, as we shall see, Barnabas travels with Paul and serves alongside him as a "co-worker." While we often highlight the work of Paul, it seems evident that the friendship with Barnabas was important to his spiritual pilgrimage. While it is impossible to measure the depth of their relationship, one can imagine that Barnabas was loyal not only to friends but also to Christ and therefore became a person Paul trusted. This part of the story ends with Saul eventually being brought to Caesarea and sent off to Tarsus, when the disciples realized that he was in danger.

Two Disciples: Aeneas and Tabitha, 9:32-43

Having seen Saul off to Tarsus, Luke now turns attention back to Peter and the mission into Judea and Syria.[13] First Peter went to Lydda, where he found "a man named Aeneas, who was paralyzed and had been bedridden for eight years. When Peter saw him, he said to him, 'Aeneas, Jesus Christ heals you; get up and make your bed!'" Immediately the man got up, and when the residents of Lydda and Sharon saw him, they all "turned to the Lord" (vv. 32-35). While Peter was still at Lydda, word came to him from believers in Joppa that "a disciple whose name was Tabitha, which in Greek is Dorcas," who was "devoted to good works and acts of charity" had become ill and died (vv. 36-37). When he arrived there, the believers had already washed her and laid the body in a room upstairs. All the widows were crying and showing the tunics and other clothes that she had made for them while she had been with them. "Peter put all of them outside, and then he knelt down and prayed." Then he turned "to the body and said, 'Tabitha, get up'" (v. 40). She opened her eyes, and seeing Peter she sat up. Luke says that he gave her his hand and helped her up. Then calling the others, he showed her to be alive. This became known throughout Joppa, and Peter stayed in Joppa for some time with Simon, a tanner.

The stories told by Luke echo stories found in Luke's Gospel (Luke 8:41-46 and 5:17-26), which may be a way of emphasizing that the followers of Jesus were, in the power of the Spirit, doing the work of Jesus. Furthermore, the stories are similar to the Old Testament stories of Elijah and Elisha and underscore that Peter is "in line with prophetic succession."[14] As we have seen in other places, the "miracle stories" are also a

---

13. It is sometimes suggested that this story reflects a turning point in Luke's account as he begins to talk about advancing the mission into Judea and Syria (Peterson, *Acts*, 319).

14. Talbert, *Reading Acts*, 91.

way of pointing to the fact that nothing, not even the power of death, can hinder the work of God as Holy Spirit. Moreover, Peter is again not seeking to draw attention to himself, nor is he merely interested in convincing new adherents to join "a movement." His ministry is in the name of Jesus and to the glory of God.

Looking more closely at the stories, some have been suggested that parallels have been drawn between the story of Tabitha and the story of Jesus raising the daughter of Jairus, a leader of the synagogue (Mark 5:21-43) with the words "Talitha cum" meaning "little girl, get up." Here, however, we do not have a child but an adult who (in a manner reminiscent of the raising of Lazarus by Jesus) has been called back to life. Tabitha was an adult, and she is named by Luke as a disciple (v. 36) who was being mourned by other adults. Dickerson underscores the point that the word, which is translated here as "devoted," is in other places translated as "full." For instance, this is the same word that is used to describe Stephen (6:8). He was "full of faith and the Holy Spirit," just as Barnabas was "full of the Holy Spirit and faith" (11:24). So here, Luke names Dorcas as a disciple and says that she was "full" of good works and acts of charity.[15] Certainly there is evidence of the work of the Holy Spirit through her, as was noted by her contemporaries in their testimony to Peter.

This section ends with Luke pointing out that Peter stayed in Joppa for some time with "a certain Simon, a tanner." The mention of Joppa may serve as a reminder of the Old Testament story of Jonah, who fled to Joppa to avoid going to Nineveh to preach to the Gentiles. Here we have Peter, who is prompted to leave Joppa to preach the gospel to the Gentiles.[16] It is worth noting that often the attention is placed on the "miracle" of healing and new life. Yet the most extraordinary fact is that Peter is in Joppa and reaching out to a woman and to a tanner. Luke seems to be emphasizing the change that is taking place in Peter's attitude toward what that might have been considered unclean. In these stories, Luke mentions that Peter had contact with someone who has been paralyzed, a woman who had been ill and died, and he goes to stay at the home of a tanner. Since mention is made that Peter was staying with a tanner, it appears that he was not concerned with keeping the purity laws. (Leviticus 11:39-40 claims that anyone who touches the carcass of an animal will be considered "unclean.")

---

15. Febbie C. Dickerson, "Acts 9:36-43, The Many Faces of Tabitha, a Womanist Reading," in Mitzi J. Smith, ed., *I Found God in Me: A Womanist Biblical Hermeneutics Reader* (Eugene, OR: Wipf and Stock, 2015), 296–312.

16. Garland, *Acts*, 105.

Perhaps Peter no longer feels that "the cleanliness laws apply to Jews and to those who associate with them."[17] In the next chapter, Peter will need to see that the purity laws do not apply when it comes to contact with Gentiles either.

Draw Your Own Conclusions

1. How do Christians today deny the inclusivity of the gospel?

2. How might our engagement with an ongoing process of daily conversion help us to change our minds about certain beliefs or customs?

3. How would you describe the characteristics of a "singular" friend? Why is such spiritual friendship important?

---

17. While Luke does not contain Mark 7:15, Talbert suggested that "some such value judgment" must underlie Peter's action in Joppa (*Reading Acts*, 92).

Acts 10

Invisible Walls, 10:1-33

Conversion is never simple. While it is easy to speak about having a change of mind and heart, the truth is that "being changed" often occurs over time rather than in an instant. As we have already noted in our discussion in chapter 9, conversion is a process that is probably never complete either. It often takes time to let go of certain ideas or practices that have long been part of our way of life. In the case of Peter, it is evident from Luke's Gospel account that Peter underwent challenges to his preconceived ideas of faith in God from the time he first met Jesus (Luke 5:1-11; 9:18-27; 22:31-34; 24:12). At Pentecost, Peter witnessed the outpouring of the Spirit and rejoiced over the work of God among all the people. He saw for himself the response of the women and men in Samaria to the proclamation of the word. He stayed at Joppa with Simon, a tanner, seemingly without any regard for ritual cleanliness. Yet he could not have imagined the further change that would take place. For while it appeared that he was open to change, Peter was still very much a person shaped by his own time and culture. He was a Jew and had been brought up to keep the traditions of the faith he was taught, even as one from Galilee. Indeed, since the early Christians (known as "people of the way" or "followers of the Nazarene") were still loyal Jews, it is of no surprise that they held to many of the practices of Judaism, i.e., regular worship in the synagogue, times of prayer, and dietary laws, and indeed many considered them a sect of Judaism until about the third century.[1]

---

1. Mikeal C. Parsons notes that Christianity seen as a movement within Judaism is the perspective of Christian, Jewish, and Roman characters in Acts and of the narrator himself (Parsons, *Acts* [Grand Rapids, MI: Baker Publishing, 2008], 162).

So that is the context for Peter's momentous step associated with Cornelius, a centurion of the Italian cohort. A Gentile, it appears that Cornelius was a God-fearer in that Luke describes him as a "devout man who feared God with all his household," and "he gave alms generously to the people and prayed constantly to God" (v. 2). One afternoon at three o'clock, he had a vision in which he saw an angel of God coming to him and calling him by name, to which he replied, "What is it, Lord"? The angel responded, "Your prayers and your alms have ascended as a memorial before God. Now send some men to Joppa for a certain Simon who is called Peter. He is lodging at the home of Simon, a tanner" (vv. 4-5). When the angel left, Cornelius called two of his slaves and sent them to Joppa with "a devout soldier" (v. 7).

The next day at noon, as they were on the way to Joppa, Peter went up on the roof to observe the time set for midday prayer, and while there he became hungry. As food was being prepared, Luke says, Peter fell into a trance and had a vision of being offered food that was unacceptable under Jewish food laws. In his dream, he heard a voice saying, "Get up, Peter, kill and eat" (v. 13). But Peter said, "By no means, Lord; for I have never eaten anything that is profane or unclean." Then the voice said, "What God has made clean, you must not call profane" (v. 15). Luke says this happened three times, and then "the thing was suddenly taken up to heaven" (v. 16).

Waking from his dream, Peter was unsure and puzzled. How was he to understand this directive not to think of things as profane or ritually unclean? As Peter puzzled over the meaning of the dream, Luke claims that Peter was told about three men looking for him. The Spirit of God said to him, "Now get up, go down, and go with them without hesitation; for I have sent them" (v. 20). So Peter went down to the men and said, "I am the one you are looking for; what is the reason for your coming?" They answered, "Cornelius, a centurion, an upright and God-fearing man, who is well spoken of by the whole Jewish nation, was directed by a holy angel to send for you to come to his house and to hear what you have to say" (vv. 21-23).

Peter invited them in and gave them lodging. The next day he went with them to see Cornelius. On his arrival, Cornelius met him and fell at his feet to worship him. Peter was quick to tell him to stand up, saying that he was "only a mortal" and not God (v. 26). Peter then went into the home of Cornelius and found a group assembled there. He told them that although it was against the Jewish law for him to associate with or visit a Gentile, God had told him not to call any person profane or unclean.

Cornelius then explained to Peter that "a man in dazzling clothes" had told him that he should send for Peter, who was in Joppa staying at the home of Simon the tanner (v. 30). Therefore, he said, "You have been kind enough to come. So now all of us are here in the presence of God to listen to all that the Lord has commanded you to say" (v. 33). Here, too, it is significant that the focus is on being in God's presence and hearing what the Lord has commanded Peter to say. There is a remarkable openness on the part of those who had gathered to hear the word.

The story is not just about looking beyond barriers; it is also a reminder that prayer may change minds and hearts. Luke claims that both Cornelius and Peter had been seeking God in prayer when they were challenged to reach beyond what they knew. Both came to a new realization of the limitless nature of the love of God, a love that they soon realized could break through any barriers men and women might erect or seek to maintain.

Reconsidering the immensity of God's love calls us to consider surmounting barriers that have often been erected by culture or even long-held religious beliefs. Yet, as Peter realized, if the gospel is to be proclaimed to others, there must be a willingness to let go of old ideas, revered traditions, and customs. Inevitably, this process of letting go may cause great discomfort and a feeling of displacement. To admit that some of our long-held views may not accord with the teachings of Jesus calls for humility, courage, and a readiness to repent. All too often, the church has been slow to reflect, unreservedly, God's all-embracing love and acceptance. Lamenting segregation and the fact that many congregations in the USA resisted integration in the 1950s, New Testament scholar Frank Stagg wrote,

> It is possible that future historians may declare the irony of ironies—that in the middle of the twentieth century, fight promoters and baseball managers did more for emancipating the negro than did churchmen. To say that they have done it for money removes none of the sting, for it is a humiliation if a pagan for money effects good which a Christian fails to effect for love. There are even evidences that segregation may make its last stand in the churches.[2]

Progress is always slow. However, if the church is to change and the gospel is to be proclaimed to all people, it must begin with individuals repenting and, in humility, seeking to make amends. A friend who grew

---

2. Frank Stagg, *The Book of Acts: The Early Struggle for an Unhindered Gospel* (Nashville: Broadman Press, 1955), 123–24.

up in a farming community in the Deep South of the United States told me that she grew up with prejudice against African Americans. When as an adult she realized the bias she had carried, she was determined to make a new beginning. There was a man, John, who had worked on the farm for many years. Since she was a young girl, my friend said that the practice had always been to serve his plate and he would eat in another place, but certainly not at the table with the rest of the family. When she recognized her own prejudice, she said that on one occasion when she was cooking the midday meal, she told her mother that John would eat at the table with them. Her mother protested, but my friend stood firm, and from that day forward John took his place at the table, and nothing was ever said about it again. It was a small step, but it was a step forward in the joy of knowing life in God.

I don't imagine that for any of us just one small step would signal complete change in our lives. All of us know how deep prejudices can go. Just when we think we are free, we realize that we continue to be bound to culture in one way or another. Even in the church we may find that at times we do not reflect the height, depth, and breadth of God's love. To the contrary, we even think of God's love in a limited way. As the hymn writer put it,

> But we make His love too narrow
> By false limits of our own;
> And we magnify His strictness
> With a zeal He will not own.[3]

Part of growing up in Christ is being willing to have all our religious and cultural norms challenged and duly changed. As Peter discovered, reaching beyond barriers that culture or religious belief have created for us is difficult and demanding. Moreover, it requires a willingness to venture, whatever the risk.

In a powerful and moving autobiographical account, Harry Bernstein described his experience growing up in a Lancashire Mill town in the north of England just before WWI. He said it was as if they had an "invisible wall" down the middle of the road where they lived: the Jews on one side and the Christians on another. While they were neighbors, they did not mix with one another. However, his sister Lily defied her parents and began

---

3. F. W. Faber, "There's a Wideness in God's Mercy," in *Baptist Praise and Worship*, music edition (Oxford: Oxford University Press, 1991), 878.

to allow a young man, Arthur, who lived just across the road to walk her home from school. Eventually, much against their parents' wishes, Arthur and Lily slipped away and married. Bernstein stayed in touch with Lily and Arthur, and he says that Arthur told him there should never be two sides to the street, claiming, "But it's all wrong. It isn't like that at all. We're not very different from one another, not different at all in fact. We're all just human beings with the same needs, the same desires, the same feelings as one another. It's all a lie about us being different."[4]

Culture will often try to erect barriers based on race, creed, religion, gender, sexual orientation, or ethnicity. As Peter discovered, it takes courage to move outside our own comfort zones. In his willingness to obey God, however, Peter demonstrated that for a follower of Jesus, nothing must hinder the proclamation of God's love to all people.

An Invitation to All, 10:34-48

Peter began his speech with the bold affirmation that he could "truly understand that God shows no partiality, but in every nation anyone who fears him and does what is right is acceptable to him" (vv. 34-35). He then proclaimed the message that Jesus Christ is Lord of all. In the speech, he once again told how Jesus came "preaching peace" but was "put to death by hanging him on a tree" (vv. 36-39). Even so, "God raised him up on the third day and allowed him to appear, not to all people, but to those who were chosen by God to be witnesses and who ate and drank with him after he rose from the dead" (vv. 40-41). Peter told the crowd how Jesus "commanded his witnesses to preach to the people and to testify that he is the one ordained by God as judge of the living and the dead" (v. 42). And then he asserted, "All the prophets testify about him that everyone who believes in him receives forgiveness of sins through his name" (v. 43).

Peter's speech boldly proclaimed that salvation was for all people not just for a select group. It was not just for the Jews but for the Gentiles, too. As he was speaking, Luke claimed, "the Holy Spirit fell upon all who heard the word" (v. 44). When the Jewish Christians saw that the gift of the Spirit was poured out also on Gentiles, they were astounded. But when Peter saw that they had received the Holy Spirit, he asked if any could withhold baptism from them. The answer was no. "So he ordered them to be baptized in the name of Jesus Christ" (v. 48). There was to be no question over the

---

4. Harry Bernstein, *The Invisible Wall* (London: Random House, 2007), 283.

matter. Moreover, it was evident that they knew that they were completely accepted by God (in a way demonstrated by Peter). He accepted their invitation to stay with them for a few days.

This is the fourth time Luke mentions the outpouring of the Spirit in Acts (see also Acts 2:1-4; 4:31; 8:17). Luke includes this scene perhaps to stress once again that conversion comes about through different forms. The story

> All that kills abundant living,
> let it from the earth be banned:
> pride of status, race or schooling,
> dogmas that obscure your plan.
> In our common quest for justice
> may we hallow brief life's span.
>
> You, Creator God, have written
> your great name on humankind;
> for our growing in your likeness
> bring the life of Christ to mind;
> that by our response and service
> earth its destiny may find.
> —Fred Kaan (1929–2009)
> Verses 4 and 5 from "For the Healing of the
> Nations," hymn in *Baptist Praise and Worship*
> (Oxford: Oxford University Press, 1991), 961.

is sometimes thought of as the conversion of Cornelius. However, as we have seen, Peter too had to turn from old beliefs and ideas, as did the Jewish believers who were amazed that the Gentiles should receive the Holy Spirit and be baptized. "God works in mysterious ways, God's wonders to perform."[5]

Draw Your Own Conclusions

1. What difference might it make if we listened to others with an acknowledgement that God is present with us, too? How might this affect conversations with friends, family, or in a community of faith where there are differences of opinion?

2. How do we accommodate those who are avowedly open to God but who see things differently from us?

---

5. Paraphrased from William Cowper's 1773 hymn "God Moves in a Mysterious Way."

3. Why is the work of the Spirit sometimes feared as a disruption to a settled faith and practice?

4. What is the connection between conversion and pilgrimage in the spiritual quest?

Acts 11

Accountability and Discernment within Community, 11:1-18

The apostles and believers in Jerusalem heard that Peter had been preaching to Gentiles and that the Gentiles, as a result, had accepted the word of God. They were troubled, however, by the news that Peter had been eating with Gentiles, as they felt that this was wrong. For them, this was not simply a matter of wanting to cling to an old custom. They believed their status and right standing before God required that they remain ritually pure. They could not accept Gentiles into table fellowship, even if they said they believed that Jesus was Lord, unless they followed the dietary laws and also practiced circumcision.

When Peter went to Jerusalem, he did not try to defend his views with a long speech. There was no attempt to try to give the apostles and believers in Jerusalem a great theological explanation; perhaps he did not have one. Rather, he simply told them the story of what happened "step by step" (v. 4). He emphasized that he, too, had been hesitant about mixing with Gentiles. He had always believed that one should stand apart. Yet he could not resist the work of the Spirit through a vision. "The Spirit told me to go with them," he said, "and not to make a distinction between them and us" (v. 12). He then described how he went to the home of Cornelius, and as he was speaking there, "the Holy Spirit fell upon them just as it had upon us at the beginning" (v. 15). Peter then claimed that he "remembered the word of the Lord, how he had said 'John baptized you with water, but you will be baptized with the Holy Spirit'" (v. 16). At this point in his story, Peter turns the question back on the apostles: "If then God gave them the same gift that he gave us when we believed in the Lord Jesus Christ, who was I that

I could hinder God?" (v. 17). The apostles had no answer to that question. Indeed, Luke simply says that they fell silent and then praised God, saying, "Then God has given even to the Gentiles the repentance that leads to life" (v. 18). This was, indeed, a watershed moment in the life of the church.

Given their strongly held beliefs on religious purification and the need for separation, it seems surprising that the apostles and believers in Jerusalem changed their minds so readily, abruptly, and unanimously. Why were they convinced that what Peter did was correct? First, the fact that Peter was willing to tell his story reflected a willingness to be accountable to his community. He did not brashly or arrogantly claim that he had discovered truth and that this was truth whether they liked it or not. Rather, it appears that he came to Jerusalem, met with the believers, and humbly told the story. Luke says that he told them "step by step." In other words, he left nothing out but explained how the events unfolded. The story of his own experience of and witness to the work of the Holy Spirit was the basis for his reasoning.

"Accountability" is an important word in spiritual formation. When an individual comes to faith in Christ, he or she is not simply declaring belief in a set of doctrines or ideas. Rather, a person is entering into relationship with Christ and with the body of Christ, the church. Those who are part of a community of faith are knit together in the love of Christ. In both joys and sorrows, they are held in relationship. In Christian

> Christianity means community through Jesus Christ and in Jesus Christ. No Christian community is more or less than this. Whether it be a brief, single encounter or the daily fellowship of years, Christian community is only this. We belong to one another only through and in Jesus Christ.
>
> —Dietrich Bonhoeffer, *Life Together* (London: SCM Press, 1976), 10.

community, this means there are no lone believers but rather that believers are always held in relationship with Christ and one another. This does not mean that accountability should be seen as an attempt by members of the community to monitor beliefs or behaviors or to make ultimate judgments concerning what is considered right or wrong. Genuine accountability begins with obedience to God and ultimately rests with God alone.

On a personal level, many Christians find it helpful to be accountable to a spiritual director or soul friend. Again, this does not mean that the person is turning the responsibility for actions or decisions over to another person. Rather, it is more about recognizing that openly talking to someone in trust about the struggles faced in seeking to follow Christ is a way of continually realigning our deepest desire to be for God. As we have already seen, many Christian writers have spoken of the need for a soul friend, or *anam čara*, to whom one may turn for advice and counsel.[1]

As Peter described his own experience honestly and with openness, he did not try to hide his hesitation to go to Cornelius or his initial abhorrence at the thought of breaking the dietary laws. However, equally important in the discernment process of the believers was the fact that the apostles appear to have listened to the story carefully. In the hearing and the telling of the story, the Spirit of God was able to move among them, and the apostles, like Peter, had a change of mind and heart. This, too, was a story of conversion. It was not just conversion of an individual but a first step in radical change within their institutional life as they had known and accepted it. This is an important picture presented by Luke and is significant in spiritual formation. Not only can individuals change, but groups also may change their minds, even to the point of repenting for past wrong. It is difficult to do, and many churches might not have the courage to acknowledge that they have been clinging to beliefs that reflect culture rather than the light and love of God. However, this passage is a challenge to Christians to continually examine the way that, individually or corporately, they may be captive to culture.

I have a friend who for many years felt that God was calling her to serve as a pastor of a church. While she wanted to be obedient to God, she did not respond at first; her initial reaction, much like Peter's, was "by no means." She had been brought up to believe that women should not preach or teach. She had never seen a woman serving as a deacon or as a pastor. She could not imagine ever serving God in that way. Over time, however, with the encouragement of other Christians around her and with an ever-present sense of calling from God, she began to see that God does not make distinctions. As Paul wrote, "There is no longer Jew or Greek, there is no longer slave or free, there is no longer male and female; for all of you are one in Christ Jesus" (Gal 3:28). In my friend's case, the dissolution of boundaries enabled her to respond to a call to serve God.

When Peter told his story of the work of God as Holy Spirit among the Gentiles and the Christians in Jerusalem listened carefully, there could be no argument. "They praised God, saying, 'Then God has given even to the Gentiles the repentance that leads to life'" (v. 18).

---

1. See the discussion in Acts 9.

Generosity of Spirit, 11:19-30

After the persecution of Stephen, as Luke reminds us, the believers had scattered to Phoenicia, Cyprus, and Antioch. While some of those who moved did not speak of their faith except to Jews, Luke makes it clear that there were a few among them who spoke to the Hellenists.[2] While Luke is adamant that this was God's work, he also insists that the spread of the gospel was with the approval and under the direction of the Christians in Jerusalem, who sent Barnabas to Antioch to meet with the believers there and to nurture them in the faith (v. 22). Here Luke notes again Barnabas's credentials and suitability for the task: it was simply that he was "a good man, full of the Holy Spirit and of faith" (v. 24). His approach was to nurture and encourage the believers in their newfound faith. "When he came and saw the grace of God," Luke says, "he rejoiced, and he exhorted them all to remain faithful to the Lord with steadfast devotion" (v. 23).

Luke indicates that while Barnabas was among them, "a great many people were brought to the Lord" (v. 24). It seems that Barnabas realized that he needed help in sharing the faith with others. So he went to Tarsus to find Paul and brought him back to Antioch. They stayed there working together for a year. Significantly, Luke says that it was in Antioch that the disciples were first called Christians (v. 26). The emphasis on the name "Christian" is worth pondering. Up to this point, the followers of Jesus have been called "saints" (9:13, 32, 41), "disciples" (6:2, 7; 9:1, 10, 26, 36), "believers" (4:32; 5:14; 10:45), the church/assembly (2:46; 5:11; 8:1, 3; 9:31; 11:22, 26), the brothers (1:15; 10:23; 11:1), and followers of "the way" (9:2).[3] Now, onlookers have given the followers of Jesus a new name that signifies that they are followers of Christ. This emphasis on claiming the name of Christ has been lost in our modern parlance. In the ancient world, to "claim the name" of the person meant that one was not only a follower of that person but had committed his or her allegiance to that individual. Today, people may say "I am Christian" and simply mean that they were brought up in a Christian home or attended a Christian school or church as a child. In other words, to say "I am a Christian" does not always signify an allegiance to Christ. To be willing to be identified in this way surely meant that early Christians had made a particular commitment.

---

2. This is further evidence that the mission to Gentiles began before Paul's journey (Talbert, *Reading Acts*, 103).

3. Talbert, *Reading Acts*, 105.

A fourth-century theologian, Gregory of Nyssa (c. 335–395), emphasized both the privilege and importance of the name when he wrote,

> Our good Master, Jesus Christ, bestowed on us a partnership in his revered name, so that we get our name from no other person connected with us, and if one happens to be rich and well-born or of lowly origin and poor, or if one has some distinction from his business or position, all such conditions are of no avail because the one authoritative name for those believing in him is that of Christian. Now, since this grace was ordained for us from above, it is necessary, first of all, for us to understand the greatness of the gift so that we can worthily thank the God who has given it to us. Then, it is necessary to show through our life that we ourselves are what the power of this great name requires us to be.[4]

Being named as a follower of Christ was not only to be considered a privilege, but with it came responsibilities, too. So when a prophet, Agabus, came from Jerusalem to Antioch and "predicted by the Spirit" that there would be a great famine over all the world, the Christians in Antioch determined that according to their ability, each would send relief to the believers in Judea (vv. 27-30). They discerned that the Holy Spirit inspired Agabus's word, and as a result they were under an undeniable imperative to act and to share.

It is noteworthy here that Luke reported the word of prophecy from Agabus as being "predicted by the Spirit." While grain shortages were a common occurrence in the Roman world, Agabus was not simply making claims based on what he had surmised from his own observation. Rather, he was being led by the Spirit to make this claim to the believers in Antioch. The fact that the believers responded not only illustrates their desire to share with one another but also indicates "their full participation in the church of the apostles" and testifies to their understanding of the unity of Jews and Gentiles as followers of Christ.[5] It shows as well their recognition that personal property was to be understood in a different way.[6]

This story highlights the immediate response of Christian people to the needs of others and once again underscores the issue of a Christian response

---

4. Gregory of Nyssa, "On Perfection," *Fathers of the Church: A New Translation* (Washington, DC: Catholic University of America, 1947), 58-95, as cited in *Ancient Commentary on Scripture*, ed. Martin, 148.

5. Talbert, *Reading Acts*, 106.

6. See the discussion in Acts 2.

to wealth. In Luke's view, material goods are never to be hoarded and kept for one's own needs; rather, a generous response is required of Christians. Over the years, I have sometimes heard Christian people say, "Charity begins at home." They mean that they must see to their own needs before the needs of others. Yet I have also seen Christians respond generously to the needs of others. I know one congregation who, when they heard of a disaster in another part of the world, immediately decided that (in addition to other personal donations) they would give all of the regular offering received by the church on that particular Sunday. It seems that they, like the Christians in Antioch, realized that if they were to claim the name of Christ, they must live with a generosity of spirit and give with glad hearts.

Draw Your Own Conclusions

1. Where should Christians draw the line between collective and personal accountability before God?

2. To what degree does spiritual formation mean knowing that "the truth will set you free"?

3. What "name" do you identify with as a follower of Christ?

Acts 12

Surrender—The Most Truly Christian Prayer, 12:1-5

Having celebrated the joy of believers working and sharing together, the story turns back to the ongoing struggle with opposing factions in Jerusalem. Luke says that King Herod "laid violent hands upon some who belonged to the church" (v. 1). James, the brother of John, was killed by the sword (which probably means that he was beheaded). Strangely, this story is told briefly. No reason is given for James's death other than the fact that he bore the name and also bore the cost of discipleship. In Luke's account, it is Passover, the feast of unleavened bread, the day when Jews celebrated deliverance from bondage in Egypt. Ironically, on this day when he should have been celebrating freedom, Peter was arrested on the orders of King Herod and handed over to four squads of soldiers to guard him.

The story of a powerful person seeking to build his power base and willing to do anything to curry favor with one group over another is never a surprise. History is riddled with the tales of tyrants and bullies who not only spread lies but often used the tactic of "divide and conquer" in order to stay in power. This seems to have been the case with Herod Agrippa I, who served as king of Judea from AD 41 to 44.[1] Although the situation seemed desperate, Luke says that while "Peter was kept in prison, the church prayed fervently to God for him" (v. 5). The sceptic might well ask, what is the point of prayer when someone is in prison and surrounded by four squads

---

1. Herod Agrippa I (c. 10 BC–AD 44), king of Judaea (AD 41–44), was a diplomat who, through his friendship with the Roman imperial family, obtained the kingdom of his grandfather, Herod I, the Great (*Encyclopaedia Britannica*, https://www.britannica.com/biography/Herod-Agrippa-I).

of soldiers? Surely, even the most fervent prayers could not change this situation. Do Christians really think that prayer can help in desperate situations? If prayer does not change things, why pray?

In his classic work, *Prayer: A Study in the History and Psychology of Religion*, Friedrich Heiler claimed that prayer is "the central phenomenon of religion, the very hearthstone of all piety."[2] After studying various forms and ways of praying, Heiler concluded by saying that in its essence, prayer is a "living communion" of people with God. He wrote, "Prayer is, therefore, a living communion of the religious man [person] with God, conceived as personal and present in experience, a communion which reflects the forms of the social relations of humanity."[3] Moreover, citing the "golden mouth" orator, John Chrysostom (c. 347–407), Heiler concluded that "there is nothing more powerful than prayer and there is nothing to be compared with it."[4]

Most people would agree that prayer is, or should be, at the heart of relationship with God. Vast tomes have been written on prayer, often with suggestions on "how to improve your prayer life." Some authors suggest that what is needed is more stillness, contemplation, and silence in the midst of busy lives. After all, they claim, how can anyone hear God speaking in the midst of the cacophony of demands in daily life? Others argue for meeting God in the midst of our busyness. Prayer can be offered at any time or any place because God is always near, though we may not always acknowledge God's presence.

Yet, no matter how many books are written about the various approaches to prayer or ways of praying, the question that remains is the one that became the title of a book by Peter Baelz, *Does God Answer Prayer?*[5] From a Christian perspective, the answer to that question is simple: God answers prayer. God is a desiring God and longs to be in relationship with those whom God loves. However, that does not mean that whatever we ask for in prayer will be given to us. Prayer is not like putting money in a slot, pushing a button, and expecting to get the bar of chocolate that we selected. Rather, we should see prayer in the context of relationship with God who loves us and in whom we may trust. Writing about prayer, Glenn

---

2. Friedrich Heiler, *Prayer: A Study in the History and Psychology of Religion* (London: Oxford University Press, 1932), xiii.

3. Heiler, *Prayer*, 358.

4. Heiler, *Prayer*, 363.

5. Peter Baelz, *Does God Answer Prayer?* (London: Darton, Longman and Todd, 1982).

Hinson claims that "surrender—putting one's life at God's disposal—is the most truly Christian prayer."[6] This was the nature of Jesus' prayer in the garden of Gethsemane. Moreover, as Hinson declares, we do not reach that point of surrender by habit; "most of us will have to grow toward a life of utter abandonment to God."[7]

We are not told the content of the community's prayer when they prayed fervently to God for Peter in prison. Did they ask that Peter be strengthened or comforted? Did they ask that he be released and spared any punishment? Did they pray that Herod would change his mind? Perhaps what mattered most was not the content of their prayers but the desires of their hearts. Our yearning is to be attuned to the yearning of God. Again, as Glenn Hinson has put it, we are to "join our love energies with the love energy of God."[8]

God Specializes in the Impossible, 12:6-17

Meanwhile, as the community prayed, Luke says that in order to ensure that he did not escape, Peter was bound with chains and slept between two soldiers (v. 6). At this point the scene becomes quite comical. Although Peter has already seen what prayer can do, he is not himself depicted as being in prayer. He is not alert, watching, or waiting on being rescued by God. He is asleep. Luke says that an angel of the Lord appeared in the cell and had to tap Peter on the side to wake him (v. 7). He does not imagine that he will be rescued from prison. The angel has to shake him from his slumber!

As if to emphasize Peter's lack of expectation of being rescued, we are told that the angel literally had to get him dressed by instructing him on what to do: "Fasten your belt and put on your sandals . . . . Wrap your cloak around you and follow me" (v. 8). In something of a daze, perhaps almost like sleepwalking, according to Luke, Peter followed the angel of the Lord and imagined that he was seeing a vision (v. 9). It was not until he found the gates opened and he was walking down a lane, after the angel left him, that he realized his actual deliverance from imprisonment.

---

6. E. Glenn Hinson, *The Reaffirmation of Prayer* (Nashville: Broadman, 1979), 119.

7. Hinson, *The Reaffirmation of Prayer*, 119.

8. This is a phrase often used by Dr. Hinson in his lectures and writing on prayer. See, for instance, E. Glenn Hinson, "On Coping with Your Anger," in *Anger Weavings: A Journal of the Spiritual Life* 9/2 (March/April 1994): 37.

Putting aside the rather comical scene of a sleepy Peter being told how to dress by an angel and then being led to freedom, one may also ponder how many times Peter looked back and recalled a moment of deliverance known only in hindsight. Perhaps this is often the way. While going through particular situations in life, we may not perceive how God is at work. Sometimes, only when we have come through a difficult period do we realize the work of God. It is often only with hindsight that we can trace the way of God in our lives or in our life together with others.

The humor of the way Peter was delivered is carried over into the next scene when Peter, having been rescued, makes his way to the house of Mary, the mother of John (whose other name was Mark), where many people had gathered to pray. Peter knocked on the outer gate, and a young woman, Rhoda, came to see who was at the gate. She was so overjoyed at hearing his voice that she rushed back to tell the others without opening the gate. The other believers gathered there immediately claimed that she must be out of her mind. They, too, had not expected an answer to their prayers—at least not quite like that. Meanwhile, Peter continued to knock. Finally, they opened the door and he came in, spoke to them, and explained that the Lord had delivered him. Then, instructing them to tell James and the believers, he went to another place.[9]

This story of escape may be Luke's attempt to reassure and to remind his community that nothing can stand in the way of God's power. Over the years, many Christians have found this difficult to believe. I am reminded of the story of an African American Baptist woman, Nannie Helen Burroughs (1879–1961). Educator, orator, social activist, civil rights worker, and Baptist leader, Burroughs worked tirelessly for a fair and equitable society. She was particularly concerned for young African American girls who faced not only racism in society but also issues of gender equality. While Burroughs endured great opposition, even from other Christians, she would not be deterred. When others told her that establishing a school for poor children would be impossible, she replied, "We specialise in the impossible."[10] Her belief was rooted in the notion that God was indeed

---

9. I. Howard Marshall suggests that James was the brother of Jesus (Marshall, *Acts*, 210–11).

10. E. L. Harrison, *The Dream and Dreamer: An Abbreviated Story of the Life of Dr. Nannie Helen Burroughs and the Nannie Helen Burroughs' School* (Washington, DC: Nannie Helen Burroughs Literature Foundation, 1966), 9, as cited in Opal V. Easter, *Nannie Helen Burroughs* (New York: Garland Publishing, 1995), 62.

able to do abundantly far more than anyone could ever imagine (see Eph 3:20-21).

The mention of two women at this point in Luke's narrative is notable. Both were clearly considered part of the fellowship of believers, though we may assume that Rhoda and Mary, the mother of John Mark, are probably different in terms of age and status. While it has been suggested that Rhoda serves rather like the figure of a "running slave" in a Greek comedy, it is not necessary to see her simply as a character that heightens the excitement or suspense of the scene.[11] Rather, both Rhoda and Mary may be recognized as members of the community of faith. Rhoda knew Peter's voice and was "overjoyed." Moreover, Ben Witherington has suggested that the prayer meeting at Mary's home may have been a women's prayer meeting, and the fact that she was holding a prayer meeting while there was opposition speaks of her courage.[12] Obviously, Peter was aware of the need for secrecy and for his own removal to another place, and tellingly, James (the Lord's brother) was not there.

Reflecting on this text, it is evident that prayer is not about throwing up our requests (or endeavoring to do so in a particular form or pattern) and then receiving the outcome that we requested. Rather it is about our surrender and our trust in God. The challenge Luke brings to us is this: Should Christians continue to believe that God answers prayer even when things seem impossible? Perhaps, as the story teaches us, we are to recall that God "specialises in the impossible." For not only is the word unfettered but also the Spirit is not barred by human (or even superhuman) forces arrayed against the gospel.

The Strength of Humility, 12:18-25

The story of Peter's escape was no doubt intended to encourage and bring hope to Luke's community. As Luke has noted elsewhere in Acts, if something is done that is only of "human origin," then it will not succeed (5:38). So the people were not to despair. While at times, tyrants rule over people, bullies do not have the last word (Luke 1:51-52). Still, the violence does not end immediately. When Herod found that Peter was missing, he called the soldiers who were supposed to be guarding him and ordered that they be put to death. Luke says that Peter left Judea and went to Caesarea.

---

11. See the discussion in Talbert, *Reading Acts*, 109.

12. Ben Witherington III, *Women and the Genesis of Christianity* (Cambridge: Cambridge University Press, 1990), 214.

Then, as if to underscore that no one should ever think of himself or herself too highly before God, Luke describes the death of Herod.[13] On an appointed day, Herod put on his royal robes and went out to address the people. The crowd that had gathered shouted, "The voice of a god and not of a mortal" (v. 22). And immediately, because he had not given the praise to God, Luke says that an angel of the Lord struck Herod down and he was eaten by worms and died. Luke intends for this story, which is similar to one found in the *History of Josephus*, to be a strong warning against thinking that anyone can ever take the place of God.[14] It is not just a warning to rulers or political tyrants who sometimes try to "lord it over" others. The boss at work, co-workers, family members—anyone who feels he or she has some measure of power—may begin to try to use that power to their own advantage. This is also an ever-present, subtle danger, even in a Christian community.

Knowing how power is often used to control or for selfish gain, and recognizing that the grasping of power is a denial of our human status before God, we see that a constant theme in Christian spirituality is the need for humility. Noting the detrimental consequences of the lack of humility on the spiritual life of a believer and on the spiritual life of a community as well, Benedict of Nursia in the fourth century offered his community some advice on the "steps of humility." Among other things, he insisted that anyone seeking humility should "keep the fear of God" always before his or her eyes and put God's will before personal will and desires. He claimed that a humble person should seek to be obedient and want to serve others; a truly humble person should always follow the common rule that Jesus gave to his disciples—to "think of others as better than oneself." Moreover, someone seeking humility must be aware of their own shortcomings and sins and confess them regularly to God.[15]

At its root, genuine humility is intentionally not thinking of oneself better than others. Or perhaps we may say that those who are humble know themselves, and they do not try to be anyone else. Writing about integrity, Thomas Merton claimed that perfect humility and perfect integrity coincide; "the two turn out to be practically the same thing."[16] Merton argued

---

13. Talbert, *Reading Acts*, 110.

14. See Josephus, *Antiquities*, 19.8.2, 349–50, as cited in Talbert, *Reading Acts*, 110.

15. Benedict, "Steps of Humility," chapter 7, *The Rule of St. Benedict*, 16–20.

16. Thomas Merton, *Seeds of Contemplation* (Wheathampstead: Burns and Oates, 1962), 75.

that a truly humble person would not be looking to see what someone owns or what they eat or drink or "what they hang on the walls of their houses."[17] Nor will they pretend to be somebody they are not. To do so, Merton claimed, is to suggest that you believe that "you know better than God who you are or who you ought to be."[18]

Merton realized that even to discuss humility is to admit that it is never possible for a person to be fully humble on earth, because the moment that person asserts that he or she is acting honestly and simply being himself or herself, that person is open to the accusation of pride. Merton warned that if you seek to be nobody but the person that God made you to be, you will be "made to feel that your honesty is only pride."[19] He wrote,

> This is a serious temptation because you can never be sure whether you are being true to your true self or only building up a defence for the false personality that is the creature of your own appetite for esteem. But the greatest humility can be learned from the anguish of keeping your balance in such a position: of continuing to be yourself without getting tough about it and without asserting your false self against the false selves of other people.[20]

In writing his autobiography, Glenn Hinson echoed the emphasis given to humility by his friend Thomas Merton. Claiming that he had learned in life that "wholeness and holiness require transparency and honesty," Hinson said that he spent many of his early years "trying to wear an image" that he thought people wanted to see.[21] As he began to read the Classics of Christian Devotion, he said that he was confronted by his "double-mindedness and play-acting." Especially, he said that when reading Søren Kierkegaard's *Purity of Heart*, he began to realize that his ability to "will the one thing" was hindered by his "false self."[22] Hinson concluded by saying that he had been helped also by the anonymous writer of the fourteenth-century work *The Cloud of Unknowing*, who defined humility as

---

17. Merton, *Seeds of Contemplation*, 76.

18. Merton, *Seeds of Contemplation*, 76.

19. Merton, *Seeds of Contemplation*, 77.

20. Merton, *Seeds of Contemplation*, 77.

21. E. Glenn Hinson, *A Miracle of Grace* (Macon, GA: Mercer University Press, 2012), 381.

22. Hinson, *A Miracle of Grace*, 381.

being able "to have a proper self-estimate, aware both of one's neediness and of God's infinite compassion."[23]

Having pointed to the dangers of asserting self over God, Luke ends Acts 12 by saying simply that "the word of God continued to advance and gain adherents" (v. 24). Barnabas and Saul then returned to Jerusalem and took with them John, whose other name was Mark (v. 25).

> Lord, You have taught us to love humility, but we have not learned. We have learned only to love the outward surface of it—the humility that makes a person charming and attractive. We sometimes pause to think about these qualities, and we often pretend that we possess them, and that we have gained them by "practicing humility."
>
> If we were really humble, we would know to what an extent we are liars!
>
> Teach me to bear a humility which shows me, without ceasing, that I am a liar and a fraud and that, even though this is so, I have an obligation to strive after truth, to be as true as I can . . . . You, Lord, were humble. But our humility consists in being proud and knowing all about it, and being crushed by the unbearable weight of it, and to be able to do so little about it . . . . For true humility is, in a way, a very real despair: a despair of myself, in order that I may hope entirely in You.
>
> —Thomas Merton, *Thoughts in Solitude*
> (Tunbridge Wells: Burns and Oates, 1958), 63–64.

Draw Your Own Conclusions

1. Is prayer more about giving ourselves to God rather than changing situations or trying to change others around us?

2. Does the sense of "specializing in the impossible" shape our understanding of God and help us to form our prayers?

3. How are humility and power opposites in Christian life and spiritual formation?

---

23. Hinson, *A Miracle of Grace*, 382.

Acts 13

The Intimacy of Relationship in Christ, 13:1-3

Acts 13 begins with a gathering for worship in Antioch. As they gathered, the group was led by prophets and teachers whose diversity is noted by Luke: "Barnabas, Simeon who was called Niger, Lucius of Cyrene, Manaen a member of the court of Herod the ruler, and Saul" (v. 1). Luke says that while they worshipped, the Holy Spirit told them to "set apart for me Barnabas and Saul for the work to which I have called them" (v. 2).

There are several observations to make from this brief scene. First, by naming the different individuals, Luke stresses that the community of faith was composed of people from different places and with different backgrounds. Second, the prompt to commission Barnabas and Saul by the laying on hands came from the Holy Spirit. They did not put themselves forward. Those who had gathered believed that this was God's will. Finally, their commissioning took place within the context of prayer and fasting. Neither Saul and Barnabas nor the church were launching out on a mission plan with set goals and objectives. They had no consultants to advise them on strategy or budget, and they did not have a long-range plan. Rather, they believed that God had called them, and after fasting and praying, the group "laid their hands on them" before sending them out (v. 3).

The practice of the laying on of hands was not unique to Christians. It was used in Judaism for "blessing, healing or the appointment of certain functions" but, according to Everett Ferguson, would "hardly constitute a basic element of Jewish practice."[1] In tracing this practice in the Christian tradition, what is perhaps more important is the way that the laying on of

---

1. Everett Ferguson, *Baptism in the Early Church: History, Theology and Liturgy in the First Five Centuries* (Grand Rapids, MI: Eerdmans, 2009), 187.

hands, or in certain circumstances the raising of hands, was associated with prayer and offering a blessing. There are examples in the Gospels of Jesus offering a blessing as he either touched or raised up his hands in blessing (cf. Mark 10:13-16; Luke 24:50).[2] There is no suggestion that by touch alone one may bring about healing or transfer power to another. Rather, the imposition of hands was seen as a prayer.[3] For Luke, this act of commissioning (with the invocation of God's blessing on Saul and Barnabas by such a diverse group of believers in Antioch) was further indication that the mission of the church was God's work.

Seeing and Not Seeing, 13:4-12

Now that the group has been sent out by the Holy Spirit, Luke offers a few details about their travel. Luke says that Saul, Barnabas, and John, who was also with them, went down to Seleucia and from there they sailed to Cyprus (v. 4). When they arrived at Salamis, they taught in the synagogues, perhaps to fulfill the idea that the gospel was to go to the Jews first. When they had gone through the whole island as far as Paphos, they encountered a Jewish false prophet, a magician named Bar-Jesus or Elymas who was with the proconsul, Sergius Paulus. This official summoned Barnabas and Saul and wanted to hear the word of God (vv. 6-7). It was a common practice at that time to have astrologers who claimed that they could give guidance by reading the stars. It appears that Saul and Barnabas immediately detected that Elymas, an aid to the proconsul, was a sorcerer and not an honest person.

The story is filled with irony. While he claimed to be able to see, namely, to prophesy and discern, and had the name Bar-Jesus (Son of Joshua or Son of the Savior), he was not a follower of Jesus, and he could not see. Rather it was Saul who had eyes to see and identified this man as a false prophet. Saul (whom Luke now says is also known as Paul) wasted no time in calling him out. He looked at Elymas intently and claimed that he was "a son of the devil," an "enemy of all righteousness, full of all deceit and villainy" (v. 10). After naming his dishonesty, Saul (from now on known as Paul) told him that he would be struck blind and would not be able to see for a time. Immediately, "mist and darkness came over him," and the man groped around and needed someone to lead him by the hand (v. 11).

---

2. Everett, Ferguson, "Laying on of Hands: Its Significance in Ordination," *The Journal of Theological Studies* 26/1, New Series (1975): 1–12, www.jstor.org/stable/23959782.

3. Ferguson, *Baptism in the Early Church*, 786.

Luke portrays this confrontation with Elymas as a powerful witness. Charles Talbert claimed that in a power-oriented society, change of faith has to be power-demonstrated.[4] In other words, the believers had to show that through the power of the Holy Spirit at work, mighty deeds could be done. Perhaps, too, Luke wanted to show that the gospel was not just accepted by the poor but also by many wealthy and powerful individuals, including ones with status. It is notable that Luke claimed that Paul was filled with the Holy Spirit and could see the man's heart. The implication is that by the power of the Spirit he could discern the man's motives and could see that he was not truthful, honest, or genuine.

Discernment is an important part of growing in Christian faith. Not only is it necessary to be able to listen to what individuals are saying, it is also important to determine whether their words reflect a commitment to God or if they are driven by other motivations. Discernment in Christian spirituality is about determining whether a person (in this case Elymas) seeks to reflect the mind of Christ or if the person's attitudes, actions, and decisions are driven by personal gain. Elymas was focused on himself and concerned that he might lose his position and status if the proconsul believed what Paul and Barnabas were saying. As it happened, the proconsul did believe when he saw what had happened (v. 12), and the truth of the gospel broke through the deception that was put in its way.

Filled with Joy and with the Holy Spirit, 13:13-52

At this point in the narrative, there seems to be a reconfiguration of the roles played by Barnabas and Paul. Previously, Barnabas seems to have taken the lead in the missionary travels. Barnabas had been a follower of Jesus longer than Paul. He was among the first to sell his field, bring the proceeds, and lay the money at the apostles' feet (4:36-37). It was Barnabas whom the apostles in Jerusalem sent to Antioch (11:22), and later he went to find Saul to bring him to Antioch (11:25). It seems that up to this point, Barnabas (perhaps as the one who had come to Christ earlier than Saul) took an appreciable role in the work of proclaiming the gospel. Now, however, there seems to be a shift in positions. Luke begins to focus on Paul as the main spokesperson on the missionary journeys. It is also at this point that John, who was also called Mark, leaves them and returns to Jerusalem. No

---

4. Talbert, *Reading Acts*, 119.

reason is given for his departure. Only later do we realize that John Mark's decision to leave them was a sore point for Paul and proved to be the cause for some dissension.

From Paphos, they set sail and came to Perga in Pamphylia and then on to Antioch in Pisidia. On the Sabbath day they went to the synagogue and sat down. After the reading of the law and prophets, the officials of the synagogue invited them to speak. It was Paul who stood up and spoke. Talbert has suggested that the sermon may be divided into several parts: The first section (vv. 16b-25) describes Jesus as the one descendant of David and the one in whom "salvation history culminates."[5] In section 2 (vv. 26-37), Paul claims that Jesus was rejected because the Jews did not understand their own Scriptures. He was crucified, taken down from the tree, and buried but was undeniably raised, testified to by many witnesses and by the Old Testament Scriptures. The final section emphasizes that in the experience of the risen Lord, we see the fulfillment of the promises of God, the promise of salvation, and the listeners are urged to believe (vv. 38-41). As they went out, they were warned that the prophet Habakkuk had foretold that scoffers would perish because of unbelief (Hab 1:5).[6]

At first there was a positive response to Paul's preaching. They invited him to return the next Sabbath (vv. 42-43). As they left, Paul and Barnabas tried to encourage the many Jews and other devout converts to Judaism who also followed them. The next Sabbath, Luke says, nearly the whole town gathered, but the unconvinced Jews were jealous. Paul and Barnabas were Jews. What Luke means is that those who were "establishment" Jews (rather than Messianists) were jealous, and they "incited the devout women of high standing and leading men of the city" to oppose Paul and Barnabas, with the result that they were driven out (v. 50).[7]

Both Paul and Barnabas spoke out boldly and claimed that it was right that the word should be given first to the Jews, but if they were not willing to accept it, it should now be given to the Gentiles. Luke says that when the Gentiles heard that the gospel was for them, too, "they were glad and praised the word of the Lord" (v. 48). Paul and Barnabas shook the dust off their feet in protest and went on to Iconium (v. 51). With that, the "disciples were filled with joy and with the Holy Spirit" (v. 52).

---

5. Talbert, *Reading Acts*, 120.

6. Talbert, *Reading Acts*, 121.

7. Talbert, *Reading Acts*, 122.

Walk with me, good and loving God, as I journey through life,
May I take your hand and be led by your Holy Spirit.
Fill me, inspire me, free me to respond generously to your call.
For I believe you desire my deepest joy,
And it is only in your company
That my soul will be satisfied
And my life will find its meaning and purpose. Amen.

—Attributed to the Sisters of Notre Dame

In the modern day, we might be tempted to judge whether the mission was "successful" by the number of people who responded. Perhaps we think that Paul and Barnabas were not given a good reception because they were effectively chased out of town. Yet here the emphasis is on the disciples being filled with joy and with the Holy Spirit. Luke reminds the reader again that success in terms of the gospel is not quantified by the world's measurements. Even in the midst of this trouble and difficulty, there is joy. The reason for this is because joy is a sign of the work of the Holy Sprit. Joy comes when there is an awareness of the presence of the Lord. Joy is knowing that in spite of trouble or difficulty, believers have done what they believe God led them to do. We sometimes confuse joy with happiness, but joy is different. That is why we may be joyful even by a bedside in the hospital or at the graveside of a loved one. There can be deep joy even as a person shakes the dust off his or her feet to the howls of a baying crowd. Like peace, joy is a hallmark of a mind "stayed upon God" (Isa 26:3).

Draw Your Own Conclusions:

1. How do we practice discernment in the church today? Can that gift be fostered?

2. What does it mean to live with an open heart and to see the heart of another?

3. Why is "success" not a term to be equated with those who are followers of Jesus?

4. What hinders joy? How do we distinguish it from contentment or satisfaction?

5. What does it mean to say with St. Augustine that "our hearts are restless until they find their rest in God"?

Acts 14

Same Old, Same Old, 14:1-7

Acts 14 begins with Luke's comment, "the same thing occurred in Iconium" (v. 1). He meant that not only did Paul and Barnabas continue to preach and "a great number of Jews and Greeks became believers" but also that some didn't accept the gospel. This caused great division among the people of the city. Luke says that even though they faced opposition, "they remained for a long time" and continued to speak "boldly for the Lord" (v. 3). It is a surprising word. If things were not going well and there was great opposition, many people would have moved on quickly. Yet, as Luke pictures the scene, Paul and Barnabas persevere in the work in spite of opposition.

Perseverance, the ability to "keep on keeping on" through all kinds of trouble for the sake of the gospel, is essential for followers of Jesus. Yet being able to keep going in the midst of trouble is not always easy, especially when day after day it seems that it is the "same old" response to the preaching and the "same old" threats, disappointments, and negative comments. Yet Luke claims that Barnabas and Paul were not willing to pack their bags and leave at the first sign of discouragement or difficulty. If this was the Lord's work and the Lord had called them to undertake it here, they were prepared to stay. The point is that genuine perseverance is not simply rolling up one's sleeves and saying " I will"; rather, it is always linked to a deep sense of trying to carry on doing what God has called us to do in the assurance that if God has led us and called us to the work, God's grace is sufficient to see us through.

Perseverance requires trust in God and also discernment that we are indeed doing what God has called us to do. In other words, perseverance is not just keeping on with the same old, same old simply because we feel that we should try to finish a job to save face. It is not keeping on because a sense of pride will not let us stop doing something or admit we never should have started it in the first place. Rather, perseverance is rooted in a deep sense that what we are doing is what God intends for us to do, and so, in God's strength, we must continue to do it until we discern that we have done all that God wants us to do. Alongside perseverance is the need for constancy, patience, and, as we have noted before, the ability to wait. It also means that while we may not be able to see the results of our labors and may appear to be unsuccessful in the world's eyes, still we continue giving ourselves to the task at hand simply because we believe this is where the Spirit has led us to be and what the Spirit wants us to do. Perseverance requires a careful balance between humility and confidence in God.

Paul and Barnabas persevered in their teaching and preaching, even as the opposition continued against them. However, when they heard that both Jews and Gentiles were stirring up trouble against them and intended to have them stoned, Luke says that the "apostles" (v. 6) fled to Lystra and Derbe, cities of Lycaonia, and to the surrounding country, where they continued to preach and teach. There has been some discussion about the use of the word "apostles" here and in verse 14. Some commentators have drawn attention to the fact that Luke usually reserved the word "apostle" for the twelve people in Jerusalem who were with Jesus during his ministry. Perhaps this reference is used in a general sense of Paul and Barnabas being "sent out" by the church at Antioch.[1]

Saying Yes, 14:8-10

In Lystra there was a man who had never walked since birth. In a parallel of the story of Peter and John healing the man by the "Beautiful Gate" in Acts 3, we find Paul looking intently at the man and then, seeing "that he had faith to be healed," calling for him to stand (v. 9). The emphasis on the man's faith may seem problematic. Did Paul mean that the man had enough faith and he was healed by his faith? What does it mean to have faith? Luke was certainly not suggesting that those who are in need of healing need only have a sufficient amount of faith! Perhaps the point of this story is not really about the healing. Rather, it may be that Luke intended for us to focus on what it means to see faith as a response to God, as total surrender to God. In this way, it could be argued that for those who follow Jesus, faith may lead us to attempt something we feel that we ourselves are unable to

---

1. Marshall, *Acts*, 233–34.

do. ~~The man believed that God (not the disciples) was calling him to stand.~~ He responded to the call. This was his faith. He simply did what he was called to do. ~~He responded to God, and that is the benchmark for Christian service and growth in grace.~~

There are times when those who want to follow Jesus feel that they do not have the ability or strength for a task. However, if we know we are called by God, Luke is suggesting that we are simply to let go and respond in faith, which is God's gift to us. ~~Faith is not something we can achieve or possess or try to hold on to in order to have a sense of security or to perform tasks. The assurance of faith comes as we continue to let go in surrender.~~

> Prayer is two-way activity. First, we speak to God, and then he speaks to us. Simply talk with God—that is the nature of prayer. How great and glorious a thing it is that the most high God in all his majesty so condescends to us poor worms of earth that we may open our mouths to talk to him, and that he delights to listen. Yet more glorious and precious by far it is that he does speak to us, and that we listen to him. . . . Always make a good and hearty "Amen," and never doubt that God hears you and says "Yes!" to your prayer. Further, always bear in mind that you are not standing or kneeling alone but the whole of Christendom is standing or kneeling with you. It is the word of God and his promise which makes good your prayer, not your own devotion.
>
> —James Atkinson, ed., *The Darkness of Faith: Daily Readings with Martin Luther* (London: Darton, Longman and Todd, 1987), 24.

Dag Hammarskjöld (1905–1961), a Swedish diplomat who served as the Secretary General of the United Nations from 1953 to 1961, wrote movingly in his diary (published after his death under the title *Markings*) of the need to surrender always to God. Reflecting on the nature of faith and the need for surrender, he wrote of the struggle that sometimes ensues when a person seeks to say "yes" to God. Drawing on the writings of a sixteenth-century Christian mystic, St. John of the Cross[2] (who claimed that "faith is the marriage of God and the soul"), Hammarskjöld noted that it is not always easy to "let go." He wrote,

Faith *is*: it cannot, therefore, be comprehended, far less identified with, the formulae in which we paraphrase what is.

---

2. St. John of the Cross (1542–1591) wrote a poem known as the "Dark Night of the Soul" and later wrote several books that reflected on the poem.

—*"en una noche oscura"* The Dark Night of the Soul—so dark that we may not even look for faith. The night in Gethsemane when the last friends left you have fallen asleep, all the others are seeking your downfall, and *God is silent*, as the marriage is consummated.[3]

Later, as he wrote of the experience of finally saying "yes" to God, he claimed,

> We act in faith—and miracles occur. In consequence, we are tempted to make the miracles the ground for our faith. The cost of such weakness is that we lose the confidence of faith. Faith *is*, faith creates, faith carries. It is not derived from, nor created, nor carried by anything except its own reality.[4]

Then, in 1958, Hammarskjöld returned to this theme of faith being God's marriage to the soul and wrote this:

> In the faith which is "God's marriage to the soul," you
> are *one* in God, and
>   God is wholly in you,
>   just as, for you, He is wholly in all you meet.
> With this faith, in prayer you descend into yourself
> to meet the Other,
>   in the steadfastness and light of this union,
>   see that all things stand, like yourself, alone before
> God,
>   and that each of your acts is an act of creation, conscious, because you
>   are a human being with human responsibility, but governed, never-
>   theless, by the power beyond human consciousness which has created
>   man [people].
> You are liberated from things, but you encounter in them an experience
> which has the purity and clarity of revelation.
>   In the faith which is "God's marriage to the soul,"
> *everything*, therefore, has a meaning.
> So live, then, that you may use what has been put into your hand . . .[5]

---

3. Dag Hammarskjöld, *Markings*, trans. Leif Sjöberg and W. H. Auden (New York: Ballentine Books, 1964), 81. See also Roger Lipsey, *Hammarskjöld, A Life* (Ann Arbor: University of Michigan Press, 2013).

4. Hammarskjöld, *Markings*, 124.

5. Hammarskjöld, *Markings*, 143.

Hammarskjöld's reflections on faith, which were written over a period of years, remind us that faith is a gift that can only be received and not possessed, a gift only known in complete surrender to God. Perhaps growing in faith is not receiving more of it but deepening in terms of discovering more of life in God as we surrender to God. The emphasis in the story of the man who was healed is not on the miracle of healing but on the fact that the man said "yes" to God in faith. We, too, are called to do the same as we follow Jesus to the place called Gethsemane and pray, "Not my will but thy will be done."

The Wounds of Discipleship, 14:11-20

Seeing that the man who had been unable to walk was now standing, and perhaps because they had heard Paul and Barnabas speaking in Greek, the people assumed that Paul and Barnabas must be gods who had come to them in human form. In their own language, they called Barnabas "Zeus" and Paul "Hermes"; they even began to make preparations to worship them!

It might have been tempting for Paul and Barnabas to take some of the credit for the healing. They might have done it quite subtly by claiming that is it God who heals but at the same time pointing out that they had noticed the man, stopped, and given him their attention. They might have even been tempted to point out that they were close to God and God had chosen to use them. But they did none of those things. As Chrysostom points out, "On all occasions they are free from the lust of glory, not only not coveting but even repudiating it when offered."[6] Indeed, Luke says that the apostles tore their clothes as a sign of their anguish and told the crowd that they were not gods but only mortals. Then, using language that clearly separated the "messengers of God from the presence of God," they explained to them that there was only one true God.[7] And then they called the people to turn away from idols and only worship God.

Even though they were hardly able to contain the excitement of the crowds, Luke claims that the mood soon changed when a group of previously antagonistic Jews from Antioch and Iconium arrived and "won over the crowds" (v. 19). Once again it should not be forgotten that Paul and Barnabas were Jews, too. The distinction to be made between them and the Jews who came to incite the crowds to stone them is that Paul and

---

6. John Chrysostom, "The Apostles Free of the Lust of Glory," in *Ancient Scripture Commentary*, ed. Martin, 176.

7. Jennings, *Acts*, 137.

Barnabas were Messianic Jews. That is, they believed that Jesus was indeed the long-awaited Messiah. But why was there terrible violence by one group of Jews against another group? It has been suggested that perhaps they were both on a similar mission in that they were reaching out to the same group of Gentiles, though with conflicting messages, and so perhaps there were territorial disputes. However, it may have simply boiled down to Christology: the non-Messianics would not accept that Jesus was the Messiah, thus creating tensions, and there is no evidence that active proselytizing was taking place besides the proclamation of Christians.[8]

In the confusion, Paul was stoned, and presuming that he was dead they dragged him out of the city (strangely, Luke does not mention Barnabas). When the disciples surrounded him, he got up and went back into the city. It is astounding that Paul would return immediately to the city. Surely having come close to death, one would not return to the people who had thrown the stones and sought his demise. Yet, as Jennings points out,

> Disciples get hurt. Disciples carry wounds and before we make them metaphysical, drawing them into spiritual alchemy, we must keep them real. We who follow Jesus are working in wounds, working with wounds, and working through wounds. . . . The shared work of disciples in strengthening and encouraging others can make the pain productive, not because we ignore the wounds but rather we come to see them in their true light. These are wounds of Christ that we share for his sake. These are marks of rejections and shame carried for the sake of this world.[9]

It is true that disciples will suffer all sorts of hurt and humiliation. After all, the gospel is at odds with much of what is accepted so easily by culture. Yet this story of such violence that ends in miraculous recovery probably reflects Luke's desire to underscore that while disciples of Christ may suffer for the sake of the gospel, the love of God is never defeated.

Encouragement, 14:21-28

Having been stoned by a crowd, most people would think it best to lie low for a while. Yet Luke says that Paul and Barnabas went to Derbe the next

---

8. See Stephen G. Wilson, "Jewish-Christian Relations 70–170 C.E.," in vol. 3 of *Anchor Bible Dictionary*, ed. D. N. Freedman (New York: Doubleday, 1992), 834–39, as cited in Talbert, *Reading Acts*, 126.

9. Jennings, *Acts*, 139.

day. They wanted to continue to encourage the believers. ~~Having preached in Derbe, they then returned to Lystra before going on to Iconium and then to Antioch~~. At every stop, they "strengthened the souls of the disciples" and encouraged the believers as they reminded them that "~~It is through many persecutions that we must enter the kingdom of God~~" (v. 22). After appointing elders in each church, "with prayer and fasting they entrusted them to the Lord in whom they had come to believe" (v. 23).

Clearly, for early believers, being part of the church was serious business. The people were not just gathering together when they felt like it. They were not volunteering to be part of a club that they had been invited to attend or where they might socialize. They had been called by God to gather together, and this calling demanded their commitment. By gathering together, they were placing themselves in the path of further trouble. There could be no hiding. Luke makes it clear that followers of Jesus must be prepared to face persecution and trouble. In the face of such threats, it is essential to foster leadership. Moreover, order is needed so that commitment may be nurtured and sustained. ~~So, according to the Jewish custom, they appointed elders in each place, though ultimately the believers were entrusted into God's pastoral oversight~~.

Having helped to encourage and organize the churches, Paul and Barnabas made their way back to Antioch. ~~They went through Pisidia and came to Pamphylia and then to Perga, where they spoke the word, and finally moved on to Attalia before sailing to Antioch~~. Arriving at Antioch, they called the church together and "~~related all that God had done with them, and how he had opened a door of faith for the Gentiles~~" (v. 27). This biblical image of opening a door illuminates the significance of it being God's work, with them as instruments in the labor of proclamation and service.

The travel to all the churches and then back to all the churches once again highlights the importance of sharing in life together and being willing to be accountable to others. Paul and Barnabas had not just taken it on themselves to serve; they were not lone missionaries who went out on their own to preach. They had been sent (again, this is perhaps why Luke uses the word "apostles" in this chapter). ~~They undertook a difficult mission and persevered in spite of conflict and opposition~~. They believed that God had "opened a door" of faith for the Gentiles and had used them to proclaim the good news.

Draw Your Own Conclusions

1. How do you understand saying "yes" to God?

2. What are the wounds of discipleship?

3. What does it meant to persevere in the strength of the Lord?

4. How do we handle opposition or misunderstanding as we seek to be about "the work of the kingdom"?

Acts 15

Discerning What Matters, 15:1-21

While Paul and Barnabas were in Antioch, some unidentified men arrived from Judea, claiming that circumcision was necessary for salvation. Paul and Barnabas did not feel that this was needed, and they "had no small dissension and debate with them" (v. 2). As with many Christian communities today, there was a difference of opinion as to what really mattered in terms of faith and practice. Some of the Jews felt that keeping the religious law, especially the practice of circumcision, was important and necessary if one was to be right with God. Barnabas and Paul, with several others, were appointed to go to Jerusalem to discuss these issues with the apostles and elders there.

When they arrived in Jerusalem, they were greeted warmly, but a group of believers who were still practicing Pharisees and felt strongly about keeping the Jewish law spoke up and claimed, "It is necessary for them to be circumcised and ordered to keep the law of Moses" (v. 5). Jennings suggests that while we may understand the conflict as a matter of cultural or theological difference, it was also on another level "an alignment of identity and story for the purpose of control."[1] Essentially, the Judean believers felt that their very identity was connected to the practice of circumcision and that if the Gentiles did not, in a sense, "become Jews" by adhering to this practice as well as following the purity laws, they could not be in fellowship with them as believers. Those, like Paul and Barnabas, who opposed the idea of demanding that Gentiles conform to Jewish law felt that to insist that they do so was to deny that salvation was God's work alone and would set limits to freedom in Christ.

---

1. Jennings, *Acts*, 140.

We may sympathize to some extent with the discomfort and sense of displacement that comes when long-held beliefs are challenged. Yet trying to force others to conform to our understanding of truth is not the way to handle difference. The alternative of simply separating ourselves from those who are not like us (because they refuse to conform) is not the answer either. As Jennings points out, to separate from others is to suggest that some form of segregation will solve problems of difference. However, while people have used spatial segregation (creating distinct geographical spheres), cultural segregation (using boundaries of language, stories, practices), or even "desperate" segregation (a sort of last-resort separation, separating with one's own group for survival), none of these forms of segregation are the answer.[2] As Jennings so aptly put it,

> Difference is best maintained, maintained in its life-giving realities, through communion with others. Only in life, shared, joined and exchanged in desire of being made permanent, can differences emerge in their deepest beauty—as invitations to the expansion of life and love. The Gentiles learn of Israel's story, enter its prayer life, learn its songs and in turn bring into Israel a world of difference that expands the contours of its life with God, and all of this through Jesus Christ, the giver of life.[3]

This is not to suggest that, especially when it comes to religious belief and customs, the "letting go" for the sake of communion with others is simple, easy, or even correct in every instance. However, as already noted, the willingness to "let go" (as long as it does not oppose conscience) is an important step in spiritual formation.

When Paul and Barnabas met with the apostles and elders in Jerusalem, after much debate Peter stood and spoke. He reminded them of his own experience of proclaiming the good news to Gentiles. He then claimed that "God, who knows the human heart, testified to them by giving them the Holy Spirit," and "in cleansing their hearts by faith he has made no distinction" between Jews and Gentiles; all are saved by grace (vv. 8-9). His words struck right to the heart of the question at issue; it highlighted the principle at stake for the gospel to remain authentic.

One can only imagine the silence in the room when Peter sat down. Surely this was a true insight. While "the door had always been open" for Gentiles to be proselytes to Judaism, in order to enjoy full status they were

---

2. Jennings, *Acts*, 146.

3. Jennings, *Acts*, 147.

expected to undergo the rite of circumcision.[4] While there were many "God-fearers," that is, Gentiles who had embraced Jewish worship and teaching (they kept the food regulations and observed the Sabbath), they were still separated from other male Jews by their lack of circumcision. The Jewish Christians claimed that circumcision could not be made a requirement for the Gentiles. They argued that there could be no requirement other than repentance and faith in the free gift of salvation through Jesus Christ. Salvation was God's work, and they were all saved by grace through faith alone.

As the whole assembly sat quietly and listened, Paul and Barnabas reported their work and told of how God had worked through them to reach the Gentiles. Finally, James, the brother of Jesus, stood up to speak. According to the historian Eusebius, James was known for his deep piety. Citing the prophets of old, according to Luke, James declared that there could be no distinction because they had claimed that the day would come when "all other people may seek the Lord—even all the Gentiles over whom my name has been called" (vv. 16-18).

In summary, the process of discernment used by the early Christians is worthy of note. They met together and openly discussed the issue. There was the opportunity to hear different sides of the argument, which included the personal experience of the believers to that point as well as various historical, theological, and pastoral viewpoints. Finally, we see from the remarks attributed to James that they also went back to Scripture for guidance, as discerned through reliance on the Spirit of God.

A Letter and a Visit, 15:22-35

Having reached a decision that the Gentile believers should not be required to practice circumcision, the council at Jerusalem decided to send several of the believers (Judas called Barsabbas, and Silas) from the congregation along with Paul and Barnabas to speak to the Christians in Antioch in order to reassure and encourage them. They also wrote a letter that was kind and conciliatory. They expressed concern that some had "gone out from us though with no instructions from us" and had disturbed them and "unsettled" their minds (v. 24). They reassured these Christians that they felt "it has seemed good to the Holy Spirit and to us to impose on you no further burden than these essentials: that you abstain from what

---

4. G. B. Caird, *The Apostolic Age* (London: Duckworth Press, 1955, rev. 1975), 29.

has been sacrificed to idols and from blood and from what is strangled and from fornication. If you keep yourselves from these, you will do well" (vv. 28-29). It has been suggested that the phrase "will do well" is important in that it makes clear that the "essentials" were not to be seen as a "form of legalism."[5] Indeed, what seems to have been important in this instance was "fellowship." The suggestion of a minimum requirement was made so the Gentiles could show respect for their Jewish brothers and sisters in Christ. However, "signs and symbols" should never be confused with the reality that is life in Christ.[6]

The believers "rejoiced at the exhortation" (v. 31). Judas and Silas stayed a while longer to strengthen and encourage the believers. Then they left to return to Jerusalem, but Paul and Barnabas remained in Antioch and taught and proclaimed the word (v. 35). Nothing is said about the way the church dealt with those who were involved in this controversy; Luke implies that they eventually accepted the overall decision of the church.

A Second Chance and a Lesson in Humility, 15:36-41

After the matter about the Gentile Christians in Antioch was settled at the council in Jerusalem, and after the Christians were visited and reassured that there should be no distinction between them, Barnabas and Saul prepared to go and visit the believers in every city where they had previously preached the gospel. This desire to check on the believers shows pastoral responsibility for those in the nascent congregations where they had preached earlier. As they prepared to go, Barnabas wanted to take John Mark, and Paul refused. In Paul's eyes, John Mark had abandoned the mission when he left them in Pamphylia and did not accompany them in their work. Luke says that the disagreement became "so sharp that they parted company" (v. 39). Barnabas took John Mark and sailed for Cyprus. Paul selected Silas and went through Syria and Cilicia strengthening the churches.

Ironically, the story in this chapter offers a look at the way a possible division was averted and settled peacefully and the way a difference of opinion led to a parting of ways. While we would like to think that every

---

5. Paul W. Walaskay, *Acts* (Louisville, KY: Westminster/John Knox Press, 1998), 149.

6. See "Acts 15:22-35," *South Asia Bible Commentary*, ed. Brian Wintle (Rajasthan: Open Doors Publications, 2015), 1490.

O Our Saviour! Of ourselves we cannot love thee, cannot follow thee,
cannot cleave to thee;
but thou didst come down
that we might love thee
didst ascend
that we might follow thee,
didst bind us round thee as thy girdle
that we might be held fast unto thee;
Thou who hast loved us, make us to love thee,
Thou who hast sought us, make us to seek thee,
Thou who, when lost, didst find us,
be thou thyself the way,
that we may find thee,
and be found in thee
our only hope, and our everlasting joy.

—E. B. Pusey (1800–1882)
The Oxford Book of Prayer, ed. George Appleton
(Oxford: OUP: 1986), 147.

division in the church can be solved by discussion, there are occasions when, as a matter of conscience, it is not possible to avoid division. In this case, it appears that Paul felt strongly that John Mark had let them down and could not be trusted. Barnabas on the other hand may have felt that everyone grows and develops spiritually in different ways. Even though John Mark had not stayed with them on an earlier occasion, perhaps Barnabas felt that he deserved a second chance. While Paul seems to become the main character in Luke's continuing narrative, as Jennings rightly puts it,

It seems that Barnabas was still ahead of Paul, trying to bring him where he needed to be in that inescapable struggle of trusting those who have or might or will fail us. Barnabas took Mark and disappeared from Luke's narrative, but he entered our future marking the path for those who would be the disciples of Jesus. That path requires trust—sometimes, often times, almost every time—of those who are marked by failure of relationship.[7]

There is a place for recognition of the brokenness in which we all share to some degree, even in our Christian faith and discipleship. As we may imagine the joy of John Mark when Barnabas gave him another chance to

7. Jennings, *Acts*, 151.

proclaim to others his love for God, we may also feel the anguish of Barnabas as he parted ways with Paul. We may understand Paul's impatience with John Mark and his reticence to trust him again. But can we imagine the courage of Barnabas as took a different path? His willingness to take a stand indicated that he was determined to be a follower of Jesus Christ, not of the Apostle Paul. Courage and desire to follow Christ alone is of central importance, especially when Christian leadership can sometimes reflect a stance of coercing and controlling rather than reflecting genuine humility in offering pastoral care and congregational direction.

Draw Your Own Conclusions

1. Why is it necessary to consider historical, theological, pastoral, and scriptural concerns when discerning the way forward personally or as a congregation?

2. Why do individuals and churches struggle with difference? When it comes to matters of deeply held principles (often formed on the basis of interpretation of Scripture), how can such differences be overcome without compromise?

3. Reflect on the importance of trust in relationship with others or with God. Why is trust so vital to Christian community? How is trust rebuilt when it has been broken?

Acts 16

The Demands of Discipleship, 16:1-4

Paul went to Derbe with Silas, who was one of the trusted and respected young men sent from the Jerusalem church to reassure the church in Antioch that circumcision was not necessary. From Derbe, they traveled to Lystra, and there they met a disciple named Timothy. He was the son of a Jewish woman who was a believer, but his father was Greek. Paul wanted Timothy to accompany them, so Luke says that Paul took him and had him circumcised. At first it appears that Paul's action seems to contradict all that he has already argued against. We read in chapter 15 that in Antioch, he and Barnabas debated vociferously with a group of believers who claimed that there was no salvation without circumcision. This led to the assembly in Jerusalem where it was agreed that circumcision was not linked to salvation and Gentiles did not need to be circumcised.

So why is Paul now taking Timothy to be circumcised? The short answer is that Timothy was not a Gentile; he was an uncircumcised Jew. His mother was a Jewish Christian and his father a Gentile, meaning that Timothy would not be accepted by fellow Jews. While circumcision was not demanded of Gentiles, it seems that uncircumcised Jews could not be tolerated. By taking Timothy to be circumcised, Paul was not suggesting that salvation was linked to this practice.[1] The principle of salvation by grace through faith had been established and was stated at the assembly (15:11). Rather, it seems that for Paul, this was a case of accommodating certain cultural practices in order to be an effective witness among certain groups of Jews without diluting the Christian faith.

---

1. Talbert, *Reading Acts*, 137.

Those who have lived and worked in other countries will be aware of the desirability of sensitivity in cross-cultural mission and the observance of customs in order not to offend. Yet there is another side to this story. As Jennings has suggested, we should not move too quickly to try to look at Paul's motives without looking more closely at Timothy, who was a Jew-Gentile-Christian.[2] As Jennings put it, Timothy "constitutes the in-between," and "his life presents the shifting plates of identity on which we all stand."[3] His willingness to submit to circumcision as an adult, therefore, was not simply a demonstration of a willingness to accommodate to culture in order to proclaim the gospel. Rather, Timothy made a choice that demonstrated the way of love that is the way of every follower of Jesus. Jennings writes,

> Timothy is registering his love for the people to whom God is sending him, and he does so in the way that discipleship demands, through his flesh, and so must we. This is the way of the Spirit. The power of in-between existence (Christian existence) is love without contradiction, and such love is always possible. It is possible for Timothy to love the Gentiles of his father and the Jews of his mother and with both and through both and in both to perform his commitment to Jesus. This is the inner logic of the Christian. We can inhabit new cultural sites of love, different languages, different holy gestures, different customs and rituals of life, and perform through the Spirit deepening love for the world and for Jesus the Christ, the savior of the world. Such loves [sic] presents no competition and no conflicted loyalties. It only gestures overwhelming addition. This is the work of the Spirit for those led by the Spirit.[4]

The way of love is the way of true discipleship, though in the church there is at times a tendency to define and limit the expressions of love to the ways we feel are socially or culturally appropriate. We forget that we are all called to embrace our "in-between" status and to be controlled by the Spirit, which will often turn our way of relating to others, and of seeing the world, upside down.

---

2. Jennings, *Acts*, 152ff.

3. Jennings, *Acts*, 153.

4. Jennings, *Acts*, 154.

The Right Time, 16:5-10

As Paul, Silas, and Timothy went out to the churches and told them about the decisions reached by the apostles and elders in Jerusalem, Luke says the churches were "strengthened in the faith and increased in numbers daily" (v. 5). Luke is keen, however, to point out that Paul, Silas, and Timothy did not have an "action plan" for their journey. They were depending on the Holy Spirit to lead them to the places they were to visit. He says that they went through the area of Phrygia and Galatia, having been "forbidden by the Holy Spirit to speak a word in Asia" (v. 6). "They attempted to go into Bithynia, but the Spirit of Jesus did not allow them" (v. 7). While no indication is given of why they felt they were hindered from speaking or how the Spirit made this clear to them, we are sharply reminded that there is "a time to speak" and "a time to be silent"; "a time to listen" and "a time to proclaim" (in the vein of Ecclesiastes 3). Luke was not laying down particular principles for evangelism. However, for those in the church who are prone to want a "five-year plan" mapped out in advance or a verifiable target for congregational achievement or growth, the overriding message of this narrative is that knowing the "right time" requires utter dependence on the Spirit and openness to the doors God will open.

They reached Troas, and during the night Paul had a vision in which a man from Macedonia pleaded with them to come and help (v. 9). After that, Luke says, "we immediately tried to cross over to Macedonia, being convinced that God had called us to proclaim the good news to them" (v. 10). This is the first time in the narrative that Luke uses the pronoun "we." Some have suggested this may indicate that Luke, our narrator, had joined the group.[5] If Paul had some malady as described in Galatians (4:13), some have even thought perhaps Luke served as his physician (Col 4:14). Luke's travelogue style here adds to the drama of the unfolding work of the Spirit leading the church to new horizons.

Welcoming Space, 16:11-15

Crossing to Macedonia by way of Troas to Samothrace, and then to Neapolis, they finally made their way to the key city of Philippi. They remained in the city for some days, and on the Sabbath they went to the gate by the river and met a group of women who had gathered there. Among them, Luke says, was a woman named Lydia from Thyatira who sold purple cloth.

---

5. See discussion in the Introduction and Polhill, *Acts*, 346.

Lydia is described as a "worshipper of God," which indicates that she had embraced Judaism (v. 14). Luke says she listened carefully to the word proclaimed by Paul, and then she and her household were baptized. Her conversion leads her to invite them to come to stay in her home, but it was not just an invitation. Luke claims that she "prevailed" upon (pressed or urged) them to stay with her. Her willingness to offer hospitality was a mark of discipleship. Their acceptance of her hospitality demonstrates that the bond in Christ between Christians knows no barriers. While here it meant lodging, the deeper significance is the notion of the welcome given.

There is far more to hospitality than simply sharing at table or offering a place of rest to others. Hospitality, as Henri Nouwen has pointed out, may best be understood as an attitude of openness revealed in the way we live and interact with others. Writing in response to the question "What does it mean to live a life in the Spirit of Jesus Christ?" Nouwen described three movements of the spiritual life. They are (1) from loneliness to solitude, (2) from hostility to hospitality, and (3) from illusion to prayer. Commenting on the second movement, Nouwen suggested that the word "hospitality" should not be limited to the idea of receiving a stranger. Rather, the "concept of hospitality can offer a new dimension to our understanding of a healing relationship and the formation of a re-creative community in a world so visibly suffering from alienation and estrangement."[6] Sometimes hospitality is simply reaching out to someone in need with food, clothing, or a place to stay. However, there is another side to hospitality that Nouwen defined as "the creation of a free space" where the stranger can become friend. Thought of in this way, hospitality transforms relationships. In order to offer space for relationships to grow, according to Nouwen, a person must have a certain "inner poverty" that allows one person to be truly open to listening to another. In this "space," the Spirit of God can draw us to the deepest bond of fellowship, and the "welcome" becomes a deeper "embrace."

From time to time in the history of the church, a person or group emerges to remind the church of the importance of hospitality for those who seek to follow in the way of Christ. Benedictine communities, which were founded in the sixth century by St. Benedict of Nursia (c. 480–543), stressed hospitality to strangers and were seen as a refuge for pilgrims and those in need. These communities were to view every person as if he/she

---

6. Henri J. M. Nouwen, *Reaching Out: The Three Movements of the Spiritual Life* (London: Collins, 1976), 65.

were Christ. More recently, the Benedictine tradition has been described as a place where there can be dialogue with others. Thus the communities provide "islands of tolerance in a sea of intolerance."[7]

In the twentieth century, the founding of the Catholic Worker Movement

> O king of stars!
> Whether my house be dark or bright,
> Never shall it be closed against any one,
> Lest Christ close His house against me.
> If there be a guest in your house
> And you conceal aught from him,
> 'Tis not the guest that will be without it,
> But Jesus, Mary's Son.
>
> —St. Moling, "Hospitality," in *A Celtic Primer*,
> compiled by Brendan O'Malley
> (Norwich: Canterbury Press, 2002), 166.

by Dorothy Day and Peter Maurin emphasized a "personalist" view, which meant that they, too, believed it was important to see Christ in others. In doing so, and in seeking to build community, Day argued that "little by little," person by person, the world would ultimately be changed.[8]

Changing Hearts and Minds, 16:16-40

From the story of Lydia, the disciple who practiced hospitality by providing welcoming space, Luke moves to the story of rejection and cramped prison quarters. A slave girl (whose name is not given) was purported to have a spirit by which she was able to predict the future. Her owners used her to tell the fortunes of people who paid them money. Luke claimed that the girl began to follow Paul and Silas around and for many days called out repeatedly, "These men are slaves of the Most High God who proclaim to you a way of salvation" (v. 17). She was right; they were slaves of God and intent on doing God's will. However, Paul grew weary with her constant calling out, so he stopped and ordered the spirit out of her. When those who owned her saw that she was changed and thus no longer a source of income, they were furious and trumped up charges against the disciples, claiming that Paul and Silas had committed treason against Rome. They had them brought before the authorities, who had them stripped, beaten with rods, and imprisoned. To show how securely they were being kept, Luke adds the detail that they were put in "the innermost cell" and their

---

7. Aaron Raverty, OSB, "Hospitality in the Benedictine Monastic Tradition," *Revista Interdisciplinar da Mobilidade Humana* [Brasília] Ano 20/38 (Jan/June 2012): 251–55, esp. 254–55.

8. Day was fond of using the phrase "little by little," which she borrowed from Thérèse of Lisieux.

feet were fastened "in the stocks" (v. 24). The work of God through them seemed to have come to an end.

However, later, about midnight, while they were singing hymns to God and praying, Luke says there was an earthquake. Their chains were unfastened, and the doors of the prison opened. The jailer was afraid that they had escaped and drew his sword in order to kill himself. But Paul called out, "Do not harm yourself, for we are all here" (v. 28). Calling for lights, the jailer rushed in and fell down trembling before Paul and Silas, asking the question: "What must I do to be saved?" They answered simply, "Believe on the Lord Jesus, and you will be saved, you and your household." According to Luke, they then "spoke the word of the Lord to him and to all who were in his house" (vv. 30-32).

After the word is proclaimed, the familiar pattern in Acts for those who come to faith in Christ is repeated: there is repentance and baptism. Since it is assumed that confession of faith and repentance happen before baptism, a question may be raised about Luke's comment that the jailer "and his entire family were baptized without delay" (v. 33). This does not necessarily imply baptism without repentance and faith. Rather, since the word was spoken to all who were in the house, perhaps we must assume that each had their own level of comprehension, repentance, and faith on their spiritual journey to that point. It may be part of Luke's intention to indicate that there is development in both faith and commitment in any disciple's life. Moreover, it is notable that Luke takes pains to emphasize that repentance was not simply expressed in words. Rather, it was demonstrated when, as Luke says, "at the same hour of night, he [the jailer] took them and washed their wounds; then he and his entire family were baptized without delay" (v. 33). He brought them into his house and set food before them. The simple reference to table fellowship underscores the emphasis on hospitality noted in the previous story. Ironically, while Paul and Silas were confined in prison, they practiced hospitality and "created space" for the jailer as they prayed, sang hymns, and refused to flee from the jail even when they had the opportunity to do so. Their openness to him is a reminder of the relational nature of Christian faith. They were not simply "evangelizing people"; rather, strangers were becoming brothers and sisters in Christ. These two showed that their deepest desire was for Christ to be made known, and the bonds of fellowship were thus forged.

The next morning the magistrates sent word that the prisoners were to be released, but Paul, according to Luke, was indignant and claimed that they were Roman citizens and should never have been beaten and imprisoned. When the magistrates learned of their citizenship, they were afraid and came to offer an apology to Paul and Silas. By demanding an apology, Paul and Silas may have hoped this would offer some protection to believers in the city after they left.[9] After leaving the prison, they went back to Lydia's home, "encouraged the brothers and sisters," and then departed (v. 40).

Draw Your Own Conclusions

1. How do you understand the demands of discipleship?

2. Consider Nouwen's emphasis on hospitality as an attitude of "creating space" for others. What hinders us from creating space within ourselves in order to listen to others?

3. Why is the church often not viewed as a "community of tolerance" in the midst of a world of intolerance?

4. What is the difference between being tolerant and condoning what might be wrong or harmful?

---

9. Garland, *Acts*, 169.

Acts 17

Turning the World Upside Down, 17:1-15

Paul and Silas leave Philippi, pass through Amphipolis and Apollonia, and stop first in Thessalonica. Here, Luke once again draws attention to regular attendance at the synagogue, saying that "as was his custom," Paul went to the synagogue on three successive Sabbath days and "argued with them from the scriptures explaining and proving that it was necessary for the Messiah to suffer and to rise from the dead" (vv. 2-3). While Paul's emphasis on the cross and resurrection would have been unpalatable to many who heard him, according to Luke some Jews believed and joined with Paul and Silas, as did a number of "devout Greeks" and "not a few of the leading women" (v. 4). It has been suggested that the reference to "leading women" indicates that they had some status in the town. Perhaps Luke wants to indicate that the gospel had a wide appeal and should not be seen as the religion of the discontented masses. Yet, while many responded to the proclamation of the gospel, as usual there was opposition, too. A mob formed and "set the city in an uproar" (v. 5). They could not find Paul and Silas, so they attacked the home of a disciple named Jason. He and other believers were dragged before the city authorities with the accusation that they were "turning the world upside down" (v. 6). Jason was accused of offering hospitality to people who were disturbing the peace.

The accusation that they were "turning the world upside down" presumably refers to the idea that they were disturbing the order of society. They were calling people to think again about their allegiances and priorities. The truth is that the gospel does turn life upside down. There can be no carrying on as usual. There is a sense, as Luke tries to describe in various ways throughout Acts, that the Spirit turns the world upside down. When a person is guided by the Spirit and led by the Spirit, the world will seem different and believers are called to make the world different. Earlier in Acts, Luke pointed out that when the power of the Spirit was at work, as people prayed the house shook (4:31). Saul's experience on the Damascus road meant that he was blinded by the light of God, and only later when he accepted the gospel did he regain his sight and receive the filling of the Spirit (9:18). When the Spirit is at work, there is a new world being created. Howard Thurman described the experience of a new life in Christ in the words of a song that was sung in the church of his childhood:

> My feet looked new
> My hands looked new,
> The world looked new,
> Leaning on the Lord.[1]

That night, Paul and Silas were sent by the Christians in Thessalonica to Beroea, and when they arrived, they immediately went to the synagogue. The Jews there "welcomed the message very eagerly and examined the scriptures" every day (v. 11). The emphasis on daily study of the Scripture, rather than just on the Sabbath, is perhaps a way of emphasizing the positive way in which the people received the word in Beroea. Luke claims that many believed, "including not a few Greek women and men of high standing" (v. 12). But when some people from Thessalonica discovered that Paul and Silas were getting a good reception in Beroea, they went over and tried to incite the crowds there. The believers in Beroea immediately sent Paul to the coast, but Silas and Timothy remained behind. Paul was conducted safely to Athens, and he sent word to Silas and Timothy that they should join him as soon as possible. Evidently Paul was the target of the opposition, and it would appear that, though he was undaunted by their attacks, he bore the brunt of their ill will.

Twice in this short text, Luke is at pains to say that the gospel appealed to people in the "upper class." This may have been Luke's effort to point out that while Jesus proclaimed the kingdom where captives are set free, this was not a radical movement trying to overthrow the social and political order by appealing to the masses. Perhaps it was also a way of stressing that the gospel is for all and that all stand in need of divine grace. Moreover, it is a reminder that those who need to be "set free" are not just the materially poor, the ill, or the oppressed. A verse from Brian Wren's hymn "Great God

---

1. Howard Thurman, *Disciplines of the Spirit*, 24.

Your Love Has Called Us Here" seems to sum up the human condition that is prevalent in the society of any age and that the gospel addresses:

> We come with self-inflicted pains
> of broken trust and chosen wrong,
> half-free, half-bound by inner chains,
> by social forces swept along,
> by powers and systems close confined
> yet seeking hope for humankind.[2]

Luke's presentation of the gospel emphasizes that whatever a person's class or economic status, everyone needs the freedom that only comes by knowing Christ as the Messiah and Lord.

Another Day, Same Gospel, 17:16-33

Paul then waited in Athens for Silas and Timothy, and it was here that we might say his eyes were opened to a new reality. For the most part, up until this point he had been concerned with arguments over whether Jesus should be rightly seen as the Messiah and whether the Jewish law needed to be kept. He had attended the synagogues and mainly proclaimed the message about Jesus in cultural settings he knew well. Now he has entered a city that is different in view of the Greek philosophical heritage. While he waited, he had time to observe the way people were living. He could see what seemed important to them, what they believed was important, and how they spent their time. According to Luke, what he saw caused him great "distress," as he felt that their understanding of the spiritual realm was completely flawed.[3]

His response was to go out to meet people, not just in the synagogue but also in the marketplace. Essentially, wherever he might go where someone would listen, Paul proclaimed the gospel. He met with some Epicurean and Stoic philosophers who accused him of being a "babbler," which was a rather unflattering reference to a person with only partial knowledge. (The word was used to depict a bird that gathered up scraps from the gutter.)[4]

---

2. Brian Wren, "Great God Your Love Has Called Us Here," words 1975, rev. 1995, Hope Publishing Company.

3. Polhill has noted that the word *paroxynō* here, sometimes translated "distressed," would be better translated as "infuriated." We get the English word "paroxysm" from this word. The point is that Paul was very angry. (See Polhill, *Acts*, 366.)

4. Marshall, *Acts*, 284.

Apparently, they thought he was a street preacher, but when they listened more closely to his ideas, they thought he was a "proclaimer of foreign divinities" and decided to listen to see what he had to say (v. 18). So they took him to the Areopagus, the place of debate, and asked him about this new teaching.

Paul's speech begins with an attempt to "build bridges" by complimenting the religious nature of the people of Athens. He noted that they had so many altars to so many gods, and even an altar to the unknown God. However, without dismissing the other gods, he said that this latter God is not unknown but the God whom he has proclaimed. The one who created all things and has given life to all human beings does not live in an altar shaped with human hands (v. 24). This God is not far from us; indeed, in him "we live and move and have our being" (v. 28). He told the listeners that while God had overlooked ignorance of God in the past, now people were called to repentance (v. 30). God had "fixed a day on which he will have the world judged in righteousness by a man whom he has appointed, and of this he has given assurance to all by raising him from the dead" (v. 31).

> O Christ, my Lord, again and again
> I have said with Mary Magdalene,
> "They have taken away my Lord
> and I know not where they have laid him."
> I have been desolate and alone.
> And thou hast found me again, and I know
> that what has died is not thou, my Lord,
> but only my idea of thee,
> the image which I have made to preserve
> what I have found, and to be my security.
> I shall make another image, O Lord,
> better than the last.
> That too must go, and all successive images,
> until I come to the blessed vision of thyself,
> O Christ, my Lord.
> —George Appleton (1902–1993), from
> *The Oxford Book of Prayer* (Oxford:
> Oxford University Press, 1985), 147

Hearing the call to repentance and especially the mention of the resurrection from the dead, Luke says that "some scoffed"; but others deferred a decision on faith by saying. "We will hear you again about this" (v. 32). At that point Paul left them, but some who heard became believers, including Dionysius the Areopagite, a woman called Damaris, and others with them. Significantly, in the narrative Luke gives us the names of many different people, and he especially notes women. In this chapter alone, he mentions Greek women, leading women, and also Demaris. Reimer suggests that

Damaris may have been a philosopher.[5] The mention of men and women from all classes is a reminder again that God makes no distinction. The incident has been seen as pivotal in Paul's approach to the gospel, but it indicates that the gospel meets with different responses according to the context.

Paul's determination to speak to anyone of every background in Athens highlights the fact that he was a persistent spokesperson for the gospel. He was not to be deterred, and the word would not be barred. Yet, as the sixteenth-century reformer Martin Luther suggested, the reception of the word was never down to the Apostle Paul. That is to say, it wasn't simply that he was a forceful or eloquent orator who could somehow compel the people to listen and respond. Rather, the word itself has power. Reflecting on the experience of the Apostle Paul, Luther claimed that Paul did not try to "kick down" the idols; rather he let the word do the work. Then reflecting on his own experience Luther claimed:

> For the Word creates heaven and earth and all things;
> the Word must do this thing and not we poor sinners.
> In short, I will preach it, teach it, write it, but I will constrain no one by force, for faith must come freely without compulsion.[6]

The emphasis on allowing the word "to work" rather than compelling people to believe challenges both the historical approach of some state/ national establishment churches and the evangelistic practices of other traditions. I had a friend who grew up in a tradition that practiced baptism by immersion. As an older adult, she told me one day that she wished she had waited to be baptized. She said that when she was baptized as a young person, it was at the prompting of a youth leader who told her and a group of friends that it was time for them to be baptized. It was many years later, however, that my friend said she had a personal experience of faith and came to believe in Jesus Christ as her personal Savior—a faith that she would have gladly professed in baptism with deep meaning. However, as Luke has indicated, baptism can come at different points on the journey of faith.

---

5. Ivoni Richter Reimer, *Women in the Acts of the Apostles* (Minneapolis: Fortress Press, 1995), 164.

6. Martin Luther, "Second Invocavit Sermon (1522)," in *Reformation Commentary on Scripture, Acts*, ed. Chung-Kim and Hains, 246.

As Luke also draws a sharp contrast between those who scoffed or said that they would listen again and those who believed, we are reminded of the need for patience, as faith must come freely and cannot be forced. We are also reminded that people are at different stages in their journey of faith. People do not come to faith in the same way, they do not come at the same time, and they certainly do not at the time that others might try to dictate.

Draw Your Own Conclusions

1. Paul's experience in Athens is a reminder of the importance of spending time with people where they live. What might this say to Christians who organize all their time around church activities?

2. How might Christians today engage with people in the marketplace?

3. How do we understand discipleship as a "work in progress"?

4. What does Paul's approach indicate about meeting people where they are in their spiritual pilgrimage?

5. Does this passage have anything to teach us about interfaith dialogue?

Acts 18

Do Not Be Afraid, 18:1-11

Paul left Athens and went to Corinth. The Corinth of Paul's time was not the classical city. The Romans destroyed Corinth in 146 BC, but it was rebuilt as a Roman colony in 46 BC. So, while the city was in Greece, it was shaped by Roman influences in culture and politics.[1] Corinth was a cosmopolitan trading center, a city that was bustling with commercial activity.

In Corinth, Paul met Priscilla and Aquila, who were Jews forced out of Rome by Claudius. Talbert claims that they may have already been believers.[2] Certainly, they welcomed Paul into their home, and because he too was a tent-maker, he worked with them in their business. While some might have thought this was rather demeaning work, it was a rabbinic ideal to practice a worldly occupation alongside the study of the law.[3] Luke says that every week they went to the synagogue, as Paul tried to "convince" both Jews and Greeks of the message of Jesus (v. 4). The implication is that in some places, the reception of the gospel was not by a burst of activity but through a long process of people being drawn by God to faith and commitment.

Silas and Timothy arrived from Macedonia and probably brought funds from the Macedonian Christians (Phil 4:6 and 2 Cor 11:7-9) that offered support and allowed Paul to preach not only on the Sabbath but also all through the week. Many of the Jews "opposed and reviled" Paul (v. 6). It must have reached such a pitch that he finally "shook the dust off

---

1. Talbert, *Reading Acts*, 158–59; Garland, *Acts*, 184.

2. Talbert, *Reading Acts*, 159.

3. Talbert, *Reading Acts*, 159. Keener also notes that he used work to spread the gospel. (Keener, *15:1–23:25*, vol. 3 of *Acts: An Exegetical Commentary* [Grand Rapids, MI: Baker Academic, 2014], 2736).

his clothes" in protest and declared that he was not responsible for them (v. 6). With that Hebrew expression of disavowal, he claimed that he would now go to the Gentiles. It was the imperative of the word that drove him to find opportunities for presenting the claims of Christ.

Paul then went to the home of Titius Justus, a Gentile worshipper of God who lived next door to the synagogue (v. 7). Paul continued to preach and teach, and many became believers and were baptized. Notably, Crispus, one of the leaders of the synagogue, became a believer, as well as his whole household (v. 8). While there was some positive response to the word, Paul must have had moments when he felt keenly the opposition to his ministry, and Luke has written the story in a way that implies this was part of costly discipleship. Luke records that one night, the Lord said to Paul in a vision, "Do not be afraid, but speak and do not be silent; for I am with you, and no one will lay a hand on you to harm you, for there are many people in this city who are my people" (vv. 9-10).

Luke did not elaborate on the cause of Paul's fear. Perhaps, with good reason, Paul was worried about his health or another physical attack or even imprisonment. Or maybe he was worn down by constant harassment and organized opposition. He may have begun to doubt his ability to convince people or was afraid that he or the churches he sought to build up might fail. Whatever the cause for his anxiety, Paul is assured of the Lord's presence with him and that he has the support of

> Hope of my heart, strength of my soul,
> help of my weakness,
> by your powerful kindness complete
> what in my powerless weakness I attempt.
> My life, the end to which I strive,
> although I have not yet attained to love you as I ought,
> still let my desire for you
> be as great as my love ought to be.
> —Anselm (1033-1109), from the *Prayers and Meditations of St Anselm with the Proslogian*, trans. Sister Benedicta Ward (Hamondsworth: Penguin Books, 1973), 93.

a Christian community. The reminder "I am with you" is an important phrase for Christians. It is easy to become anxious or afraid and to forget this singular truth that the presence of God is ever near.

Emphasis on the presence of God was an important theme in the spirituality of Brother Lawrence (1614–1691), a monk who worked in a monastery kitchen in Paris in the seventeenth century. He believed that for Christians, above all it was important to "practice the Lord's presence" all the time. Claiming that that there was no time or place where one could not experience the presence of God, he suggested that every activity, every thought, could be God-directed—so much so that while working in the kitchen washing pans, he said he could feel as close to the Lord as he did when at worship. In a collection of his letters and writings, which were published under the title *Practicing the Presence of God*, Brother Lawrence claimed,

> The most holy practice, the nearest to daily life, and the most essential for the spiritual life, is the practice of the presence of God, that is to find joy in his divine company and to make it a habit of life, speaking humbly and conversing lovingly with him at all times, every moment, without rule or restriction, above all at times of temptation, distress, dryness or revulsion, and even of faithlessness and sin. We should apply ourselves continually, so that all our actions become small occasions of fellowship with God . . . .[4]

This idea of knowing God's nearness was also a central theme in the spirituality of the eighteenth-century Quaker John Woolman (1720–1772). As with Brother Lawrence, so for Woolman, it seems that the discovery of God in life was to be revealed in the simplicity of life itself. By this Woolman meant that the more he detached himself from things that he had once assumed gave him life, the more he discovered that life was not found in these things but in God alone. Woolman lived in colonial America at a time when many sought to gain from the slave trade and the subjugation of lands and property of the indigenous population. Refusing to benefit from the slave trade in any way, Woolman would not dye his clothes with indigo or use any products that had come from slave labor. In his journal he wrote of the danger of wealth, claiming, "The collecting of riches, covering the body with fine wrought, costly apparel, and having magnificent furniture, operate against universal love and tend to feed self, so that it belongs not to the children of light to desire these things."[5] Woolman, like Brother Lawrence and countless others through the ages, argued that simplicity of life is an outward reflection of inward obedience to God. It is also in simplicity that a person learns to trust in God for everything and in such daily trust that one knows the presence and power of God.

---

4. Brother Lawrence, in *The Practice of the Presence of God* (London: Hodder and Stoughton, 1984), 68.

5. John Woolman, "A Plea for the Poor (1793)," in *The Journal of John Woolman and a Plea for the Poor* (Secaucus, NJ: Citadel Press, 1961), 236–37.

The Baying Crowd, 18:12-17

In the midst of a city where he faced opposition, Paul sought to be obedient
to the call of God and must have been encouraged and strengthened by the
word of the Lord to him. Luke tells us "he stayed there a year and six months
teaching the word of God among them" (v. 11). However, when Gallio was
the proconsul of Achaia, the Jews who opposed Paul tried once again to
have him silenced. Luke says that they made a "united attack" on Paul
and brought him before the tribunal (v. 12). They accused him of trying
to persuade people to worship God in ways that were not in accordance
with the Jewish law and tradition. Gallio did not want to get involved.
He deemed that this was a matter for the Jews to sort out for themselves.
So the crowd seized "Sosthenes, the official of the synagogue" and beat
him.[6] There is some question over who delivered this apparently random
beating. Luke does not identify the reason for the attack. However, Talbert
claimed that it was most probably an "expression of pagan anti-semitism"
and would not have been an isolated incident. In effect, "The Roman ruler
in Corinth ignores mob violence against Jews after having prevented their
violence against Paul."[7] In other words, the mob was probably Gentiles
seizing an opportunity vent their anti-Jewish feelings.[8] Whatever the reason
for the mob violence, although they beat Sosthenes in front of the tribunal,
Gallio paid no attention.

This story is yet another reminder (and there are many throughout
Acts) that the followers of Jesus can expect opposition. What is interesting
about this account is that no mention is made of Paul speaking. Perhaps the
Proconsul dismissed the case before he had opportunity to speak. On the
other hand, sometimes there is no need to offer words. The ability to stand
silently in truth has long been upheld as a sign of genuine humility—not
the sort of false humility that stands with head down, thinking, "I don't
deserve this treatment" or "I am so much better than all of these people"
but humility that always stands for truth and seeks to live in submission
to God. In the Rule of St. Benedict, one of the steps to humility for a
believer is the suggestion that "even under difficult, unfavorable, or even
unjust conditions, his [her] heart quietly embraces suffering and endures

---

6. It does appear that Sosthenes was a Messianist (1 Cor 1:1) (Williams, *A Commentary on the Acts of the Apostles*, 212).

7. Talbert, *Reading Acts*, 163.

8. Garland, *Acts*, 187.

it without weakening or seeking escape."[9] This description seems to depict the attitude of Christ, who refused to defend himself when he stood before his accusers and Pilate (Luke 23:3). It may have been the attitude that Paul was displaying, too, and this provides another example of the Christian calling to live in imitation of Christ.

Outward Appearances, 18:18-23

After staying for some time in Corinth, Paul set sail for Syria, accompanied by Priscilla and Aquila. At Cenchreae, Paul had his hair cut to show that he had taken a Nazarite vow. Again this may have been a reflection of Paul's desire to show that he had not abandoned his Jewish heritage. When they arrived at Ephesus, Luke says that Paul left Priscilla and Aquila there, but first he went to the synagogue to have a discussion with the Jews. They asked him to stay. Though he declined to do so, he said he would return if God willed it.

Paul's willingness to move on, even as people wanted him to stay, is another reminder that he sought to follow the leadership of God as Holy Spirit. Perhaps it was also a realization that the people needed time to reflect on their desire to follow Christ. Beyond the initial enthusiasm of an experience of conversion, there is a place for due consolidation of the believer in faith and practice, and this, too, is always a part of the spiritual journey. While it might have been easy to present a convincing argument and even to whip up enthusiasm in a crowd, genuine commitment to Christ requires attentiveness to the Spirit in order to know the next step of the journey. It was so for the Apostle Paul, and it is so for others, too.

Leaving Ephesus, Paul went up to Jerusalem and "greeted the church, and then went down to Antioch," and thereafter he "went from place to place through the region of Galatia and Phrygia, strengthening all the disciples" (vv. 22-23). It appears that Paul's whole purpose was to be among the people. He realized that those who were believers needed encouragement, too. It was not a matter of simply trying to make new disciples; he also wanted to encourage those who had made a commitment and were seeking to follow the risen Lord. The importance of ongoing support in discipleship is never to be ignored. The Christian life is one of continual growth for those who want to be open to the Spirit, and Luke implies that everyone needs support and encouragement along the way.

---

9. *Rule of St. Benedict*, 18.

Writing of the need to give attention to spiritual formation and growth, and for pastors to be focused on caring for people rather than "running a church," Eugene Peterson suggested that there is a great deal of difference between seeing the church as a business and wanting to help people grow spiritually. Those who see their work as "running a church," according to Peterson, ask questions like these: "What do we do?" "How can we get things going again"? Those who are interested in the "cure of souls" (caring for people) ask, "What has God been doing here?" "What traces of grace can I see in this life?" "What history of love can I read in this group?" "What has God set in motion that I can get in on?"[10]

Significantly, Peterson claimed that there is a critical difference between those who see themselves "running a church" and those who are involved in caring for people. He put it this way:

> In running the church, I seize the initiative. I take charge. I take responsibility for motivation and recruitment, for showing the way, for getting things started. If I don't, things drift. I am aware of the tendency to apathy, the human susceptibility to indolence, and I use my leadership position to counter it.
>
> By contrast, the cure of souls is a cultivated awareness that God has already seized the initiative . . . . The cure of souls is not indifferent to the realities of human lethargy, naïve about congregational recalcitrance, or inattentive to neurotic cussedness. But there is a disciplined, determined conviction that everything (and I mean, precisely, everything) we do is a response to God's first work, his initiating act.[11]

The desire of the Apostle Paul to personally visit the congregations (and his ministry of sending letters to them) indicates his desire to help them in the continuing process of spiritual formation.

A Lesson in Humility, 18:24-28

Paul was not the only one who was trying to encourage believers to continue to grow in their faith. Luke says that in Ephesus there was a Jew named Apollos who was a native of Alexandria. He was an eloquent professor of the faith and well versed in the Scriptures. He had been well taught and had a burning enthusiasm for the things of Jesus. However, for reasons

---

10. Peterson, *Contemplative Pastor*, 61.

11. Peterson, *Contemplative Pastor*, 60–61.

Luke does not explain, Apollos only knew "the baptism of John" (v. 25). He began to speak boldly in the synagogue, and when they heard him, Priscilla and Aquila took him to one side and "explained the Way of God to him more accurately" (v. 26).

The story is a firm reminder of the need for spiritual guidance in the life of faith. It is necessary for those who seek to guide as much as it is for those whom they endeavor to help. How easy it would have been for Apollos to take offense and refuse to listen to them. However, he had the humility to realize that, as a follower of the Way, he was not fully formed in the faith. When he wanted to go to from Ephesus to Achaia, they encouraged him and commended him in writing to the disciples there. On his arrival, Luke says "he greatly helped those who through grace had become believers, for he powerfully refuted the Jews in public, showing by the scriptures that the Messiah is Jesus" (vv. 27-28).

Draw Your Own Conclusions

1. How do you think Christians today might practice the presence of God?

2. What hinders us from growing in humility? What is the difference in true and false humility? How might a greater emphasis on humility change relationships in the church?

3. Why is it important to have an "informed faith" as we are being formed in discipleship?

4. Is it possible to defend faith using Scripture without demeaning those who believe differently or have no belief?

5. How much of our spiritual growth is a "shared quest" in the life of a congregation of believers?

6. What makes for genuine encouragement in the life of the Spirit?

7. What is it about the church that sets it apart from being just a business, a charity, or a community organization?

Acts 19

The Inclusive Spirit, 19:1-10

While Apollos was in Corinth, Paul went back to Ephesus. Curiously, after the episode with Apollos (Acts 18), Paul came across some believers who had only been baptized into the "baptism of John," and they had never heard of the Holy Spirit. Paul explained that John's baptism was for repentance, but they needed to be baptized in the name of Jesus Christ and receive the Holy Spirit. He baptized them, "laid his hands on them," and Luke says that then they "spoke in tongues and prophesied" (v. 6). This appears to be a reenactment of the day of Pentecost, since they spoke in actual languages (not in unknown tongues such as Paul discusses in 1 Cor 12-14).[1] The fact that Jews and Gentiles received the Holy Spirit was a reminder of how God celebrates difference and at the same time brings people together in genuine community. Moreover, the emphasis on receiving the Spirit when they experienced the "laying on of hands" testifies to the freedom of the Spirit, which will not be limited by any human power.[2] It was not their action that initiated the action of God but their openness to the sovereign freedom of God as Holy Spirit.

As already noted, while the act of the "laying on of hands" did not indicate any transfer of power or authority from one individual to another, the practice was widely associated with prayer and blessing.[3] In terms of spiritual formation, this practice is also a sign of fellowship and intimacy as a gathered community of brothers and sisters in Christ, as well as a symbolic act of genuine embrace, love, respect, and acceptance. Reflecting

---

1. Garland, *Acts*, 194.

2. Talbert, *Reading Acts*, 167.

3. See discussion in Acts 13.

on this practice, I am reminded of a story told by Coretta Scott King, the wife of Martin Luther King Jr. Apparently, when it was announced that Dr. King had won the Nobel Peace Prize in 1964, he was in the hospital having tests and also resting and recuperating from a busy schedule. While he was in the hospital, Dr. King was visited by the Roman Catholic Archbishop Paul John Hallinan of Atlanta. Coretta King told of the visit by Hallinan to her husband:

> Bishop Hallinan offered his congratulations and then said to Martin, "May I give you my blessing?" Martin said, "Of course," and the Archbishop recited a traditional blessing and made the sign of the cross. Martin responded, then to his surprise, the Archbishop sank to his knees beside the bed and quietly said, "May I receive your blessing?" Later Martin told me how humbled he felt and how beautiful it was that a Roman Catholic Archbishop would receive the blessing of a Baptist preacher named Martin Luther.[4]

Paul went to the synagogue and for three months preached and tried to convince people "about the kingdom of God" (v. 8). Many refused to believe, and some "spoke evil of the Way," so he left them (as he had determined to do earlier) and went to the lecture hall of Tyrannus, where he argued daily (v. 9). He stayed in Ephesus for two years (his second long stay on this particular journey around the churches), so Luke claimed that "all the residents of Asia, both Jews and Greeks, heard the word of the Lord" (vv. 9-10). Once again Luke notes Paul's persistence in proclaiming the word "in season and out of season." The ability to persevere is never simply the result of our determination or strength in discipleship. Paul was not able to stay two years in the midst of considerable opposition under his own strength. Rather, his ability to "keep on keeping on" was the result of God's faithfulness to him, not merely the Apostle's faithfulness.

A Fire of Repentance, 19:11-20

In spite of opposition, Luke claims that God continued to do extraordinary things through Paul. Luke says that "handkerchiefs or aprons that had touched his skin" were brought to those who were sick and "their diseases left them" (v. 12). Naturally, it should not be assumed that the items

---

4. Coretta Scott King, *My Life with Martin Luther King Jr.* (London: Hodder and Stoughton, 1969), 17.

themselves had any power. Rather, Luke is trying to point to the fact that God was working through Paul in an extraordinary way and quite beyond the Apostle's own capabilities. This was God's work, and Luke's emphasis is on Paul's witness to God or, perhaps better, God's love expressed through Paul as he endeavored to share God's love with others.

As sometimes happens, when people saw the healing that took place through Paul, they assumed that he possessed the power and they wanted to have this power, too. Luke claims that some itinerant Jewish exorcists tried to use the name of the Lord, saying, "I adjure you by the Jesus whom Paul proclaims" (v. 13). Also, Luke says that the seven sons of a Jewish high priest, Sceva, were trying to imitate Paul and were (as exorcists) trying to do things in the name of Jesus, but they were not successful (vv. 13-14). Luke seems to be suggesting that they did not have a personal experience of God and were not seeking to bring help to people in God's name. Luke says that an evil spirit leapt out of the man and claimed, "Jesus I know and Paul I know; but who are you?" (v. 15). It has been suggested that Luke's picture of these seven being attacked by the spirit and running away naked is not simply to make a public spectacle of them but to offer a comic scene for Luke's Christian readers on the futility of such deception using the sacred name.[5] Perhaps Luke was suggesting that instead of being afraid of those who opposed them, believers should realize how foolish and laughable it is to think it is possible to imitate or manipulate the power of God. The underlying message is that they were left humiliated and exposed, and in that sense they must be pitied, too.

Luke was emphasizing once again that only God can master evil. Through Paul, the people realized that God was the only source of good. Many believed, and they turned away from magic. Some publicly denounced it and publicly burned their books. Luke mentions the cost of the books perhaps to underscore that this newfound faith was worth far more than material wealth. The public spectacle of burning the books was also a demonstration of repentance. While some people might say it is not necessary to publicly denounce their old ways, Luke indicates that this was not simply an activity the new believers used to draw attention to themselves. Rather, the willingness of individuals to renounce publicly things that they had formerly considered important was an outward sign of an inward desire to turn to God. According to Luke, the result was that "the word of the Lord grew mightily and prevailed" (v. 20).

---

5. Garland, *Acts*, 198.

The Anger of a Crowd, 19:21-41

After this, Paul "resolved in the Spirit to go to through Macedonia and Achaia" and then to Jerusalem before finally heading to Rome (v. 21). In some ways, this description of his travel plans suggests an emphasis on pilgrimage. Luke does not tell us, but it may be inferred that Paul wanted to go to Jerusalem to take the believers the gift collected for poor Christians.[6] Perhaps this was a way of emphasizing the unity in Christ alone between the Jews and the Gentiles. It was also a way of highlighting the responsibility Christians have for one another, especially for those in need. Most probably as a means of preparing the way, Paul "sent two of his helpers," Timothy and Erastus, to Macedonia while he stayed longer in Asia (v. 22). The Apostle would himself go, but only as prompted by the Spirit. For now, his journeying continued in that one place.

While Paul remained in Ephesus a little longer, it became clear that as a disciple of Christ and a person who repeatedly proclaimed the importance of turning from idols to worship a living God, Paul was increasingly seen as a troublemaker. Luke gives us an example in his narrative of a riot that broke out in Ephesus after a silversmith named Demetrius (who made his money creating silver shrines to the goddess Artemis) grew concerned that Paul's teachings that "gods made with hands are not gods" was causing

> "For the sake of the gospel," O God, that is my plea.
>
> For the sake of the gospel help me to lay aside all pettiness and meanness of spirit.
>
> For the sake of the gospel let me find ways to overcome conflict and divisions.
>
> Yet for the sake of the gospel may I not substitute what is not gospel for the gospel or compromise the gospel out of fear or betray the gospel out of self-interest.
>
> For the sake of the gospel help me to stand fast for the gospel.
>
> For the sake of the gospel help me to be faithful to the gospel.
>
> And, finally, O God, for the sake of the gospel enable me, above all, to distinguish what is gospel from what is not the gospel.
>
> For the sake of the gospel enable me to discern the line I must never cross.
>
> For the sake of the gospel enable me to know when to yield and when to stand fast.
>
> Through Jesus Christ, your gospel. Amen.
>
> —E. Glenn Hinson, "Reconciliation and Resistance," in *Standing Fast*, Weavings 15/6 (November/December 2000): 46.

---

6. See Romans 15:25-28.

him to lose business (v. 26). Demetrius stirred up others to oppose Paul, and soon an irate crowd gathered against the Christians. They seized two of Paul's travel companions from Macedonia, Gaius and Aristarchus, and took them to the theater as the crowd shouted over and over, "Great is Artemis of the Ephesians!" (v. 28). Luke is referring to the crowd's frenzied defense of their local cultus, the great shrine of the goddess Artemis, which was a significant feature of the city.

Luke claims that Paul wanted to go himself and speak to the crowd, but the disciples stopped him, and he was even urged by other officials of the province of Asia not to go to the theater where there was a near riot. It appeared that the mob had gained the upper hand when, first, Alexander, "whom the Jews had pushed forward," tried and failed to get the crowd to listen (v. 33). He attempted to speak, but when they realized that he was a Jew, the mob dismissed him and shouted for two hours, "Great is Artemis of the Ephesians!" (v. 34). When at last the town clerk was able to silence the crowd, he warned them that they were in danger of being charged with rioting and suggested that any lawful complaints that Demetrius and the other artisans had should be formally brought to a court for a proconsul's judgment.

As we read the narrative and reflect on the angry crowd dispersing to their separate homes, in imagination we may stand near and overhear the conversations of those who gathered. In anger, we imagine them swearing and saying to one another, "We will not stand for it. We will not allow these people to ruin our business. How dare these upstarts try to convince people to stop worshipping the gods they have always worshipped by saying that there is only one God."

Luke's emphasis on the shouts of the crowd and the rising anger of a mob in Ephesus heightens our awareness that, as followers of Jesus Christ, Paul and the other believers were increasingly in danger. People felt threatened because the teachings about Jesus seemed to be turning the world upside down. The validity of their local cult was called into question as the gospel challenged the predominant culture.

Although Paul felt responsible and wanted to show leadership by going to the theater himself to speak, at the urging of others he did not go. Perhaps this was Luke's way of saying that others could present a robust defense and needed to stand for the faith. It is also a reminder that this was not about Paul, though he figures prominently in the rest of the travel narrative. Yet, while he assumes the role of the Christian pilgrim following in the way of Jesus to Jerusalem and then to Rome, as we shall see, the story is ultimately not about Paul. It is about the power of God at work over the forces of society. It is about the liberating activity of the Spirit of God by whose actions believers are able to point out evil and falsehood in the culture of the day.

Draw Your Own Conclusions

1. What are the signs of repentance? How important are outward signs of inward change?

2. How do we determine the best way to defend the gospel against misunderstanding and misrepresentation?

3. What are the "idols" that challenge believers today?

Acts 20

The Encouragement of Friends, 20:1-6

Paul now prepares to embark on the journey he had planned to Macedonia, Achaia, and then on to Jerusalem before heading to Rome. The journey begins as a pilgrimage of encouragement as well as an opportunity for him to say farewell to the believers. Saying goodbye to friends is never easy, especially those with whom one has a relationship in Christ. Paul had shared time with them, and, as they had faced opposition together, no doubt there was a mutual bond of love and care between them that had been strengthened. Yet Paul's willingness to leave them was another demonstration that this was God's work and not his own work. There is no place for possessiveness or territorial demands in the ministry of the kingdom.

He felt that the Spirit was leading him to leave, and he knew that the time had come. So, after the furor in the theater, Paul sent for the disciples in Ephesus and encouraged them before leaving for Macedonia. He went through to Greece, where he stayed for three months, and then he was about to set sail for Syria when he heard of a plot against him by the Jews. So he decided to go back through Macedonia again. Luke gives the names of his travel companions, all of whom appear to have represented Paul's work among "Gentiles" in Macedonia, Galatia, and Asia. The seven names are Sopater son of Pyrrhus from Beroea, Aristarchus and Secundus from Thessalonica, Gaius from Derbe, and Timothy, Tychicus, and Trophimus from Asia (v. 4).

By listing the names of Paul's companions, Luke highlights the fact that the gospel has spread to many places. Paul, who first appeared as Saul in the narrative and had hunted down the Christians, now had quite a diverse group of Jews and Gentiles, men and women of different ages and social status, as his friends in Christ. As the pilgrimage to Jerusalem and ultimately to Rome continues, Luke is pointing to the spread of Christian faith and reminding us that the love of God is not only able to change people but also draws people together. In Christ, enemies may become friends and strangers become companions on the Way. As we are reminded over and over in Acts, there are no barriers to such shared love in Christ; even those who have held opposing views find common ground. This is surely the "fellowship" alluded to in Acts 2:42.

Interestingly, here in the text Luke says of the travel companions, "we sailed from Philippi after the days of Unleavened Bread, and in five days we joined them in Troas, where we stayed for seven days" (v. 6). While the use of the word "we" may suggest that Luke had rejoined Paul's group, it also serves to draw the reader more closely into the narrative.[1] As Luke well knew, in a sense, believers are always to be on pilgrimage, journeying forward in faith. This theme of pilgrimage has been taken up many times in the history of the church, most notably in the allegory *The Pilgrim's Progress* written by John Bunyan (1628–1688), the Puritan preacher from Bedford. In this work, the main character, Christian, embarks on a journey from the "City of Destruction" to the "Celestial City," and along the way he encounters many difficulties, trials, and temptations. In this allegorical tale, he also meets many characters, such as "Obstinate" and "Pliable" and "Hopeful," and on the way he contends with places like the "Slough of Despond" and the "Hill of Difficulty." Bunyan's purpose was obviously to call believers to reflect on the costly nature of the Christian life. Throughout Acts, this has been Luke's purpose as well. On this final part of the pilgrimage, as Luke recounts Paul's journey to Jerusalem and Rome, Luke shapes the narrative to remind us of how difficult the overall journey of the Christian life can be. The obstacles are many, but believers can know that they are being led in the strength and power of the Spirit, whatever the personal cost or the hardship faced on the way.

A Drowsy Disciple, 20:7-12

Staying in Troas, Luke says that they met to break bread on the first day of the week with the believers. This may be an early reference to the Christian custom of sharing the Lord's Supper on a Sunday.[2] Since Paul planned to leave the next day, he took the opportunity to teach and encourage the

---

1. See discussion in the chapters on Acts 1 and 16.

2. Marshall, *Acts*, 325.

believers in Troas until midnight. The night meeting may have been in part an effort to avoid the authorities who were harassing them. Luke claims that there were lamps lit within the building and that one man, Eutychus, was sitting in a window and became drowsy as Paul spoke.[3] Unfortunately, Eutychus "began to drift off into a deep sleep" and then fell out of the window. While many assumed he was dead, Paul went to him and, "bending over him took him in his arms" and told them not to worry, that he was alive. Indeed, his recovery was seen as a miracle, and perhaps Luke was merely playing down the miraculous side of the incident when he claimed that those who took the boy away were "not a little comforted" (v. 12).

The story is similar to the narrative of Peter healing Tabitha (9:40), and it has been suggested that it is reminiscent of the Old Testament stories of Elijah and Elisha. The implication is that Paul should be seen in line with the prophets of old.[4] On the other hand, it has also been suggested that maybe Luke was reminding the followers of Jesus not to be like the disciples who slept when they should have been watching and praying (Luke 22:45). While it is difficult to know what Luke intended by this story, it may have simply been a way of underscoring how God used Paul. He, like Peter and the prophets before them, was chosen by God to do God's work, and he would use every moment he had to do so. After "breaking bread," the vigil lasted until dawn.

On a human level, anyone who has attended a late-night meeting or listened to a long-winded preacher can empathize with the plight of the drowsy disciple. While we may want to point to Eutychus's inability to stay awake and highlight the need for attentiveness among disciples, it is equally important to note that sometimes we may feel too tired to think, to listen, to give ourselves meaningfully to devotion, or to give our attention to prayerfulness. Commenting on such occasions, Mother Maribel (1887–1970), a sister in a religious order in Wantage in the twentieth century, suggested that even "dog-tired" we could pray. She wrote,

> Dog-tiredness is such a lovely prayer, really, if only we would recognize it as such. Sometimes I hear, "I'm so dog-tired when I get to chapel, I can't pray". But what does it matter? We don't matter. Our Lord can pray just

---

3. Luke injects some humor here, since the name Eutychus means "good fortune" or "lucky" (Witherington, *Acts*, 607).

4. 1 Kings 17:19-22; 2 Kings 4:34-35.

as well through a dog-tired body and mind as through a well-rested one, better perhaps.[5]

The Sorrow of Parting, 20:13-36

Paul's companions went ahead of him and they set sail for Assos. Paul arrived there on foot, and then they set sail to go to Mitylene and to Chios. Next, they touched down at Samos and the day after arrived at Miletus. They had sailed past Ephesus to save time because Paul wanted to get to Jerusalem, if possible, by the day of Pentecost. When they stopped in Miletus, Paul called for the Ephesian elders to meet him in what turned out to be an emotional farewell, as described in Luke's summary of what was spoken there.

Paul's speech to them was not a defense of the gospel or of his ministry. Rather, the purpose of this farewell speech was to encourage them to continue in the faith.[6] He appealed to them to continue the work he had begun among them. He exhorted and encouraged them to follow in the way he had shown them, especially reminding them that they must—if they would be true to Christ—persevere even through trials and difficulties. Using himself as an example, he claimed that he had not been a people pleaser and had not tried to say or do things to keep people on his side. Rather, his main concern was to call people to repentance and to point to the joy he had discovered for himself in relationship with Jesus Christ. The gospel he proclaimed was about nothing less, hence the gravity of his appeal to them to stay faithful.

Turning to their responsibilities, he reminded the Ephesian elders of their duty to keep watch over themselves and the flock. He claimed that "savage wolves" would come among them and even some from within would "come distorting the truth" (v. 29). They must be on guard against all types of deception. Then, he highlighted what Luke seems to have considered one of the greatest temptations: wealth. Paul reminded them that he coveted no one's gold or silver. Rather he worked with his own hands to support himself, and he cared for the weak (v. 35). The believers,

---

5. Sister Janet, CSMV, *Mother Maribel of Wantage* (London: SPCK, 1972), 65, as cited in Lavinia Byrne, ed., *The Hidden Tradition: Women's Spiritual Writings Rediscovered* (London: SPCK, 1991), 113. Mother Maribel, an Anglican nun and a sculptor and artist, was the Mother General of the Community of St. Mary the Virgin in Wantage (England, UK) from 1940 to 1953.

6. Soards, *The Speeches in Acts*, 105.

too, must support the weak and remember, "it is more blessed to give than to receive" (v. 35). Finally, Paul made it clear that while he did not want to say goodbye, he had to leave them because he was "captive to the Spirit" (v. 22). This emphasis on the Spirit is the mantra repeated throughout Acts in one way or another. In this final pilgrimage of Paul toward Jerusalem and Rome, Luke will continue to stress that the work of Paul, as indeed of all

For all who have enriched our lives,
whom we have loved and known,
for saints alive among us still
by whom our faith is honed,
we thank you, God, who came and comes
through women, children, men,
to share the highs and lows of life:
God for us, now as then.

For all who with disarming love
have led us to explore
the risk of reasoning and doubt,
new realms not known before,
we thank you, God, who came and comes
to free us from our past,
from ghettos of rigid mind,
from truths unfit to last.
—Verses 1 and 2 of the hymn by Fred Kaan
© 1996. Hope Publishing Company.
(Carol Stream, IL).

disciples, is God's work. Paul was not making plans of his own but was seeking to go forward in obedience to God, captive to the Holy Spirit. As for the Ephesian elders, it was their duty, as those appointed to share pastoral oversight of some kind, to maintain care for the people and openness to the Spirit.

The themes in the speech are a recitation of the qualities Paul has already claimed are essential for those who seek to follow Christ: perseverance, care for others, proclaiming the gospel to everyone, and openness to Jews and Greeks. He also warned them of pitfalls: trials, opposition from others, false witnesses coming among them to distort the truth, and the lure of wealth—the problems that they had already faced, which would continue to take many guises.

The final dramatic scene is one that Luke, it seems, intends to be etched on the minds and hearts of his readers. Paul has told the believers that he did not count his life as anything (he has died to self) and said that he only wanted to "finish my course" and "the ministry that I received from the Lord Jesus, to testify to the good news of God's grace" (v. 24). Then, Paul kneeled down with the elders from Ephesus, and they wept and prayed together. It is a picture of genuine fellowship in Christ. Paul and the Christians in Miletus, along with the elders from Ephesus, were bound together in the deep bond of love that is known only in Christ. ~~Knowing that they would probably never see Paul again,~~ from a human standpoint they did not want him to leave. Yet, acknowledging the spiritual imperative, they also knew that servants of Christ must continue on the way and that they themselves needed to continue looking to the Spirit for guidance.

Draw Your Own Conclusions

1. How might Christians show encouragement to one another?

2. What are some of the pitfalls to faith?

3. Reflect on Bunyan's pilgrim journey. How might we relate to the idea of Christian pilgrimage today?

Acts 21

To Be a Pilgrim, 21:1-15

The journey to Jerusalem continues. Having bid farewell to the Ephesian elders, Paul and his companions set sail for Cos. As was the custom of the day, they boarded ships that were going in the direction in which they wished to travel. From there, they went to Rhodes and then to Patara. They then boarded a ship bound for Phoenicia. They set sail for Syria and landed at Tyre because the ship needed to unload cargo there. Luke says that they "looked up the disciples and stayed there for seven days" (v. 4). Then, for a second time, we are told of a poignant parting scene as men, women, and children escorted them down to the boat. They all knelt on the beach and prayed as they said farewell.

Luke does not tell us the content of the prayer, though we can imagine that there was thanksgiving to God for all that was shared with Paul and perhaps prayers for Paul and his companions as they continued on their travels. While we sometimes think of prayer merely in terms of petition for ourselves or others and often offer prayer using a particular pattern, there are examples of prayer in the Judeo-Christian tradition that are more spontaneous. The Psalms, for instance, include prayers that are cries of praise and thanksgiving as well as those that offer expressions of deep anguish, including imprecatory prayers that pointedly ask God to act. There are also examples of prayer being offered even while attending to mundane matters, with reference down to the smallest detail in life.

In the fifth and sixth centuries in Ireland, Scotland, Wales, Cornwall, and Brittany, Christians offered prayer while attending to the simple tasks of daily life, like lighting a morning fire, doing the washing, or even milking a cow. Significantly, these Christians, whom we now refer to

as part of the Celtic tradition, emphasized pilgrimage for Christ's sake.[1]
Some of them, like Columba, came from Ireland to Scotland in the
sixth century and helped establish a community at Iona. St. Aidan went
from Iona to Lindisfarne in Northumbria (now often referred to as Holy
Island) in the seventh century and established a community of faith
there. As these believers established communities and travelled to proclaim
the gospel, tradition has it that they, too, had prayers of blessing for the
travellers as well as those going about daily tasks. Wherever they went, there
was the keen sense of seeking to obey God and abiding always (even on
voyages or journeys) in the presence of God. There was also an awareness
of the ways that their faith might be challenged. As the well-known verses
attributed to St. Patrick put it,

> I arise today through
> God's strength to pilot me, God's might to uphold me,
> God's wisdom to guide me, God's eye to see before me,
> God's ear to hear me, God's word to speak for me,
> God's hand to guard me, God's way to lie before me,
> God's shield to protect me, God's host to secure me—
>   against snares of devils,
>   against temptations and vices,
>   against inclinations of nature,
>   against everyone who shall wish me
>   ill, far and near,
>   alone and in a crowd . . .
> Christ, be with me, Christ before me, Christ behind me,
> Christ in me, Christ beneath me, Christ above me,
> Christ on my right, Christ on my left, Christ where I lie, Christ where
> I sit,
> Christ where I arise, Christ in the heart of every man who thinks of me,
> Christ in the mouth of every man who speaks of me,
> Christ in every eye that sees me, Christ in every ear that hears me.
>   Salvation is of the Lord.
>   Salvation is of the Lord.

---

1. For a discussion of the "Celtic tradition," see Esther de Waal, *A World Made Whole:
Rediscovering the Celtic Tradition* (London: Harper and Collins, 1991); Ian Bradley, *Colonies
of Heaven: Celtic Models for Today's Church* (London: Darton, Longman and Todd, 2000);
Celtic Spirituality, *The Classics of Western Spirituality*, trans. and introduced by Oliver Davies
(New York: Paulist Press, 1999).

Salvation is of the Christ.
May your salvation, O Lord, be ever with us.[2]

Having had prayer with his friends from Tyre, Paul and his companions went to Ptolemais and greeted the believers (v. 7). They stayed a day before going to Caesarea. There Paul and his companions went and stayed at the house of Philip, one of the seven (described as "the evangelist"). "He had four unmarried daughters who had the gift of prophecy" (v. 9). While they were there, a prophet from Judea, named Agabus, came and took Paul's belt, using it to bind his own hands and feet, and warned Paul that this would happen to him at the hands of the Jews if he went to Jerusalem. Unsurprisingly, the people there urged him not to go. Yet Paul was adamant. He would not be won over by an emotional appeal. In a scene reminiscent of the journey of Jesus toward Jerusalem before he was arrested and then crucified, Paul claimed, "For I am ready not only to be bound but even to die in Jerusalem for the name of the Lord Jesus" (v. 13). Luke then says that since they were unable to persuade him, "we remained silent except to say, 'the Lord's will be done'" (v. 14). Though there are times to speak, this was a time for silence and for quiet acceptance of God's call and due resignation to God's will.

By giving details of their travel and highlighting the warning of Agabus, Luke is stressing once again the costliness of following in the way of Christ. Just as Jesus "set his face" toward Jerusalem, so Paul was determined to go to Jerusalem. He had already been warned of the dangers, but the issue was not his safety; it was his desire to be obedient to the will of God.[3] He was a follower of Christ. Whatever the dangers, he must go. However hard it might be to leave cherished things or people behind, he must willingly relinquish all of it for Christ's sake (Luke 9:57-62).

Accompanying Paul on this journey to Jerusalem, we too are reminded that Christian pilgrimage takes us to many different places. We meet with people we know and love and who are of like mind. We also rub shoulders with those who would betray us or wish us harm. We meet selfish people, braggarts, and those who are focused on material gain. We also form deep relationships in the bond of God's love. In their own way, good or bad, there are people or things that distract us from following in the way of

---

2. This is an abridged version of a longer prayer attributed to St. Patrick. For the longer version see *Celtic Spirituality*, 118–20.

3. Paul was warned three times of the dangers in 20:22-24, 21:4; and 21:10-11.

Christ. Every Christian must aim to follow Christ, to be led by the Spirit, and to stay focused on the journey.

As we have already seen, the idea of staying on the journey and following always in the way of Christ in spite of difficulty is a major theme of Christian spirituality. Evelyn Underhill, an early twentieth-century Christian, believed that waiting through difficulty is part of our participation in the passion of Christ. She pointed out that just as the Lord's quiet time was Gethsemane, so we must have waiting moments before we make "a great spiritual effort."[4] She argued that Christians must reflect on the pain and conflict that Christ faced. Then, harking back to the journey of Christian in Bunyan's *Pilgrim's Progress*, she described some of the trouble that must be endured:

> If there is a Christian form of discipline, it is based neither on will-power nor on a morality of things to be given up. Far from being an end in itself, it is a humble response to a love . . . .
> There are days when it is hard to keep going. But without perseverance our commitment wastes away. Remaining faithful even more in times of dryness than when faith breaks spontaneously into prayer. Keeping in mind the times that were filled with a Presence.
> The only remedy for formalism and routine lies in remaining true to a resolution we have made, and in this way, fervour and adoration will spring up once again.
> —*Brother Roger of Taizé:*
> *His Love Is a Fire: Central Writings*
> *with Extracts from His Journals*
> (London: Geoffrey Chapman
> Mowbray, 1988/1990), 22

> Weariness and desolation of spirit, the complete disappearance of everything that could minister to spiritual self-love, humiliating falls and bitter deprivations, the apparent failure even of faith, buffetings of Satan renewed when we least expected, long sojourn in the solitary valley where Christian "was so confounded that he did not know his own voice": these are all part of that long process, which sometimes seems like a plodding journey and sometimes like a swaying battle, through which the mighty purposes of the Divine Charity are fulfilled in human souls.[5]

---

4. Evelyn Underhill, *School of Charity* (London: Longmans, Green and Co., 1934), 61.

5. Underhill, *School of Charity*, 62.

All of this and more, Underhill claimed, is part of Christian faith. Having reflected on the struggle ahead, the Christian is called to respond, even though the way may be difficult. She added,

> Little wonder that the Christian must be sturdy about it; fit for all weathers, and indifferent to his [her] interior ups and downs. Umbrellas, mackintoshes, and digestive tabloids [*sic*] are not issued to genuine travellers on this way. Comfort and safety-first must give place to courage and love, if we are to become—as we should be—the travelling agents of the Divine Charity. If the road on which we find ourselves is narrow, with a bad surface and many sudden gradients, it is probably the right route. The obvious and convenient by-pass which skirts the worst hill also by-passes the city set upon the hill: the City of Contemplation of the Love of God. It gives a very nice general view to the pious motorist; but those who enter the City must put up with the bad approach. After a certain point the right road is marked "unfit for motors," and the traveller must go forward alone.[6]

Bowing and Bending, 21:16-26

Paul arrived in Jerusalem in much the same way that he did earlier, as narrated in Acts 15. He was welcomed warmly when he visited James, and then he met with all the elders to report on the things God did among the Gentiles. Hearing Paul's report, they were pleased and praised God. However, they immediately turned their attention to the danger that awaited Paul. While the issue about Gentiles not having to keep the Jewish law when they became believers was settled, many Jewish believers felt that Paul had told Messianic Jews that they did not need to keep the law either. It was rumored that Paul was a Jew who did not keep the law. This was not true. As Luke has already pointed out, Paul encouraged Timothy to be circumcised (16:3); Paul also took a Nazarite vow (18:18), and he went to Jerusalem in time to be there for the Pentecost celebration (20:16).

Still it seems that rumors flew about, so the Jerusalem council suggested that Paul should accompany four men who were preparing for the rite of purification. (Their heads were shaved, which would imply that they were taking the Nazarite vow.) If Paul accompanied the men for this rite, it would be a public display of his loyalty to the Jewish faith and, perhaps, go some way toward quelling the gossip about Paul. He agreed and went to the

---

6. Underhill, *School of Charity*, 62.

temple with the four men. In doing this, it appears that Luke is suggesting that Paul was "acting in an accommodating way to foster the unity of the church."[7] However, Paul's desire to keep the peace and work for unity raises issues about how far one should go for the sake of unity. Is it possible to foster unity without sacrificing conscience? When is compromise acceptable for the greater good?

The twentieth-century philosopher and theologian Howard Thurman (1899–1981) spoke eloquently of the need to work for unity among all people. Brought up in Daytona, Florida, in the early twentieth century, Thurman knew the suffering that comes when one race mistreats another. His own grandmother had been a slave, and he experienced for himself the ugliness of racial prejudice. He endured racial segregation and knew how it separates and harms not just one group of people but society as a whole. Yet, throughout his life, he felt a call to try both to break down the barriers and to build bridges between people. In 1944, he felt called by God to leave his work as Dean of Rankin Chapel and Professor of Theology at Howard University and move, with his family, to San Francisco to serve as minister of the Church for the Fellowship of All Peoples. In this church, members pledged to "share in the spiritual growth and ethical awareness of men and women of varied national, cultural, racial, and creedal heritage united in a religious fellowship."[8]

Thurman experienced a number of hurdles as he set about trying to bring people together. It was not easy in the 1940s for an African American man to be accepted in the wider community as a Christian minister to people of all races. Yet, because he believed that he was called by God to be there to witness to the love of God in Jesus Christ, he began to build relationships with people in the fellowship and outside the church, too. The result was the growth of a community where people began to see and love one another as people. His faith was personal. As he put it, from his earliest years he had known that "Jesus was more of a religious subject than religious object."[9] Yet, as he grew in his faith, he described a deepening awareness of the need to simply stay on one journey. In his autobiography, *With Head and Heart*, he wrote,

---

7. Talbert, *Reading Acts*, 186.

8. Howard Thurman, *With Head and Heart* (London: Harcourt Brace and Company, 1979), 143.

9. Thurman, *With Head and Heart*, 266.

The older I have grown, the more it is clear that what I needed to hold me to my path was the sure knowledge that I was committed to a single journey with but a single goal—a way toward life. In formal and religious terms this meant for me the disclosure of the Will of God. And from this flowed an inescapable necessity: to be totally involved. What I did with my life had to be secure in the inclusive sense that only the word "total" can signify.[10]

Thurman seems to describe a life of freedom discovered only when one is on the path of obedience to God and open to others. He described, for instance, being invited to give a "vesper address" at Olivet College in Michigan in 1926. He said that a few minutes before the service, the person who had invited him said quite casually, "By the way, Howard, I neglected to tell you that many of the people at the vesper this afternoon will be Jewish."[11] Thurman's comment on this occasion speaks of the change and transformation he had discovered in his own life in God:

In that moment I suddenly imagined that I was a Jew. What would be my reaction, my thoughts! Instantly I felt a sensitivity I had never known and have never forgotten. I reshaped my address with that imaginative leap. It was a fresh, new moment in my life, the residue of which has never left me.[12]

Closed Doors, 21:27-40

Paul's decision to accompany the four men to the temple for the ritual ceremony may not have been simply an attempt to accommodate the culture and therefore "keep the peace." It seems likely that he, too, had discovered a freedom that comes by being on a "single journey" with but a "single goal." However, Paul was not successful in convincing the determined opposition of his faith and openness. Some of the antagonistic Jews stirred up the crowd against him. They had seen Trophimus, an Ephesian, with him in the city, and they had wrongly assumed that Paul had brought him into the temple. They accused Paul of teaching against the Jewish law and the temple. Moreover, they said he had brought a Greek into the temple and so

---

10. Thurman, *With Head and Heart*, 266.

11. Thurman, *With Head and Heart*, 266.

12. Thurman, *With Head and Heart*, 266–67.

defiled it. The crowd was incensed. They seized Paul and dragged him out. The doors to the temple were shut, which signaled it was shut to outsiders.

The crowd began to beat Paul and tried to kill him. The uproar came to the attention of the Roman authorities, and they rushed to calm the disturbance. The officials assumed that Paul must be an Egyptian outlaw who had caused trouble earlier. They tried to calm the crowd and to ask who he was, but Luke records (harking back to the rejection of Jesus) that the people were shouting "away with him" (v. 36). Finally, the soldiers had to carry Paul out. Once he was out and being taken to the barracks, Paul spoke to the man in Greek and asked if he could say something. He identified himself as a Jew and a citizen of Tarsus in Cilicia and asked for permission to speak. When the people were quiet, he addressed them in the Hebrew language.

Draw Your Own Conclusions

1. Reflect on the prayer attributed to St. Patrick. Is praying at all times still possible in life today? What might hinder prayer in the smaller, ordinary tasks of life?

2. How might Christians seek to shape their witness to Christ in order to reach out to others?

3. What does it mean to reflect on Jesus as more of a "subject" than an "object"?

Acts 22

A Testimony, 22:1-30

Paul stood to speak to the mob, and once they grew quiet he addressed them in the Hebrew dialect, presumably ~~Aramaic~~.[1] It has been suggested that this was the ~~first of six defense speeches~~. However, this speech was not simply a defense; it was also an ~~attempt to once again offer his testimony~~. Luke is trying to make the case that ~~Paul was a faithful Jew~~, and faithful to the Jewish traditions, even as he was also a follower of Jesus Christ, always ready to account for his faith.

According to Luke, Paul told those who had gathered that he was ~~brought up in the strictest tradition of Judaism~~, at the feet of a teacher named ~~Gamaliel~~ (v. 3). Such was his adherence to Jewish law that, previously, he had persecuted those who were followers of Jesus, rounding up both men and women who claimed to be followers of "the Way" and putting them in prison (v. 4). Having ~~established his credentials as a loyal adherent~~ to the ~~Jewish faith~~, Luke records that Paul then gave an account of his conversion ~~to Christian faith on the Damascus road~~. This is the second time that Luke relates how Paul (Saul) was on the way to Damascus to persecute Christians when, blinded by a great light, he fell to the ground. He claimed that a voice then said to him, "Saul, Saul why are you persecuting me?" "Who are you Lord?" asked Saul. To which came the reply: "I am Jesus of Nazareth whom you are persecuting." "What am I to do Lord?" Saul asked (v. 8). According to Luke, he was then instructed, "Get up and go to Damascus; there you will be told everything that has been assigned to you to do" (v. 10). The narrative then recounts the help that Saul received from Ananias, who was a "devout man according to the law and well spoken of

---

1. Garland, *Acts*, 234.

by all the Jews living there" (v. 12). Finally, Luke's account of Paul's speech includes how Paul was visited by Ananias, who called him "Brother Saul" and then "commissioned" him to proclaim the gospel with these words:

> The God of our ancestors has chosen you to know his will, to see the Righteous One and to hear his voice; for you will be his witness to all the world of what you have seen and heard. And now why do you delay? Get up, be baptized, and have your sins washed away, calling on his name. (vv. 14-15)

The basic elements of Paul's testimony, as indicated by Luke, are the same as we find in Acts 9. In each case, Paul is keen to stress that at every stage, God was guiding him. He was not making choices on his own. He did not simply decide to begin to follow Jesus. Rather, he was confronted by the Lord and called to follow. Luke then says that Paul told how he had returned to Jerusalem and was praying at the temple when he claimed he fell into a trance and saw Jesus, who said that he should "hurry and get out of Jerusalem" because the Jews would not receive his testimony. Luke says Paul pointed out that he knew at this point that he was being sent to the Gentiles (v. 21). Unlike the account in chapter 9, here Luke uses the personal word of command to indicate Paul's decision to go to the Gentiles with the gospel.

Through the years, some Christians have used Paul's experience as a pattern for conversion.[2] While Luke did not intend for it to become a set pattern to be followed by everyone, it does seem that we can draw some identifiable aspects of an encounter with the Lord from Luke's account of the conversion of Paul. First, he was "called out" and, in a sense, surprised by God in a dramatic encounter. Second, Paul was brought to his knees before God, and in the story it says that he was blinded and then led by the hand to Damascus. This detail seems to be Luke's reminder that an encounter with God draws attention to the frailty and need of human beings and to the place of "submission" as true openness to God. Finally, in Luke's view, a personal experience with Christ will leave a person unable to look at the world in the same way and unable to carry on with life in the usual way. At this stage, and as an expression of the recognition of their sin, a person must repent, or "turn around," be baptized, and then seek to live

---

2. See discussion in Acts 9.

in obedience to God, demonstrated in daily life and in association with the community of faith.

> I fled Him, down the nights and down the days;
> I fled Him, down the arches of the years;
> I fled Him, down the labyrinthine ways
> Of my own mind; and in the mist of tears
> I hid from Him, and under running laughter.
>   Up vistaed hopes I sped;
>   And shot, precipitated,
> Adown Titanic glooms of chasmèd fears,
>   From those strong Feet that followed, followed after.
>   But with unhurrying chase,
>   And unperturbèd pace,
>   Deliberate speed, majestic instancy,
>   They beat—and a Voice beat
>   More instant than the Feet—
> 'All things betray thee, who betrayest Me . . .'
>   —First verse of "The Hound of Heaven"
>   by Francis Thompson (1859–1907)

In thinking about Paul's emphasis on obedience throughout this testimony, we might note again that obedience to God is a theme often highlighted by Christian spiritual writers. Indeed, obedience is associated with "letting go," relinquishing control, and "submitting to the authority of another." While we may talk about obedience to God and seeking God's will, the truth is that human beings as a whole are not naturally compliant, which is probably why so many spiritual writers return to the theme of obedience over and over.

One simple but profound discussion of the meaning of obedience to those seeking to live as Followers of the Way was presented by an American Quaker Thomas Kelly (1893–1941) in his work, *A Testament of Devotion*. Kelly grew up living on a farm in Southwestern Ohio and during that time attended Quaker meetings with his parents. As a young man, he went to college initially to study science, but then he became enthralled with philosophy and dreamed of making his mark in the world of academia. Douglas Steere, who wrote a biographical essay of Kelly's life, claimed that even after he had married and was teaching in a Quaker College, Kelly was restless and always seemed to want to achieve higher status and recognition in the academic world.[3] In the autumn of 1937, however, Steere claimed that something happened to Kelly and he changed as a person. The things that had seemed to matter to him were no longer his focus. Steere put it this way: "No one knows exactly what happened, but a strained period in his life was over. He moved toward adequacy. A fissure in him seemed to close, cliffs caved in and filled up a chasm, and what was divided grew together within him."[4] Others who knew him recognized that while he had possessed "knowledge about" God, now it seemed that he had "an acquaintance with" God.[5] In a lecture to a Quaker meeting in 1938, Kelly encouraged people to believe that God could be found:

> To you in this room who are seekers, to you, young and old who have toiled all night and caught nothing, but who want to launch out into the deeps and let down your nets for a draught, I want to speak as simply, as tenderly, as clearly as I can. For God *can* be found. There *is* a last rock for your souls, a resting place of absolute peace and joy and power and radiance and security. There is a Divine Center into which your life can slip, a new and absolute orientation in God, a Center where you live with Him and out of which you see all of life, through new and radiant vision, tinged with new sorrows and pangs, new joys unspeakable and full of glory.[6]

By all accounts, it seems that Thomas Kelly had experienced another step in his life with God and for God. It was another step in the conversion process. He knew that this was not the end of the journey. Alluding to the poem of Francis Thompson, Kelly claimed that it is possible to have an experience that leaves a person no doubt that the "Eternal Lover of the world, the Hound of Heaven is utterly, utterly real, and that life must henceforth be determined by that Real."[7] When individuals have discovered God or, perhaps better, discovered that God has been longing for relationship with them, the next step according to Kelly is obedience. He wrote,

---

3. Thomas R. Kelly, *A Testament of Devotion with a Biographical Memoir by Douglas V. Steere* (New York: Harper and Row, 1941), 8ff.

4. Kelly, *A Testament of Devotion*, 18.

5. Kelly, *A Testament of Devotion*, 19.

6. Kelly, *A Testament of Devotion*, 18–19.

7. Kelly, *A Testament of Devotion*, 57. The poem by Francis Thompson (1859–1907) likens God to the "Hound of Heaven" baying at our heels.

"But holy and listening and alert obedience remains, as the core and kernel of a God-intoxicated life, as the abiding pattern of sober, workaday living."[8]

While many people imagine that obedience is a passive activity, Kelly claimed that we are to be active and seek to subject our will to the divine will. He acknowledged that this is not easy but takes place over time as we "wrestle" with our own desires. To aid in the process (it is a process, not a one-time event) Kelly offered "steps to obedience." The first step, he claimed, is to have "the flaming vision of the wonder of life" with God and for God. The second step is a willingness to begin in the present moment— just "begin where you are," "obey now." The third step in obedience to God, according to Kelly, is a willingness to start over again and again. He wrote, "If you slip and stumble and forget God for an hour, and assert your old proud self, and rely upon your own clever wisdom, don't spend too much time in anguished regrets and self-accusations but begin again, just where you are." Finally, Kelly claimed that the last step to holy obedience is a willingness to live in the "passive voice." In other words, Kelly says, "Relax. Take hands off. Submit yourself to God. Learn to live in the passive voice . . . ." "Don't grit your teeth and clench your fists and say, 'I will! I will!' . . . For 'I will' spells not obedience."[9] Significantly, Kelly claimed that there are many "fruits" of holy obedience, but importantly, in addition to humility and simplicity, Kelly said that obedience to God will inevitably be "an entrance into suffering."[10]

Writing during the period of World War II, Kelly was acutely aware of the number of people who were suffering as a result of the conflict. Yet the suffering he spoke of—as a result of "holy obedience"—was not suffering that may be avoided or removed. Rather he was referring to what Dietrich Bonhoeffer called the "cost of discipleship."[11] Claiming that seeing "the cross as dogma is painless speculation," Kelly argued that suffering comes to us as we seek to do the tasks of love that God has put into our hearts.[12]

It seems evident from reading *A Testament of Devotion* that Kelly, like the Apostle Paul, had come to a turning point in his life. His experience was not exactly like that of Paul. Every person is unique and has his or her own encounter with God. However, it is interesting that Kelly seems to

---

8. Kelly, *A Testament of Devotion*, 58.

9. Kelly, *A Testament of Devotion*, 60–61.

10. Kelly, *A Testament of Devotion*, 67.

11. See discussion in Acts 7.

12. Kelly, *A Testament of Devotion*, 71.

draw parallels between his "Damascene experience" and the experience of
the Apostle Paul described by Luke. Kelly wrote,

> But humility rests upon holy blindedness [*sic*] like the blindedness of
> him who looks steadily into the sun. For wherever he turns his eyes on
> earth, there he sees only the sun. The God-blinded soul sees naught of
> self, naught of personal degradation or of personal eminence, but only
> the Holy Will working impersonally through him, through others, as one
> objective Life and Power. But what trinkets we have sought after in life,
> the pursuit of what petty trifles has wasted our years as we have minis-
> tered to the enhancement of our own little selves! And what needless
> anguishes we have suffered because *our* little selves were defeated, were
> not flattered, were not cozened and petted! But the blinding God blots
> out this self and gives humility and true selfhood as wholly full of Him.[13]

Kelly, like many others, was drawing on the analogy of "seeing, but not
seeing," which is used by Luke a number of times in his Gospel as well as in
Acts. By highlighting Paul's testimony of being blinded and then recovering
sight, Luke seems to urge the Jews who were antagonistic to open their
eyes to God in a new way. At this point in the narrative, however, while
the crowd appeared to listen to Paul's testimony, Luke says that the people
became angry and began to shout, "Away with such a fellow from the earth!
For he should not be allowed to live" (v. 22). It may have been that they
were outraged by the mere mention of the Gentiles, or perhaps Luke was
pointing to the fact that since they were not seeing, they were "full of darkness" (Luke 11:33–36).

The crowd, according to Luke, became so incensed that they would
have murdered Paul, but the centurions were holding him. At this point the
tribune said Paul should be brought to the barracks and flogged in order
to find out why the people were so angry with him. However, when they
had tied him up and were preparing to flog him, Paul asked a centurion
standing by if it was legal "to flog a Roman citizen who is uncondemned"
(v. 25). It wasn't legal; no Roman citizen was to be scourged before a trial
and conviction. The centurion went to tell the tribune that Paul was a
Roman citizen and could not be flogged. The next day, the tribune released
Paul and had him brought before the chief priests and the council.

This story highlights Paul's desire to put aside claims of any status,
rank, or position that previously formed his identity and worth as a person.

---

13. Kelly, *A Testament of Devotion*, 62–63.

While he made the point that he had reason to boast of very good credentials, and he had used them to track down and arrest Christians, now he no longer cared about these things. For him, what was of most importance was his desire to be obedient to God. Paul realized that his personhood did not depend on the human recognition that awards, personal achievement, and cultural status might bring. It is telling that when Paul found himself at the mercy of state officials, in order to avoid being flogged he did not hesitate to use his credentials as a Roman citizen. Clearly, however, he was not trying to use his status to impress or to gain power over anyone else, nor did he shrink from suffering in other contexts (cf. Gal 6:17). He used his rights as a citizen to enable him to be given the opportunity to fulfill his calling to go to Rome.

Draw Your Own Conclusions

1. Is there a difference between a personal testimony and a defense of the faith?

2. How can judgments be made about claims regarding "a call from God," "a word from the Lord," or "prophetic speech"?

3. How would you describe obedience to God?

4. Is there a template for conversion that might be inferred from this or other stories in Acts? Why or why not?

Acts 23

A Very Bad Day, 23:1-11

As noted earlier, there are evident parallels between the journey Jesus made to Jerusalem and Paul's final journey to Jerusalem and then to Rome. Just as Jesus had "set his face" to Jerusalem (Luke 9:51), so, too, Paul was determined to go to Jerusalem. Now he stands before the Sanhedrin to face the accusations against him. Entering into the narrative, we must take our place as observers in the room. The atmosphere is highly charged as Paul stands before his accusers. Paul looks intently at them and then speaks. "Brothers," he says "up to this day, I have lived my life with a clear conscience before God" (v. 1). The high priest standing nearby has Paul struck on the mouth, presumably because he addressed the assembly as equals, calling them "brothers." Quick-tempered, Paul replies angrily, "God will strike you, you whitewashed wall! Are you sitting there to judge me according to the law, and yet in violation of the law you order me to be struck?" (v. 3). The metaphor of a whitewashed wall is taken from Ezekiel 13:8-15 and suggests that the high priest is not being truthful.[1]

People around Paul rebuked him for speaking to the high priest in this way. He apologized and claimed that he did not know this man was the high priest. This again could be construed as an insult because Paul seems to suggest that the high priest should have been recognizable as such! Another alternative may be that Paul had poor eyesight (see Gal 4:13-15).

As Luke relates the account, it does not appear that Paul has gotten off to a good start in his speech with the council. Things seem to be going from bad to worse. Then, perhaps to distract attention away from himself, Paul

---

1. The metaphor is taken from Ezekiel 13:8-15, where prophets are denounced by God for promising peace when there is no peace. They are likened to flimsy walls built and covered with whitewash to make them appear solid (Garland, *Acts*, 24).

appealed to the Pharisees that he, too, was a Pharisee, a son of Pharisees, and he was on trial for declaring the hope of the resurrection of the dead (v. 6). Again Luke presents a comical scene as the ploy works. The Pharisees immediately began to debate with the Sadducees the validity of believing in the resurrection of the dead. They argued so fiercely that some scribes (teachers who were Pharisees) within the group rose up and said, "We find nothing wrong with this man. What if a spirit or an angel has spoken to him?" (v. 9). Luke ironically adds an aside to explain that the Sadducees believed there was no "resurrection, or angel, or spirit; but the Pharisees acknowledge all three" (v .8). Luke also indicates that those who were Pharisees did not condemn Paul.

Luke concludes the account by stating that the argument grew so fierce that the tribune feared the mob would "tear Paul to pieces." So he ordered soldiers to take Paul back to the barracks (v. 10). That night, after a very bad day, Luke says that the Lord stood near to Paul and said, "Keep up your courage! For just as you have testified for me in Jerusalem, so you must bear witness also in Rome" (v. 11). These were words of encouragement and hope as well as affirmation of Paul's sense of call amid what seemed like an impossible situation. While the trouble is not always immediately removed, Luke seems to offer a reminder that God comes to those who continue to ask and seek. Indeed, to everyone who knocks the door will be opened (Luke 11:10).

Sometimes the devoted Christian life is depicted as trouble free. Appealing to the human desire for a "good life," it is sometimes suggested that believers need only "come to Jesus and you will be blessed with a happy life and riches untold." The truth is that every person will face trials and difficulties, but especially those who choose to follow in the way of Jesus. After all, we

Finally, there must be a matured and maturing sense of Presence. This sense of Presence must be a reality at the personal level as well as on the social, naturalistic, and cosmic levels. To state it in the simplest language of religion, modern man [woman] must know that he [she] is a child of God and that the God of life in all its parts and the God of the human heart are one and the same. Such an assurance will vitalize the sense of self, and highlight the sense of history, with the warmth of a great confidence. Thus, we shall look out upon life with quiet eyes and work on our tasks with the conviction and detachment of Eternity.

—Howard Thurman, *Deep is the Hunger*
(New York: Harper and Row, 1951;
repr., Richmond, IN:
Friends United Press, 2000), 144.

follow one who came to serve (Luke 22:27). Trouble, hardship, and suffering are part of any life, and no Christian is exempt. Whether our trouble is due to our own poor choices or whether it involves facing illness or loss or confronting disappointment, often what we need more than anything is the courage to go on believing. Courage is not an attitude or outlook that we can devise or manufacture. Genuine courage is closely linked to the assurance of God's presence. Many have testified to a renewed sense of courage when they became aware of the reality of God—not simply in worship, not just in good moments, but in the midst of trouble, too. Our courage is the outworking of our trust in Christ and is to be distinguished from human bravery or heroism.

The fourteenth-century English mystic Mother Julian (1342–c. 1416) of Norwich lived in a time of great turmoil. Due to social inequity and exploitation of the poor, there were food shortages and riots. It was also the age of the Black Death, when many people died as the bubonic plague swept devastatingly across Europe. Mother Julian lived a solitary life alongside the Church of St. Julian at Conisford, near Norwich, and it was here that she gave herself to a life of prayer. She particularly prayed that she would know the sufferings of Christ and identify with Christ in his suffering. Around the age of thirty as she lay stricken with a near-fatal illness, she had several visions of Christ in which she was comforted, and these "revelations" gave her courage and hope. She survived the illness and later pondered the meaning of these visions. What she saw was written down and is available to us today as the *Revelations of Divine Love*. In her reflections on the experience of identifying with the suffering of Christ, at one point she claimed that she was given an assurance of God's presence and peace.

> These words, "You will not be overcome", were said very insistently and emphatically to give me confidence and strength for every trouble that may come. He did not say "You will not have a rough time; you will not be burdened; you will not have to face difficulties", he said "You will not be overcome". God wants us to pay attention to these words so that we can always be strong and confident, through good and bad times. God loves us and delights in us, so he wants us to love and delight in him and trust him implicitly. So all will be well.[2]

---

2. Mother Julian, *Revelations of Divine Love* (London: Hodder and Stoughton, 1987), 142.

Courage, in distinction from fortitude, comes from the realization that no matter how many bad days we may have, God does not abandon us but comes and stands alongside us. All down through the ages people have had moments when they felt that God directly intervened to bring them courage they might not have had otherwise and to remind them that they would not be overcome. Martin Luther King Jr., Baptist leader and Civil Rights activist, told of one occasion when he felt broken. He had endured a difficult day, and he was increasingly worried about the threats that he and his family had received. On this night the phone rang and an angry voice on the other end threatened him again. At this point, King claimed that he felt "all of my fears had come down on me at once." As he struggled with his mixed emotions, he came to a decisive moment in his life:

> With my head in my hands, I bowed over the kitchen table and prayed aloud. The words I spoke to God that midnight are still vivid in my memory: "Lord, I'm down here trying to do what's right. I think I'm right. I am here taking a stand for what I believe is right. But Lord, I must confess that I'm weak now, I'm faltering. I'm losing my courage. Now, I am afraid. And I can't let the people see me like this because if they see me weak and losing my courage, they will begin to get weak. The people are looking to me for leadership, and if I stand before them without strength and courage, they too will falter. I am at the end of my powers. I have nothing left. I've come to the point where I can't face it alone."
>
> It seemed as though I could hear the quiet assurance of an inner voice saying: "Martin Luther, stand up for righteousness. Stand up for justice. Stand up for truth. And lo, I will be with you. Even until the end of the world."[3]

Plots and Counterplots, 23:12-35

The strength of the local opposition to Paul is revealed when Luke says that more than forty Jews joined in a conspiracy to have Paul killed. Such was their determination to stop Paul that they vowed not to eat or drink until they had killed him (vv. 12-14). They hatched a plot to have him brought to the Sanhedrin again for a more thorough investigation, as they

---

3. Martin Luther King Jr., "The Violence of Desperate Men," chapter 8 in *The Autobiography of Martin Luther King Jr.*, ed. Claybourn E. Carson (New York: Grand Central Publishing, 2001). Available online at the Martin Luther King Jr. Research and Education Institute, Stanford University, https://kinginstitute.stanford.edu/king-papers/publications/autobiography-martin-luther-king-jr-contents/chapter-8-violence-desperate.

planned for him to be ambushed and killed by a mob. Luke then surprises us by revealing that Paul had a nephew (otherwise unknown to us) who heard of the plot and informed his uncle. Paul had the young man taken to the tribune to tell him of the plot. The tribune then decided to send Paul under guard to Felix the governor, writing a letter seeking to portray himself in the best possible light. The tribune did not say that he had put Paul in chains and was about to have him flogged. Rather he claimed that Paul, a Roman citizen, was in danger at the hands of a mob and that he had rescued him. He wrote that hearing that there was a plot against Paul, he was therefore sending him to be examined by Felix. Paul was taken to Felix, and when Felix realized that Paul was from Cilicia, he claimed that he would deal with his case when his accusers arrived. Paul was then taken to Herod's headquarters, the governor's residence, to be kept safely under guard. As the story progresses, there is an increasing sense that Paul will be required to stand alone, though confident in the assurance that, as he sought to be obedient to God and as the Holy Spirit guided him, he would not be overcome.

Draw Your Own Conclusions

1. Where might our own faith and witness lead us into danger today?

2. What are the means by which we come to know God's presence among us, in particular when facing difficulty?

3. Why is it important to see the difference between everyday hardships and the difficulties we must bear for the sake of the gospel?

Acts 24

Incarceration and Conversation, 24:1-27

Along with an accompanying letter written by the tribune, Lysias, soldiers delivered Paul to Felix, the governor at Caesarea. The letter outlined the fact that Paul was seized by some Jews who were annoyed because they did not think he was keeping their religious laws. Upon receiving the letter, Felix said that he would hear the case when Paul's accusers arrived. Five days later, the high priest Ananias, along with some of the elders and Tertullus, an attorney who was a professional orator, came from Jerusalem to Caesarea to testify against Paul before Felix (v. 1). Luke claims that Tertullus, who does not appear to have been a Jew, began by complimenting Felix. To gain the favor of Felix, though contrary to the claims of history, Tertullus sought to ingratiate himself by saying that Felix had brought peace and reforms to the land.[1] He then accused Paul of being a disturber of the peace. He claimed that Paul was seized because he had profaned the temple and that he was a ringleader of the sect of Nazarenes, "a pestilent fellow, and an agitator among all the Jews throughout the world" (v. 5).

According to Luke, Paul then offered his defense and stated that he had not denied or contravened his Jewish faith. He had worshipped regularly, and on his recent visit to Jerusalem, contrary to their allegations, he had not caused a disturbance in the synagogue or the temple (v. 12). In the narrative provided by Luke, Paul claimed that he believed in the resurrection of

---

1. Antonius Felix was procurator of Judea from AD 52/53 to 59/60. He was a former slave of Mark Antony's daughter. After he became a freedman, he rose to power. His brother Pallas was financial secretary to the emperor Nero. He was not acclaimed as a good leader; rather he was unjust and cruel. Tacitus, the Roman historian, claimed that Felix "wielded royal authority with the disposition of a slave." (See Garland, *Acts*, 254; Caird, *The Apostolic Age*, 34).

the dead, and he believed that Christianity was the fulfillment of all that the prophets had foretold—indeed, the true fulfillment of the Jewish faith (v. 14). Felix, Luke says, was well informed about "the Way" and decided to keep Paul in custody and under guard, though Felix stipulated that Paul should have some liberty and that his friends should not be prevented from meeting his needs. Paul was then kept under guard for two years, probably because Felix wanted him to pay money to secure his release. In the end, Felix was succeeded by Porcius Festus, Luke says that because Felix wanted to gain favor with the Jews, he left Paul in prison.

Two years of conversation. Two years of uncertainty. Two years of incarceration and reflection with little, if any, hope of release. Paul could do nothing but wait. He was living in what today we might call the "meantime." It is a place that most people know well. The meantime is an interval, the time between one occurrence and another. It is the period between the "now and the not yet." In many ways, we humans spend most of our lives in the meantime. We live between birth and death, but we also measure time in that way, too: between birthday and birthday or event and event. Sometimes we even think of relationships in that way as we live between argument and reconciliation, between the "it is begun and it is finished."

This was, in effect, Paul's position during the period of incarceration awaiting trial. He was living in the time between when he was taken into custody and the time that a decision would be made about his future: whether he would be released and given his freedom or kept imprisoned indefinitely or even put to death. In this "meantime living," while he waited to see what his fate would be, it appears that Paul was treated rather like a "puppet on a string," as over a two-year period Felix sent for him often to have conversation, even including his Jewish wife Drusilla. Luke does not elaborate on the content of the conversations but merely claims that they spoke about topics like "justice, self-control, and the coming judgment" (v. 25). This is a curious set of topics for a conversation between a secular governor and a person imprisoned for his faith, themes that Luke, no doubt, thought essential to Christian faith and life.

While we recognize that our living is in the liminality of the meantime, there are times when it may become an uncomfortable place to be, especially when the uncertainty is brought about by loss and grief. Whatever form these might take for us, most of us prefer certainty and security to vulnerability and apprehension. Yet we are often called to live in this meantime space, and, strangely, this "in-between time" is often the place of discernment and spiritual growth. While Luke's narrative does not give us

any information about how this
two-year interval may have affected
Paul, it is possible that some of his
correspondence with the churches
(known or unknown) may have originated during this time, as with other
occasions of imprisonment. Moreover, we may imagine that, during
this meantime experience, Paul had
the opportunity to develop a distinct
feature of Christian spirituality:
patience.

> My Lord, I have nothing to do
> in this world,
> but to seek and serve thee;
> I have nothing to do with a
> heart and its affections,
> but to breathe after thee.
> I have nothing to do with my
> tongue and pen,
> but to speak to thee and for
> thee,
> and to publish thy glory and
> thy will!
>   —Richard Baxter,
> *Dying Thoughts upon Philippians 1:23*
>   (1683) (London: Hall, Virtue
>   and Co., 1850), 240.

In modern parlance, a patient
person is seen as one who is tolerant
and able to bear with others and
remain even-tempered, especially in
situations of prolonged waiting. A patient person may be regarded as a
person who is able to live without allowing restlessness or external circumstances to determine his or her attitudes or actions. In short, to be patient
is to live diligently and steadfastly in the moment, whatever the circumstances. From a Christian point of view, patience is sometimes referred to
as forbearance, and it is viewed as one expression of the fruit of the Spirit
alongside love, joy, peace, kindness, goodness, faithfulness, gentleness, and
self-control (Gal 5:22-23).

Having patience in the service of Christ is a theme that emerges in
many of the Christian spiritual writings, partly, it may be judged, because
we are an impatient people. Even when it comes to the spiritual life, we
want to see results. In some Christian circles there is a tendency to speak far
more of "seeing growth" as counting new Christians (usually measured by
numbers) rather than as people being formed and becoming wholly Christian. When it comes to the spiritual life, there is occasionally a tendency to
try to tackle spiritual disciplines much like we would approach tasks that
need to be done around the house or in the workplace. We just want to
"get on with it" and "tick the jobs off the list," and most of all, we want to
see what we would regard as measurable or calculable progress. However,
all of the classical spiritual writers claim that to be formed in the likeness of
Christ is not only a slow process but also takes a slowing down of mind and
body and, most importantly, a determination to simply rest in the moment.
The spiritual life is not measurable and cannot be quantified by the amount

of time spent reading the Bible, the number of hours spent praying, or even the number of worship services attended! Rather, those who seek to be "formed in the likeness of Christ" must not only "let go" of our tendency to count the number of hours spent doing what we consider to be "spiritual things" but also learn more and more to abide with God in the moment.

St. Augustine discovered the need for resting in God's presence when he wrote the oft-quoted prayer, "for you have made us for yourself, and our heart is restless until it rests in you."[2] Throughout the centuries, many people have identified with Augustine's words. I suppose that the description of "restless hearts" is a good summary of impatience with others, with ourselves, and sometimes with God, too. The only answer to our "restless longing" is to discover what it means to live in the present, patiently waiting on God and with God as we trust in God and entrust everything into God's good care and keeping.

In his book *School for Prayer*, the Orthodox writer Archbishop Anthony Bloom[3] described how, in learning to draw near to God in prayer, we also need to give attention to our way of thinking about time. In a chapter titled "Managing Time," he pointed to the way people often look back or look forward and don't spend enough time just being in the present. He wrote,

> Usually we think or we behave as though the present was an imaginary line, very very thin indeed, between the past and the future, and we roll from the past into the future, continually passing this line in the same way as you can roll an egg on a cloth. If you do this, it runs continuously, it is nowhere at any moment, there is no present, because it is always in the future.[4]

As Bloom went on to explain, closely connected with learning to stand in the present moment without focusing too much on either the past or the future is the ability to be still and quiet and yet, simultaneously, alert and attentive. It is a delicate balance to achieve.

---

2. St. Augustine, *Confessions*, 43.

3. Anthony Bloom was also known as Metropolitan Anthony of Sourozh (1914–2003). A well-known writer and broadcaster, he was Archbishop of the Russian Orthodox Church in Great Britain and Ireland from 1962–1974.

4. Anthony Bloom, *School for Prayer* (London: Darton, Longman and Todd, 1970/1978), 51.

It is essential to be alert and alive, and at the same time still and relaxed . . . this very difficult balance between the kind of alertness that will allow you with a completely open mind, completely free from preju-dice, from expectation, to receive the impact of anything that will come your way, and at the same time this stillness that will allow you to receive the impact without dreaming into it the picture of your own presence that will be destructive of it.[5]

Bloom's point here was that patience is formed as we establish ourselves in the present by being open to God's presence. We are not to live in regret about the past, constantly replaying all that has been. Nor are we to look too far into the future with worry or care. Rather, we are to stop and know God's presence in the stillness and, in so doing, gain a right perspective on both the past and the future.

In order to explain this approach further, Archbishop Bloom told a story about a woman whom he met shortly after he was ordained. It was Christmas time, and he visited a care home where he encountered this elderly woman whom he said lived to be 102 years of age. On this day, the woman came and asked his advice about prayer. She said that she had been trying for years to pray but had never experienced God's presence in prayer. What could she do? Bloom told her that after breakfast each day she should go to her room and sit for fifteen minutes. First, she should just sit quietly and "take stock of her room"; in other words, she needed to notice her surroundings. She was not to think at all about what she thought she needed to do, whether any cleaning or sorting of items. She must just sit. Next, he told her, "And then take your knitting and for fifteen minutes knit before the face of God, but I forbid you to say one word of prayer. You just knit and try to enjoy the peace of your room."[6]

Apparently, the woman did not think this was very "pious advice," but after some time when Bloom met her again, she told him that she had followed his advice, and when she put aside the "busyness" of life and let go of any effort to try to use the time, she discovered silence that she described as "not the absence of noise" but "the presence of something." She then said, "All of a sudden I perceived that the silence was a presence. At the heart of the silence was Him who is all stillness, all peace, all poise."[7]

---

5. Bloom, *School for Prayer*, 59.

6. Bloom, *School for Prayer*, 60.

7. Bloom, *School for Prayer*, 61.

This story describes an experience of a newfound freedom: the freedom that comes through God's gift of relationship that is known through prayer. The discovery of such freedom, as the Apostle Paul had already realized, requires detachment from things that were once held to be important. It also requires patience and a readiness to accept the meantime as it is—a gift of grace. The Apostle Paul was probably not "knitting before the face of God" in the two years Felix held him in custody. Yet we can imagine that he had time to reflect on the importance of knowing the presence of God in every present moment, as he waited patiently on the Spirit to show him the next step on the journey to Rome. Whether or not he had achieved anything, such as convincing Felix or writing letters, this was not "wasted time."

Draw Your Own Conclusions

1. How can living in the meantime give new perspective to church life?

2. What hinders us from finding "our rest" in God?

3. Is there ever such a thing as "wasted" time? Should we speak of "killing time"?

Acts 25

Single-minded and Solitary, 25:1-27

In the previous chapter of Acts, we found that Felix kept Paul under guard for two years. While he was given some freedom of movement and allowed the care of friends, it is clear that Paul lived in what we have described as the "meantime."[1] He lived in a period of liminality over which he had little control. Three days after Festus (who succeeded Felix) arrived in the province, Luke says that he went to Jerusalem, where Jewish leaders "gave him a report against Paul" (vv. 1-2). They tried to convince Festus to have Paul brought to Jerusalem. (Their plan was to have Paul ambushed and killed on the way.) Festus told them he would hear the case in Caesarea and suggested that they should come and make their accusations there (v. 5).

When Festus left Jerusalem (just days later), Luke claims that he went to Caesarea, and the very next day he ordered that Paul should be brought to him (v. 6). The Jews who opposed Paul had come from Jerusalem and surrounded, him "bringing many serious charges against him which they could not prove" (v. 7). Luke claims that Paul defended himself by saying, "I have in no way committed an offense against the law of the Jews, or against the temple, or against the emperor" (v. 8). Wanting to gain favor with the Jews who were opposing Paul, Festus asked Paul if he wanted to go to Jerusalem to be tried there. Paul again flatly denied that he had done anything wrong and claimed that he wanted to appeal to the emperor. Luke says that after consulting with his council, Festus replied with a flourish, "You have appealed to the emperor; to the emperor you will go" (v. 12). Strangely, therefore, Luke declares that by the agency of an empire and in

---

1. See discussion in Acts 24.

fulfillment of the Scriptures, the will of God is wrought: Paul will indeed be brought to Rome (cf. Gen 45:8; Isa 45:1).

Trites has noted Luke's use of legal scenes and language as a way of presenting a convincing witness. Especially in the trial scenes of Paul (Acts 22–26), it appears that the same legal language is used to mount a defense. In doing so, Luke may have been trying to provide an example of a way of defending the faith for Christians of his day. He also wanted to make it clear that Christian faith was not a threat to the Jewish religion or to Roman law, and it posed no menace to orderly society.[2] Significantly, Luke's portrayal of Paul is also a reminder of another quality needed by those who are seeking to live for Christ in the meantime: single-mindedness.

The quality of single-mindedness, which we might think of as being focused, determined, or resolved to achieve a goal, is sometimes negatively associated with being strong-willed or even what some commonly refer to as being "pigheaded." In short, it is sometimes seen as a rigid determination to get one's own way. Yet, in terms of Christian living, to be single-minded is not to be focused on achieving a particular individual goal. Rather it is about being focused on Christ in order to "press on toward the goal for the prize of the heavenly call of God in Christ Jesus" (Phil 3:14). This kind of single-mindedness is what many Christian spiritual writers have identified as purity of heart and mind. A fifteenth-century spiritual classic titled *The Imitation of Christ*, attributed to Thomas à Kempis (c. 1380–1471), claims that simplicity of purpose and purity of mind are imperative if a person is to discover real freedom in Christ:

> There are two wings that raise a man [person] above earthly things— simplicity and purity. Simplicity must inspire his [her] purpose, and purity his [her] affection. Simplicity reaches out after God; purity discovers and enjoys Him. No good deed will prove an obstacle to you if you are inwardly free from uncontrolled desires. And if you are free from uncontrolled desires, and seek nothing but the Will of God and the good of your neighbor, you will enjoy this inner freedom.[3]

In the nineteenth century, this emphasis on single-mindedness as "purity of heart" was also described by Danish philosopher Søren

---

2. Alison Trites, "The Importance of Legal Scenes and Legal Language in the Book of Acts," *Novum Testamentum* 16/4 (1974): 278–84.

3. Thomas à Kempis, *The Imitation of Christ* (Harmondsworth: Penguin Books, 1952/1982), 72.

Kierkegaard (1813–1855) as the ability to "will the one thing," namely the Good.[4] Moreover, Kierkegaard stressed that to will the Good requires that an individual should be willing to suffer all for the sake of the Good. For Kierkegaard, it was important that every person should take responsibility for being a "solitary individual" before God. There could be no pointing to someone else to pass the blame for one's actions or words. Rather every person, according to Kierkegaard, must acknowledge his or her sole responsibility because, as he put it, "In eternity, the individual, yes, you, my listener, and I as individuals will each be asked solely about himself [herself] as an individual and about the individual details in his [her] life."[5]

Kierkegaard's emphasis on the individual is not to deny the place of community in Christian spirituality. Rather, it seems that he was emphasizing that every person must face up to individual accountability. We are not to point fingers and ask if someone else has obeyed God. Nor are we to seek to put blame on another person for our inability to walk in the way of Christ. Kierkegaard is well aware of what he calls "barriers to willing the one thing" and names some of the distractions to single-mindedness: "seeking a reward," "willing out of fear or punishment," "egocentric service of the Good," and "commitment to a certain degree."[6] Claiming that none of these are really an example of true purity of heart, he argues that it is up to each individual to constantly ask whether he or she has, indeed, followed in the way of Christ.

> Most kind Jesus, grant me Your grace, I pray; let it dwell in me, work in me, and abide in me to the end. Grant me always to will and desire whatever is most pleasing and acceptable to You. Let Your will be mine, and let my will ever follow and be conformed wholly to Your own. Let me ever will and not will in union with Yourself, and be unable to will otherwise than You will or do not will. Grant that I may die to all things in this world, and for Your sake love to be despised and unknown. Grant me, above all else, to rest in You, that my heart may find its peace in You alone; for You are the heart's true peace, its sole abiding place, and outside Yourself all is hard and restless. In this true peace that is in You, the sole, supreme, and eternal Good, I will dwell and take my rest. Amen.
>
> Thomas à Kempis, *The Imitation of Christ*
> (Harmondsworth: Penguin, 1952/1982), 113.

---

4. Søren Kierkegaard, *Purity of Heart* (New York: Harper and Row, 1938/1956), 53.

5. Kierkegaard, *Purity of Heart*, 212.

6. The barriers are noted in chapters 3 to 7. See Kierkegaard, *Purity of Heart*, 7.

Luke would have agreed. While throughout the narrative he certainly emphasizes the role of community and the place of soul friends in the spiritual life, in these last chapters of Acts, as we accompany Paul on the way, we are mindful that Paul is to make his own personal defense of the gospel. Paul is to give an account of himself. Paul is to be single-minded and to set his face to follow in the way of Christ, and in so doing to provide an example for others to do the same.

As we stand and look on the scene, however, it is evident that while Paul seeks to be single-minded, his fight is not just against "flesh and blood" but also against what would later be described as "principalities and powers" (Eph 6:12). In this case he has been confronted not only by the authority of those who represent a certain approach to Judaism that he has now, as a Messianic Jew, left behind but also by the imperial powers of the Roman government. Will he remain steadfast when faced with the onslaught of such power? The temptation when confronted by power is to try to show greater power, to somehow seek to overcome the threat of being overtaken by the assertion of rights, powers, or privileges or, conversely, to bow to the power before us and so to become a slave to the very things we have rejected. While Paul had successfully remained single-minded in his confrontation with his Jewish antagonists, he was still facing the Roman powers and had to keep his singular resolve for Christ. He remained steadfast against any temptation to "buy his way" out of captivity with Felix (24:26). Yet, at this point in the narrative, it remains to be seen if he would indeed go to the emperor, as seemed now inevitable, or if he would seek a way to be released from captivity.

As Luke has recorded it, a few days after Paul was told by Festus that because he had appealed to the emperor he would be taken to the emperor, King Agrippa with his wife Bernice came to visit Festus in Caesarea. Knowing that Paul had not committed a crime against Rome but that he was caught up in a matter of differing religious opinions, Festus decided to present the matter to King Agrippa and to seek his opinion. According to Luke, King Agrippa claimed that he wanted to hear Paul for himself (v. 22).

The next day Paul appeared before Agrippa and his wife Bernice. Luke emphasizes the stark contrast between Paul and Agrippa as he describes the fact that Agrippa and his wife Bernice "came with great pomp, and they entered the audience hall with the military tribunes and the prominent men of the city" (v. 23). Then Paul, a prisoner for Christ, was brought in and Luke says that Festus explained again to Agrippa that the Jewish community had charged Paul with not keeping their religious laws. They had asked

Festus to have Paul put to death, but Paul had appealed to his "Imperial Majesty," so Festus had decided to send him to the emperor. Yet Festus had no idea what he could say to the emperor because he did not know how to charge Paul and hence had nothing to write to the emperor (vv. 25-26). All eyes turned to Paul to see what he would do when confronted again by such power. Would he give in under pressure or out of fear of punishment? Or would he stand ready to suffer for the sake of Christ? In the eyes of the world, he was not free, but, as will become apparent, since he remained steadfast and single-minded, in Christ he was free indeed. Moreover, all the governments of the world do not have authority over the Word of God, a constant theme throughout Acts and, indeed, the note on which the book will conclude.

Draw Your Own Conclusions

1. When is it wrong to seek to accommodate those who are "set against" us?

2. What resources might we rely on when confronting "principalities and powers"?

3. How would you describe what it means to "will the one thing"?

Acts 26

With Head and Heart, 26:1-32

As we observe the courtroom scene, Luke says that Paul's defense, which is directed toward Agrippa and not Festus, begins with Paul stretching out his hand like an orator.[1] Once again Paul claims that he is a good Jew and that he has always followed the Jewish law. He claims that he has done nothing wrong and suggests that he is on trial for believing in the promises to Israel's ancestors.[2] Then, as if to underscore the point, Luke claims that three times Paul mentions the hope that is part of Judaism and points out that he is being accused by the Jews for believing in the very hope that is so central to Jewish faith (vv. 6-7). As Luke describes the scene, it is obvious to Paul that Jesus is the Messiah, the one who has been promised of old. For him the hope has been fulfilled in the resurrection of Jesus from the dead, and that is why Paul exclaims, "Why is it thought incredible by any of you that God raises the dead" (v. 8)? Or, to put it in the words of the question that was first posed to the disciples of Jesus, "Why were they so foolish and slow to believe all that the prophets had declared?" (Luke 24:25).

Returning to his credentials as a faithful Jew, Paul stresses that from his youth, he has belonged to the strictest sect of Judaism and has lived as a Pharisee (v. 5). As to his zeal for keeping the Jewish Law, Paul claims that he previously not only hunted down Christians but also "cast his vote against them when they were being condemned to death" (v. 10). According to Luke, Paul claims, "Indeed, I myself was convinced that I ought to do many things against the name of Jesus of Nazareth" (v. 9). "By punishing them often in all the synagogues I tried to force them to blaspheme; and

---

1. Witherington, *Acts*, 738.
2. Garland, *Acts*, 267.

since I was so furiously enraged at them, I pursued them even to foreign cities" (v. 11). Having affirmed Paul's Jewish credentials, Luke's account shifts now to examine Paul's change of mind, as for the third time in Acts the story of Paul's conversion on the Damascus road is recounted.

Over the years, the repetition of the conversion story (though with some variations) in Acts has been a matter of interest in Pauline studies. Why tell the story three times and in different ways? One suggestion is that Luke simply wanted to emphasize the importance of conversion and, as a storyteller, added or subtracted various details as rhetorical flourishes. It is more likely that Luke, an experienced narrator, was shaping the story each time for a purpose. Garland has suggested that if the three conversion narratives in Acts are compared, it appears that Luke is highlighting different but equally important themes. In the first account, Luke seems to focus on the close ties of Christ with believers, while in the second account he underscores the continuity of Christian faith with Judaism.[3] In this third account, Garland points out that light is mentioned three times, which may suggest that Luke was emphasizing spiritual illumination. Witherington, too, claims that throughout Acts (as in other places in the New Testament), there is an emphasis on a movement from darkness to light that may be a metaphor for salvation.[4] Given what appears to have been Luke's overall purpose of focusing on the "personal" nature of discipleship as a journey in the final chapters of Acts, it is possible that he shaped the conversion narrative to fit with this plan.[5]

The emphasis on personal relationship with the risen Lord is highlighted first by the addition of the fact that Paul claimed, in this testimony of his conversion, that the Risen Lord spoke to him in Aramaic and said to him, "It hurts you to kick against the goads" (v. 14). A goad was a pointed stick that today we might liken to a cattle prod. It was used to guide animals that were yoked to a farm implement, and because the animal did not like to be prodded it would often try to kick at the goad. It is suggested that the phrase was used proverbially to mean that someone was "kicking against destiny."[6] Luke seems to have been pointing out that

---

3. Garland, *Acts*, 270.

4. Witherington, *Acts*, 745.

5. Polhill makes the point that in all three accounts, only Paul "experienced" the event (Polhill, *Acts*, 502).

6. Garland, *Acts*, 267. Joseph A. Fitzmyer says that in Greek the proverb expresses that it is "idle or useless to resist divine influence in future conduct" (*The Acts of the Apostles*, The Anchor Yale Bible [New Haven: Yale University Press, 1998], 758–59).

Paul was not only being called personally by name but was also already known by God and specially chosen by God for a task; God had singled him out and "called" him to carry out his divine purposes. Moreover, the fact that Paul did not make any mention of Ananias's help when he gave his testimony to Agrippa most certainly points to Luke's aim to emphasize again the idea of the importance of a personal relationship with Christ.[7] As already noted, Luke's focus in these last chapters of Acts is on the theme of discipleship and the qualities needed for those who seek to follow Christ. By telling Paul's story in this way, Luke underscored that discipleship is first and foremost a matter between an individual and God. While the community of believers has a vital place, each believer has her or his direct relationship with the Lord.

Having related the nature of his experience with the risen Christ, Paul then claimed that Jesus Christ told him he was sent to the Gentiles in order "to open their eyes so they may turn from darkness to light and from the power of Satan to God, so that they may receive forgiveness of sins and a place among those who are sanctified by faith in me [Christ]" (v. 18). Having declared his calling to proclaim the gospel, Paul said that he had not been disobedient to "the heavenly vision" but had proclaimed "in Damascus, then in Jerusalem, and throughout the countryside of Judea, and also to the Gentiles, that they should repent and turn to God and do deeds consistent with repentance" (v. 20). Luke says Paul claimed that the Jews in the temple had seized him for this reason and that they had tried to kill him (v. 21). Paul concluded his speech by aligning himself again with Jewish thought, claiming that what he believed was what the prophets and Moses had said would take place, that "the Messiah must suffer, and that, by being the first to rise from the dead, he would proclaim light both to our people and to the Gentiles" (v. 23).

In this account, it appears that two important themes in Christian discipleship—experience and doctrine—are brought to the fore in a careful balancing act. Luke does this by drawing attention first to the teaching of Judaism, focusing on the long-held hope of the people of God and their belief in the promises of God passed down in Scripture. This enables Luke to underscore the fact that Christian faith is not simply based on unsubstantiated personal religious experiences but is firmly rooted in the belief that Jesus was the fulfillment of all the promises of God found in the Jewish Scriptures. Alongside this focus on belief or doctrine is the personal account

---

7. Garland, *Acts*, 267.

of the Apostle Paul's experience with the risen Lord. As we have seen, in all three conversion accounts, Luke highlights that Paul had an encounter with the living Lord; he repented of his sin, was baptized, and made the confession that "Jesus Christ is Lord." The emphasis on both doctrine and experience, according to Luke, is necessary, and thus these two facets of the faith have been part of the narrative Luke provides throughout Acts.

Through the centuries, men and women have sometimes struggled to keep doctrine and experience in balance. At times Christians have wanted to emphasize orthodoxy (correct belief) over ortho-

> Through all the changing scenes of life,
> in trouble and in joy,
> the praises of my God shall still
> my heart and tongue employ.
>
> Oh, magnify the Lord with me;
> with me exalt his name;
> when in distress to him I called,
> he to my rescue came.
>
> The hosts of God encamp around
> the dwellings of the just;
> protection he affords to all
> who make his name their trust.
>
> Oh, make but trial of his love,
> experience will decide
> how blest are they, and only they,
> who in his truth confide.
>
> Fear him, you saints, and you will then
> have nothing else to fear;
> make but his service your delight,
> your wants shall be his care.
> —Nahum Tate (1652–1715) and Nicholas Brady
> (1659–1726), *Baptist Praise and Worship*
> (Oxford: OUP, 1991), 827 (selected verses).

praxy (correct action). When this happens, there is often an emphasis on "keeping rules" and abiding by religious traditions. Those who emphasize doctrine in this way are often accused of placing too much emphasis on intellectual propositions and not enough on personal experience with the living Lord and the proclamation of the good news of Jesus to others. On the other hand, too much emphasis on an experience of faith has led to criticisms of people being led by their emotions rather than having a firm grounding in Scripture and in the long-held beliefs of Christian faith.

The struggle for balance between doctrine and experience has played out many times in the history of the church. For example, in the seventeenth century, in his work *Pia Desideria* (Pious Desires), Philip Jacob Spener (1635–1705) claimed that reform was needed in the Lutheran church in Germany. Specifically, he argued that more attention should be given to encouraging others to have a personal relationship with the living God rather than simply focusing on doctrinal correctness. He wrote,

> Let us remember that in the last judgment we shall not be asked how learned we were or whether we displayed our learning before the world; to what extent we enjoyed the favor of men [people] and knew how to keep it; with what honors we were exalted and how great a reputation in the world we left behind us; or how many treasures of earthly goods we amassed for our children and thereby drew a curse upon ourselves. Instead we shall be asked how faithfully and with how childlike a heart we sought to further the kingdom of God; with how pure and godly a teaching and how worthy an example we tried to edify our hearers amid the scorn of the world, denial of self, taking up the cross and imitation of our Savior; with what zeal we opposed not only error but also wickedness of life; or with what constancy and cheerfulness we endured persecution or adversity thrust upon us by the manifestly godless world or by false brethren [believers], and amid such suffering praised our God.[8]

Spener's complaint, along with that of others in the Pietist movement, was that too much attention was given to intellectual understanding of the faith and doctrinal wrangling, and not enough was devoted to the affective side of faith. In other words, the focus was on a religion of the "head" and not enough on that of the "heart." The Pietist movement emphasized that Christian faith must be reflected in "head, heart and hands," that is, that there should be a balance between the emphasis on doctrine, experience, and the practical outworking of faith in terms of sharing with others.

A similar call for reform occurred in Britain among the Puritans in the seventeenth century and, again, in the writings and hymns of those involved in what became known as the Evangelical Revival of the eighteenth century. In North America, an expression of the revival known as the First Great Awakening was associated with the ministry of Jonathan Edwards (1703–1758) in New England. Edwards was vilified by many of his day and became embroiled in controversy for not only allowing but also, in the eyes of many, encouraging what they called "enthusiasm" and emotionalism in worship. Edwards defended his work by insisting that these emotional expressions were all part of the "surprising work of God." Moreover, he wrote a classic work titled *Religious Affections* in which he

---

8. Philip Jacob Spener, *Pia Desideria*, trans. Theodore G. Tappert (Philadelphia: Fortress Press, 1946/1974), 36–37.

addressed the question, What is the nature of true religion? His reply was that "true religion, in great part, consists in holy affections."[9]

There are many other examples, past and present, of spiritual guides highlighting the struggle to find the right balance between doctrine and experience in Christian faith and practice. However, it should be noted that, while seeking a balance between the two, earlier writers and hymnists did not ignore the importance of Scripture or deny the place of doctrine and tradition. For them, the balance was to be discovered as one grounded one's faith in Scripture. Hence, many of the hymns of an earlier period were based on Scripture and reflect the importance of sound doctrine, reasonable experience, and the outworking of faith in relationship with others. For instance, the words of this hymn by the renowned eighteenth-century Nonconformist pastor Isaac Watts (1674–1748) speak of knowing, experiencing, and sharing the love of God made known in the death and resurrection of Jesus Christ.

> When I survey the wondrous Cross
> on which the Prince of glory died,
> my richest gain I count but Loss,
> and pour contempt on all my pride.
>
> Forbid it, Lord, that I should boast,
> save in the death of Christ my God:
> all the vain things that charm me most,
> I sacrifice them to his blood.
>
> See from his head, his hands, his feet,
> sorrow and love flow mingled down!
> did e'er such love and sorrow meet?
> or thorns compose so rich a crown?
>
> Were the whole realm of nature mine,
> that were an offering far too small;
> love so amazing, so divine,
> demands my soul, my life, my all.[10]

---

9. Jonathan Edwards, *A Treatise Concerning Religious Affections* (New Haven: Yale University Press, 1959), 95.

10. Isaac Watts, "When I Survey," *Baptist Praise and Worship* (Oxford: Oxford University Press, 1992), 349.

The emphasis on the love of God is central to finding the balance between doctrine and experience in any expression of Christian faith. For, whatever one may consider an appropriate balance between doctrine and experience, Christian faith teaches that the possibility of encounter and relationship with God is open to people through the love of God made known in the life, death, and resurrection of Jesus Christ. The way that people may encounter the love of God, or the way that such love in relationship through Christ finds expression in worship and action, is open to debate.

What matters most, and what seemed to be of concern to Luke, was the emphasis on a personal encounter with the living God that led to genuine repentance and, under the guidance of the Holy Spirit, a determination to proclaim the name of Jesus to everyone whatever the cost. Certainly, this was the witness of Paul, and according to Luke he even took the opportunity to boldly witness to Agrippa, appealing to him to believe in Christ. Agrippa was shocked at Paul's boldness but not offended by his broad appeal (far from self-aggrandizement) that all should become like him, except without the chains (v. 29)! Paul's witness to everyone who would listen—jailers and kings, Jews and Gentiles, politicians and ordinary people—points to the fact that the gospel is for all, regardless of their social status or culture. As the meeting with Agrippa ends, it is obvious that Paul was not guilty of high crimes or misdemeanors. As King Agrippa was leaving with his wife, Bernice, Festus, and others who had been sitting with them, they passed comment on the case and there was agreement among them that "This man is doing nothing to deserve death or imprisonment" (v. 31). According to Luke, Agrippa then said to Festus, "This man could have been set free if he had not appealed to the emperor" (v. 32). Here, Luke ironically points to the divine destiny in store for the Apostle, despite the inclinations of state or regional politics or personalities.

Draw Your Own Conclusions

1. How is "true religion" best defined?

2. How do you think a balance is achieved between "head, heart, and hands" in the Christian life?

3. Which do you think is more important in the Christian life, orthodoxy or orthopraxy?

Acts 27

In Peril on the Sea, 27:1-44

Having presented his case before King Agrippa, Luke claimed that it was agreed that even though the Apostle Paul was not guilty of a crime, because he had requested to go before the emperor he would go to Rome. Luke, who would have been familiar with the popularity of a sea tale, takes some time to relate this dramatic story of the trip to Rome, offers details of the various ports where the ship stopped, and describes the increasingly bad weather the travelers faced. Since Luke continues to tell the story using the plural pronoun "we," it is an invitation for us to join the group and imagine ourselves on the voyage with Paul and his fellow prisoners.

The day has come for the journey to Rome to begin, and with Paul and the other prisoners placed under the care of a centurion named Julius, we board the ship with Luke and Aristarchus, a Macedonian from Thessalonica (Col 4:10 and Phlm 1:24), heading toward "ports along the coast of Asia" (vv. 1-2). It appears that this will be a long and arduous journey, so it is good that, when the boat puts in at Sidon, the centurion (as Luke tells us) allows Paul's friends to care for him, though there is no further explanation of what that entailed.

As we put out to sea from Sidon and sail for Cyprus in unfavorable winds (v. 4), we have the feeling that this will not be an easy journey. After sailing across the sea that is off Cilicia and Pamphylia, the ship arrives at Myra in Lycia (v. 5). Here the centurion finds a ship bound for Italy, and we are put on board. It is slow going for a number of days until we arrive, with difficulty, off Cnidus, go "under the lee of Crete off Salome," and finally come to Fair Havens, "near the city of Lasea" (vv. 7-8).

There must have been a huge sigh of relief among the sailors as they arrived in port safely, though Luke simply says that "the Fast had already gone by" (the Day of Atonement) and sailing was now deemed dangerous (v. 9).[1] Given the fact that the weather was not favorable for travel, it would seem only sensible to make the decision not to put back out to sea for a few months. According to Luke, Paul suggested to the centurion that it was too dangerous to try to sail further, but the centurion did not listen to his advice, following the majority view instead, and the ship left again to head for Phoenix, a more favorable wintering port on the other side of Crete (vv. 9-12).

As Luke describes the journey, it seems doomed; the storm clouds became more ominous, and, as Paul had predicted, the ship was caught in a terrible storm at sea. The boat was pounded by the storm to the point that the travellers threw some cargo overboard. They took another desperate measure on the third day, throwing some of the ship's tackle overboard as well (vv. 13-19). At this point it appears that all was lost. Luke captures the mood in these words: "When neither sun nor stars appeared for many days, and no small tempest raged, all hope of our being saved was at last abandoned" (v. 20). Just when everyone was losing hope, Paul (who could not resist saying "I told you so") addressed the ship's crew, telling them that they should have listened to him and not set sail from Crete, but now they must not be afraid. He announced that there would be no loss of life, though the ship would be lost (vv. 21-22). Luke says Paul then related how an angel of God had told him not to be afraid, that he must "stand before the emperor," and that, indeed, all those who were travelling in the boat with him would be granted safety. So Paul told them, "keep up your courage, men, for I have faith in God that it will be exactly as I have been told" (vv. 23-25).

On the fourteenth day, at about midnight, they suspected that they were getting near to land and were afraid the boat might run up on the rocks. Some of the sailors wanted to try to save themselves by escaping from the ship. Paul realized what they were doing and warned the centurion, claiming that in order to ensure everyone's safety, the sailors had to stay on the ship. The soldiers cut the ropes to the boats so the sailors had to remain on the ship (vv. 30-32). In the midst of the plotting, scheming, and intrigue, Luke says that Paul spoke to everyone on the boat and urged them to eat some food. While they have not eaten during the storm due to anxiety over their fate, Paul claimed that now they must eat and be

---

1. The Day of Atonement was in September or October depending on where it fell in the lunar calendar (Garland, *Acts*, 274).

strengthened, for "none of you will lose a hair from your heads" (v. 34). Then, as told by Luke, Paul took bread and, in the presence of everyone, gave thanks to God and began to eat (v. 35). While they were not yet out of danger, this was intended as a very public demonstration of Paul's trust in God and his belief that God would see all two hundred and seventy-six of them through the trouble. Encouraged by his action, everyone ate. Then they lightened the ship by throwing the wheat into the sea, perhaps as another sure sign of confidence in Paul's assurance that God would provide for them.

Luke reports that the next morning, they could see "a bay with a beach" (v. 39). While no one recognized the land, they decided to try, if possible, to run the ship ashore. Before they reached the shore, the ship struck a reef and started to break up (vv. 39-41). The soldiers suggested killing the prisoners to prevent them from escaping, but the centurion wished to save Paul and prevented them from carrying out their plan (vv. 42-43). Everyone on board the ship made it safely to land, the island of Malta.

Reaching this stage on such a harrowing journey (one of the many that Paul apparently faced; see 2 Cor 11:23-28), allows us to stop for reflection. Any journey accentuates the sense of disorientation or ambiguity we often experience when we live in the meantime (in the liminal time between one event and another).[2] However, Luke's dramatic tale of the voyage at sea, which ended with a shipwreck, offers us a chance to think particularly about what is needed if we are to navigate the difficult experiences that inevitably come in life. The story of Paul on the ship to Rome is not simply a tale of a dangerous physical journey; rather Luke is probably alluding to the pilgrimage of a Christian disciple.[3] In doing this, as we have already seen, he is presenting the opportunity to reflect on the

> O Living God,
> we who are partly living,
> scarcely hoping,
> and fitfully caring,
> pray to you now
> to make us fully alive.
> Give us the vitality, awareness
> and commitment
> that we see in Jesus Christ,
> through the power of his
> death and resurrection.
> We ask this in his Name.
> Amen.
>
> —John V. Taylor, *A Matter of Life and Death* (London: SCM Press, 1986), 33.

---

2. See discussion in Acts 24.

3. Susan Marie Praeder, "Acts 27:1–28:16: Sea Voyages in Ancient Literature and the Theology of Luke-Acts," in *The Catholic Biblical Quarterly* 46/4 (October 1984): 683–706, https://www.jstor.org/stable/43716795.

challenges faced by anyone seeking to follow in the way of Christ, staying faithful and trusting no matter what adversity happens on the journey.

In this story, the heightened anxiety of the near-death experiences on the ship and especially Paul's display of confidence and trust as he turned to God, gave thanks, and broke bread serve as a reminder of the confidence and trust that disciples must show at every stage on the journey. While the similarity of the breaking of bread with the occasions when Jesus broke bread with his disciples is notable, this scene is not to be interpreted as Paul sharing in the Lord's Supper with the group. Rather, Luke may be pointing to the need for those who truly seek to follow in the way of Christ to show hospitality to others and to share table fellowship with everyone (Luke 19:1-9), even those who might be prepared to abandon us or even put us to death (Luke 6:27-36).

Luke's passing comment that after they had broken bread and "satisfied their hunger, they lightened the ship by throwing the wheat into the sea" (v. 38) is particularly significant when thinking about Christian pilgrimage. While this act may be viewed as a clear reference to securing the ship's safety by making it lighter and more buoyant as they approached the shore, when thinking of spiritual formation it also serves as a reminder of the need for "detachment."

In Christian spirituality, "detachment" is associated with "letting go" of certain things or relationships that might hinder a person's relationship to God. While detachment is sometimes viewed negatively as a sort of abnegation or denial of self or the world, the idea of detachment may be seen in a positive sense as being so single-minded for God that other things find their rightful place. It has been suggested that detachment is "an act of spiritual freedom."[4] In other words, a person becomes so attuned to God that he or she is free to do what God wants without worrying about the views of others or the norms and pressures of society. In other words, "spiritual detachment" allows a person to make choices "out of freedom and not compulsion, fear or routine."[5] These choices relate to every area of a Christian's life and lead to a simplicity of life that reflects the desire of a follower of Jesus to always seek first the will and way of God.

In the early1980s, Richard Foster reflected on the way detachment and simplicity go hand in hand in a popular study titled *Freedom of Simplicity*.

---

4. Howard Gray, "Detachment," in *The New SCM Dictionary of Christian Spirituality*, ed. Philip Sheldrake (London: SCM Press, 2005), 234–35.

5. Gray, "Detachment," 234.

In the preface to the book, he noted that the subject of Christian simplicity is, paradoxically, complex. Pointing to a scriptural foundation as well as drawing from examples within Christian history, Foster argued that simplicity is "part and parcel" of a call to be a follower of Jesus Christ.[6] Simplicity is not merely a matter of outwardly adopting a pious minimalist approach to living. Nor is it solely about reflecting on ecological or ethical concerns and seeking to adjust our style of life accordingly. From a Christian standpoint, simplicity should reflect the heart and mind of the believer who truly wants to follow in the way of Jesus. Simplicity, as Foster noted, will also express a certain "detachment" from the opinions, values, and choices of society.

Noting the call of Jesus not to worry about your life, what you will eat or what you will drink or what you will wear, but to "strive for the kingdom" (Luke 12:22-34), Christian spiritual writers have often reflected on the need for detachment and simplicity of life. In the fourth century, men and women who became known as the Desert Fathers and Mothers fled to the desert in Egypt in order to live with simplicity toward God. They felt that the world had become so entrapped in materialism that the only way they could be free to truly follow Christ was to flee from the world. Thomas Merton wrote that what they desired most was "their own true self, in Christ."[7] "In order to do this," he wrote, "they had to reject completely the false, formal self, fabricated under social compulsion in the world."[8] While today it may seem too harsh to draw a sharp dichotomy between being "in the world" and yet not "of the world," the early Desert Mothers and Fathers had no difficulty in making this distinction. They felt that neither culture nor the attachments to people or possessions should affect their desire to live for Christ. Foster aptly described the attitude of those who fled to the desert in this way:

> They were seeking to revive true Christian devotion and simplicity of life by intense renunciation. Their experience has particular relevance, because modern society is uncomfortably like the world they attacked so vigorously. Their world asked, "How can I get more?" The Desert Fathers asked, "What can I do without?" Their world asked, "How can I find myself?" The Desert Fathers asked, "How can I lose myself?" Their world

---

6. Richard Foster, *Freedom of Simplicity* (London: Harper and Row, 1981), 183.

7. Thomas Merton, *The Wisdom of the Desert* (New York: New Direction, 1960), 5.

8. Merton, *The Wisdom of the Desert*, 6.

asked, "How can I win friends and influence people?" The Desert Fathers asked, "How can I love God?"[9]

One of the best known of those who fled to the desert to pursue holiness and simplicity of life was St. Anthony (251–356). The story is told that when he was a young man he heard the text from Matthew's Gospel read: "Go, sell what you possess and give to the poor . . . and come and follow me" (Matt 19:21). Leaving the church, he immediately gave away his land and sold his possessions and went to live initially at the edge of the village. Eventually, he went to the desert, where he stayed for twenty years living the solitary life.

Similar stories are told of other men and women who then went to the desert in order to renounce the things that might hinder them in their desire to live simply for God. Many who chose this life supported themselves by weaving baskets or mats out of palm leaves or reeds and trading them in towns. However, their work was simply for subsistence, and their main desire was to give themselves to God in prayer. They often described the desert experience as a time in which they had to face, and often wrestle with, certain "demons" that tried to hinder them from living for God alone. The "demons" were what we might today refer to as "obscure forces" that human beings often bear within themselves.[10] Describing the desert struggles, Louis Bouyer wrote,

> The ascetics of whom we are speaking, following the sacred authors and certainly Christ himself, recognized this fact: solitude alone allows man [people] to discover, and so to face, all the obscure forces that he [she] bears in himself [herself]. The man [person] who does not know how to be alone, does not know either (and secretly does not wish to know) what conflicts there are in the depths of his [her] heart, conflicts which he [she] feels that he [she] is incapable of untangling, even of touching. Solitude is a terrible trial, for it serves to crack open and burst apart the shell of our superficial securities. It opens out to us the unknown abyss that we all carry within us . . . [in solitude] it is not only the depths of our own soul, unknown to us that we discover, but the obscure powers that are

---

9. Foster, *Freedom of Simplicity*, 56. It should be noted that while Foster refers to Desert Fathers, there were women (Desert Mothers) who also embarked on this way of life. For information on their sayings, lives, and stories see Laura Swan, *The Forgotten Desert Mothers* (New York: Paulist Press, 2001).

10. Louis Bouyer, *A History of Christian Spirituality: The Spirituality of the New Testament and the Fathers*, vol. 1 (Kent: Burns and Oates, 1968), 313.

lurking there, whose slaves we must inevitably remain so long as we are unaware of them. In truth, this awareness would destroy us, if it were not illuminated by faith. Only Christ can open out to us with impunity "the mystery of iniquity", because he alone, *in* us today as *for* us in the past can confront it successfully.[11]

Having confronted their own inner "demons," the Desert Fathers and Mothers became well known, respected, and sought after for their wise counsel and keen sense of discernment. The sayings of both men and women ascetics have been recorded and handed down through history in the form of short sayings and stories. In a book that, as the title suggests, reflects on *The Wisdom of the Desert*, the twentieth-century writer, theologian, poet, and Trappist monk Thomas Merton claimed that the Desert Fathers and Mothers who detached themselves from society may be compared to those who were fleeing a shipwreck from which each single person had to swim for his or her life.[12] Merton claimed that "they did not mean to save themselves." Merton wrote,

> They knew that they were helpless to do any good for others as long as they floundered about in the wreckage. But once they got a foothold on solid ground, things were different. Then they had not only the power but even the obligation to pull the whole world to safety after them.[13]

While, as Merton pointed out, it would be too much to claim that we need to try to form another movement exactly like that of the Desert Fathers and Mothers in order to try to "reproduce simplicity, austerity and prayer of these primitive souls," yet he wrote,

> We must be as thorough and as ruthless in our determination to break all spiritual chains, and cast off the domination of alien compulsions, to find our true selves, to discover and develop our inalienable spiritual liberty and use it to build, on earth, the Kingdom of God.[14]

The Apostle Paul was very aware of the need to put aside anything that might prevent him from being single-minded for Christ. Detachment,

---

11. Bouyer, *A History of Christian Spirituality*, vol. 1, 313.

12. Merton, *The Wisdom of the Desert*, 3.

13. Merton, *The Wisdom of the Desert*, 23.

14. Merton, *The Wisdom of the Desert*, 24.

however, like the whole of spiritual formation, is an ongoing process. So, when he was finally brought to shore after the ordeal at sea, he knew that many challenges to his faith would continue to confront him as he made his way to Rome.

Draw Your Own Conclusions

1. A line in the hymn "Amazing Grace" by John Newton says "through many dangers, toils and snares." Is there any indication here as to how, through a difficult pilgrimage, the Lord brings us safely home?

2. How might we ensure that "detachment" does not become a "work" in which we might boast?

3. How do we ensure that the desire to be single-minded for God does not lead to the neglect of others or disregard for the needs of the wider community?

Acts 28

A Safe Haven, 28:1-10

The land that they had seen from the ship was Malta. After the travellers reached land safely, Luke claims that the people of the island were welcoming, and since it was rainy and cold, the islanders started a fire and "welcomed" Paul and the others around it (v. 2). Paul had gathered wood and was putting it on the fire when, according to Luke, a viper attached itself to Paul's hand (v. 3). The people thought this must be a sign that Paul was a criminal, and they waited for him to die from the snakebite. However, he was unharmed, and when he did not even become ill from the bite, they thought he must be a god.[1] Luke says that one of the leading men on the island, named Publius, took Paul and his companions to his home and offered hospitality for three days. During this time, the father of Publius became ill. Paul went and prayed, "putting his hands on him," and the man was healed (v. 8). Other people then brought those who had diseases to Paul in order that they, too, might be healed. According to Luke's narrative, Paul and the others stayed there for three months, and during that time they had "many honors bestowed" on them. When they were about to sail, the islanders generously put provisions on board the ship for them (v. 10).

As recorded by Luke, this brief, unintended stopover in Malta points again to the support and help that is gained from others. While Christian pilgrims are sometimes required to walk a solitary way, we are never alone. In addition to knowing the presence and power of God, we can find others

---

1. It has been noted that today there are no poisonous snakes on Malta. However, this may not have been the case in the first century. There has been lots of discussion over the type of snake this might have been with no firm conclusion. See Craig Keener, *24:1–28:31*, volume 4 of *Acts: An Exegetical Commentary* (Grand Rapids, MI: Baker Academic, 1025), 3670–78; Polhill, *Acts*, 530–32.

who offer encouragement and help us along the way. Moreover, here, as well as in other places in Acts, Luke pays tribute to the mutuality of relationship. While Paul and his companions were offered hospitality and care, Paul in particular also reached out to bring comfort and help to others. The healing of diseases in this instance, as noted elsewhere, is the work of God through Paul and not accomplished by any power that Paul possessed. It is a practical demonstration of the gospel proclaimed.

Furthering the discussion of detachment in the previous chapter, it is notable that here Luke offers a reminder that, while followers of Jesus may at times be required to withdraw from the world, the needs of the world are always before us and are to be a matter of prayer and practical concern, too. In one of her letters of spiritual direction, Evelyn Underhill counseled someone she thought was not giving enough attention to the needs of others by saying,

> I hope you are going to get hold of a little personal work amongst the poor when you can? As for the inclination to cut connection with other people, *that* must be fought tooth and nail, please. Go out as much as you can, and enter into the interests of others, however twaddley. They are all part of life, remember: and life, for you, is *divine*.[2]

Underhill's point was that there must be balance in the life of the Christian. The balance is discovered as a person seeks to learn what it means to follow the command, "You shall love the Lord your God with all your heart, and with all your soul, and with all your strength, and with all your mind; and your neighbor as yourself" (Luke 10:27). It is sometimes difficult to love God and to love people, as Underhill well knew. Writing again to the same person, she counseled,

> Oh, *do* turn to, and do and be things for and to your fellow creatures for a bit. Devote yourself to that. Don't be afraid of "surface interests." Christ will be with you in those sorts of surface interests if they are whole-heartedly undertaken for His sake, and *not for your own soul's sake*.[3]

Underhill's advice is to the point. Devoting ourselves to God will always draw us to a greater awareness of the needs and concerns of others.

---

2. Evelyn Underhill, *The Letters of Evelyn Underhill* (London: Longmans, Green and Company, 1943/1944), 97.

3. Underhill, *The Letters of Evelyn Underhill*, 98.

While Luke does not mention that Paul preached to the people in Malta, it may be assumed that he would have found opportunities to proclaim the love of God to them, just as he reached out to pray and lay hands on those who were ill and in need. As at Lystra (with Barnabas), he would have strongly disavowed any suggestion that he was a god, pointing instead to the Lord in whose name he presumably offered the laying on of hands for healing (Acts 14:8ff).

Witnessing without Hindrance, 28:11-31

After three months, Paul and his travel companions set sail for Rome in a ship that had "wintered" in Malta (v. 11). According to Luke, they went to Syracuse for three days and then to Rhegium and on to Puteoli, where they found other believers. At their invitation, the travellers stayed there for seven days (v. 14). Finally, according to Luke, Paul (and whoever was with him then) arrived in Rome. When the believers from there heard of his arrival, they came to meet Paul and those with him. On seeing them, Paul "thanked God and took courage" (v. 15). Perhaps this was Luke's reminder once again that every believer needs the encouragement of a wider fellowship of friends in Christ. Reaching Rome and immediately finding brothers and sisters of the faith with whom Paul might worship and share life in Christ would indeed have enabled him to "take courage."

Luke's further note that Paul was allowed to live by himself with a soldier, who was guarding him, draws attention to a relative sense of safety and peace for a time (v. 16). In other words, Paul was not being hunted down or treated like a criminal; it appears that he was given time, and some degree of space, to carry out his calling to proclaim the good news of Jesus Christ in Rome.

Three days after his arrival, Paul called together the local leaders of the Jews and explained his situation to them. According to Luke, Paul told them that while he had done nothing against the Jewish law, he had been arrested and handed over to the Romans. He then explained how the Romans wanted to release him, but the Jews who opposed him wanted him to be put to death. According to Luke's narrative, Paul claimed that while there was no case against him, he had appealed to the emperor in order to try to settle the case, and that was why he was now in Rome. Luke says that Paul then appealed to the Jewish leaders in Rome by saying, "For this reason therefore I have asked to see you and speak with you, since it is for the sake of the hope of Israel that I am bound with this chain" (v. 20).

The Jewish leaders assured Paul that they had not gotten any letters from Judea, and no one had come to Rome to speak against Paul. But they said they would like to hear more about the followers of Jesus because "with regard to this sect we know that everywhere it is spoken against" (v. 22). They then established a time when they might meet Paul at his lodgings, and great numbers came to hear him. Luke says that "from morning until evening he explained the matter to them, testifying to the kingdom of God and trying to convince them about Jesus both from the law of Moses and from the prophets" (v. 23). Not surprisingly, some were convinced and some were not. Luke concludes that Paul made one further statement as they were leaving. Quoting from Scripture, he said that the Holy Spirit was right in saying to their ancestors through the prophet Isaiah,

> Go to this people and say,
> you will indeed listen, but never understand,
> you will indeed look, but never perceive,
> For this people's heart has grown dull,
> and their ears are hard of hearing,
> and they have shut their eyes;
> so that they might not look with their eyes
> and listen with their ears,
> and understand with their heart
> and turn—and I would heal them. (vv. 26-27)

The words leave no doubt as to the position of the Jews who rejected Jesus as the Messiah. However, according to Luke, Paul concluded this speech with a final clarifying statement: "Let it be known to you then that this salvation of God has been sent to the Gentiles; they will listen" (v. 28). It is notable that in this last statement, attributed to Paul, a clear distinction is made between the Jews who believe and accept the gospel and those who don't. By reporting that Paul said "your ancestors" rather than "our ancestors," as he did when speaking to the Jews in Antioch of Pisidia (13:17), Luke may be suggesting that now an "irrevocable split has occurred," and, as Garland put it, "Those who reject the gospel belong to the line of ancestors who disavow God's purposes and the hope of Israel."[4]

Luke does not offer any reference to a further response from the Jews in Rome. Rather, he simply comments that Paul lived in Rome for "two whole years at his own expense, and welcomed all who came to him, proclaiming

---

4. Garland, *Acts*, 283.

the kingdom of God and teaching about the Lord Jesus with all boldness and without hindrance" (v. 30). With a deceptively undramatic close, Luke's narrative reaches a crescendo in that the Apostle's ministry, and that of the wider church of which he was a key representative, continued unabated. While his journey to appear in Rome before Caesar had ended, the progress of the gospel was unending. Keener has suggested that the open ending may serve a rhetorical function in that it projects the "unstoppable progress of the gospel into the long-range future."[5]

Luke's narrative ends, rather mystifyingly, with an elusive reference to the ongoing ministry presumably not just to the Jews but also to the Gentiles in the capital city of the empire. While the final speech in Acts indicates that Paul's proclamation was met by a mixed response, we may assume that he continued to proclaim the story of the life, death, and resurrection of Jesus. We are not told what happened to Paul after this time, but it has been suggested that he remained in custody until his case was resolved perhaps around AD 62.[6] Hence, it is possible that Paul was allowed to continue preaching and, perhaps, even eventually released from imprisonment.[7] If he were released after the two-year period of incarceration, it is speculated that he may have travelled to Spain, but there is no firm evidence for this suggestion.[8] After the burning of Rome in AD 64, the emperor Nero blamed Christians for the fire and began to persecute them. It is suggested that Paul may have been executed by beheading (as was the punishment for Roman citizens) sometime between AD 65 and 68.[9]

Significantly, in this last speech by Paul, Luke has included a reference to "the hope of Israel," a phrase that was also highlighted by Luke in the closing chapter of the Gospel account. In the Gospel of Luke, the two disciples on the road to Emmaus lamented that they had "hoped that Jesus was the one to redeem Israel" (Luke 24:21). Then, in this final chapter of Acts, Luke claims that Paul said that he was "in chains for the sake of the hope of

---

5. Keener, *Acts: An Exegetical Commentary*, 4:3760–61.

6. Ben Witherington III, *The Paul Quest: The Renewed Search for the Jew of Tarsus* (Downers Grove, IL: Intervarsity, 1998), 325.

7. Garland, *Acts*, 283; Witherington, *The Paul Quest*, 326.

8. Witherington, *The Paul Quest*, 326. See also Jerome Murphy-O'Connor, *Paul: A Critical Life* (Oxford: Clarendon, 1996), 356–65, and Adolf Deissmann, *Paul: A Study of Social and Religious History* (New York: Harper and Brothers, 1957), 248.

9. Witherington, *The Paul Quest*, 326. He also offers a chronology for Paul (327ff) that includes suggestions for possible dating for the epistles of Paul, though the author admits that this is highly speculative.

All my hope on God is founded;
all my trust he does renew.
Through all change and chance he
  guides me,
only good and only true.
God unknown,
he alone
calls my heart to be his own.

God's great goodness lasts forever,
deep his wisdom, passing thought:
splendour, light, and life attend him,
beauty springing out of nought.
Evermore,
from his store
new-born worlds rise and adore.

Day by day the Almighty giver
does his gracious gifts bestow;
God's good will is for our pleasure,
leading us wher'er we go.
See love stand
at his hand;
and joy wait on his command.

Still from earth to God eternal
sacrifice of praise be done,
high above all praises praising
for the gift of Christ his Son.
Hear Christ call
one and all:
those who follow shall not fall.
—Robert Bridges (1844–1930)
based on hymn by Joachim Neander (1650–
1680) in *Baptist Praise and Worship*
(Oxford: Oxford Unversity Press, 1991), 485
(selected verses).

Israel" (v. 20). In both instances, Luke, whom we have suggested was most probably a Jew writing to Jews, is stressing that "hope" no longer rested on a promise that had not been fulfilled. Rather, in Jesus, the promise of the Messiah has come. This is the good news: Jesus Christ is the Messiah, the promised one, and in him is the hope of all people. This hope, however, is not only to be seen as the fulfillment of God's promise; rather, in Christ there is the hope of a new creation that is characterized by the love of God not only revealed supremely in the cross and the resurrection but also to be revealed at the "parousia" or the return of Christ.[10]

Crucially, it should be noted here that while Christians often refer to the parousia as the final, end-time, "second coming" of Christ, "parousia" does not mean the return of someone who has departed.[11] Rather, as Jürgen Moltmann has pointed out, "parousia" may also mean "imminent arrival" or "presence" and

---

10. Jürgen Moltmann, *Theology of Hope* (London: SCM Press, 1967/1978), 227.

11. Moltmann, *Theology of Hope*, 227.

points to the fact that while the (future) "parousia" of Christ is different from the present reality of knowing Christ, it is also intimately and inextricably connected to it. Karl Barth expressed this coming of Christ as an "unveiling," "the revelation of what already is." He wrote,

> What is the future bringing? Not once more a turning point in history, but the revelation of that which is. It is the future, but the future of that which the church *remembers*, of that which has already taken place once and for all. The Alpha and the Omega are the same thing.[12]

Moltmann has argued that understanding the parousia as both an unveiling and a fulfillment is important if we are to understand that the future coming/parousia of Christ is "not a mere repetition of his history, and not only an unveiling of it, but something which has so far not yet happened through Christ."[13] As Moltmann put it,

> The Christian expectation is directed to no other than the Christ who has come, but it expects something new from him, something that has not happened so far: it awaits the fulfillment of the promised righteousness of God in all things, the fulfillment of the resurrection of the dead that is promised in his resurrection, the fulfillment of the lordship of the crucified one over all things that is promised in his exaltation. The visible and painful experience of the unredeemed state of the world is not for Christians, as for Jews, an argument against belief in the Messiah's having come, but constitutes the burning question in their prayers for the future of the Redeemer who has come. . . . Faith in Jesus as the Christ is not the end of hope, it is the confidence in which we hope.[14]

The whole subject of "hope in Christ" was and still is difficult to grasp. Sometimes people speak of hope as if it were "wishful thinking," as if they are looking forward to some future change or occurrence but are not sure if it will happen. However, the hope that Christians proclaim in Jesus Christ is not some vague notion based on a wistful longing. Rather it is grounded in the present reality of relationship with Jesus Christ and looks forward to the final fulfillment of all that God longs for: the redemption of all

---

12. Karl Barth, *Dogmatik im Grundriss (1947)*, 158f (ET. *Dogmatics in Outline*, 1949, 134f) as cited by Moltmann, *Theology of Hope*, 228.

13. Moltmann, *Theology of Hope*, 228–29.

14. Moltmann, *Theology of Hope*, 229.

creation. This hope is not seen fully now. For as the Apostle Paul would write in his Epistle to the Romans, "Now in hope we were saved. Now hope that is seen is not hope. For who hopes for what is seen? But if we hope for what we do not see, we wait for it with patience" (Rom 8:24-25).

And so, with such theological clarity and yet with historical ambiguity, this is where we leave Paul as Luke's narrative ends: the Apostle in Rome (and, in a sense, all Christians everywhere) waiting patiently in hope. While humanly speaking we might desire a conclusion that brings everything neatly to an end, Luke's conclusion is once again a reminder that for those who are followers of the Way, the pilgrimage is open-ended. As Luke has reminded us time and time again, those who follow Jesus must be prepared to live "in the meantime"—in the time between the "now" and the "not yet." We do so in the knowledge of the love of God that has been revealed supremely in the life, death, and resurrection of Jesus Christ, and as those who are guided and comforted by the Holy Spirit. Luke's ending here deliberately suggests that as we seek to follow Jesus now and journey on in the pilgrim way one with another, we confess that we do not see the way ahead clearly. What we do see is the hope of Israel, and indeed of all creation, set before us as those who acknowledge, in the words of the Apostle Paul, Jesus Christ as the "Amen" to all of God's promises, and the Spirit is given in our hearts as a first installment (2 Cor 1:20-21).

Draw Your Own Conclusions

1. What might be considered "hindrances" to sharing Christian faith today?

2. How does gathering with other believers enable Christians to "take courage"?

3. What is the difference in Christian hope and wishful thinking?

Epilogue

The Continuing Journey of Spiritual Formation: Remembering and Waiting

In many ways, the story of Acts ends as it began, with an emphasis on waiting. Through the power of story, and with Luke as a remarkable narrator, we have had the opportunity to accompany and to observe the witness of those who sought to be obedient followers of Jesus Christ. In the first part of Acts, our engagement with the word encouraged us to stand alongside the first apostles as Jesus ascended into heaven; we then made our way back to Jerusalem to join together with them in prayer. On the day of Pentecost, we imagined the awe and wonder of the disciples as they first experienced the power of the Holy Spirit. We then gathered with the early disciples and reflected on sharing life with others who are in Christ. We went with Peter and John to the temple and observed how they "looked intently" at the man who was begging by the gate. When the man was healed, we rejoiced as he stood for the first time and then entered the temple "walking and leaping and praising God."

When Peter and John stood before the council, we listened as they gave their testimony and boldly declared that they would not be silenced. They had to speak of Jesus and "could not keep from proclaiming all they had seen and heard." We watched as Stephen, "a man full of faith and the Holy Spirit," was arrested, tried, and put to death for his faith. As the persecution of the believers increased and they were scattered to other places, we listened to Luke's account of Philip preaching in Samaria and then observed his obedience to the call to go to a deserted place to meet an Ethiopian eunuch. As Philip then found himself in Azotus, our attention was turned to a man named Saul who, according to Luke, had stood with approval and watched as Stephen was stoned to death. We then met Saul on the road to Damascus and witnessed his encounter with the risen Christ. Here we were made aware that conversion is not a one-time event as we reflected on the obedience of Ananias, who in spite of his fear responded to God's call to go to Saul and received him as a brother in the Lord.

As Saul went to Jerusalem, we then turned our attention back to Peter and to Christians in Joppa. Luke made it plain that the gospel really is for all, as we realized that through the power of the Spirit Peter brought healing to Tabitha (Dorcas) and then stayed at the home of Simon, a tanner. While staying in Joppa, Peter was led to see that "God shows no partiality" and that he, too, must reach out to everyone with the good news of Jesus. Directed by God, he went to Cornelius, and then after the gift of the Holy Spirit was poured out on the Gentiles, he said that they too should be baptized in the name of Jesus Christ. He then returned to Jerusalem to report to the apostles and believers there.

As the gospel began to spread to other places, the communities of faith began to grow. While initially those who were scattered because of the persecution of Stephen only proclaimed the word to Jews, the good news was soon spread more widely. Saul and Barnabas were sent out by the church at Antioch. They then set sail on the first of what turned out to be (at least in Luke's account) three "missionary journeys" that Saul (now known as the Apostle Paul) made before he ended up in Jerusalem, where he was arrested before being taken to Rome to await trial before the emperor, a right that he claimed as a Roman citizen.

While the first half of Luke's narration focused on the development of the church, the later chapters beckoned us to reflect on the qualities needed by those who are seeking to follow in the way Christ. Luke presented Paul as an example of a follower of Jesus. Three times we were told about his encounter with the risen Christ on the road to Damascus. While we were left in no doubt of his faults and failings, Luke gave us an opportunity to accompany Paul as he tried to proclaim the gospel to others. At every stage of the narrative, Luke reminded us that both conversion and formation in the faith is God's work. Indeed, Luke emphasized over and over again that having personally encountered the risen Christ as Son of God, and having repented of sin and turned to the Lord in faith, the believer must then depend on God as Holy Spirit to lead and guide. As we enter the narrative, we wait and watch, but we are also drawn to remember what God has already done, and in remembering we are drawn closer to the Lord in the here and now, whatever that might mean for each reader.

If the first part of Acts was written to show us the potential for genuine Christian community, the second part was framed to remind us of the continued struggle for authenticity, as a Christian believer must face of all kinds of opposition from empire and culture. It has always been so. Writing of the growth of the church in the first few centuries after Acts was written, Alan Kreider claimed that it might best be described as "patient ferment."[1] The early believers did not try to manipulate the work of the Holy Spirit. They did not plan elaborate programs or spend time thinking about big budgets. But they increased in number as they gave themselves to practicing the virtue of patience or, as Kreider put it, sought to create a habitus (which includes attitudes, skills, and dispositions) of patient ferment. Some of the ways that early Christians created this habitus, according to Kreider, included meeting frequently with other believers, having certain postures to express thanksgiving or to recall the saving work of Christ in worship, eating together and sharing certain expressions of the peace, memorizing texts of Scripture, visiting the poor, sick, or those in prison, exercising hospitality and giving generously to the needs of others, being truthful and practicing discernment, maintaining sexual purity, observing disciplines that would limit impatient behavior, being willing to lose out (not practicing litigation or coercing others), and facing death without fear.[2]

These practices and the emphasis on patient ferment seem to echo the ideals that Luke emphasized in his account of the growth of the church in Acts. Moreover, this emphasis on patience, alongside waiting and remembering, is crucial to the continuing picture of spiritual formation. Throughout Acts, as we have listened to stories of people being encouraged to gather, to wait and to pray, to listen and to respond, we have been reminded that we do not control the Spirit of God. We do not know what tomorrow will bring; rather we live always in a liminal existence, which we have labeled the "meantime," and Luke stresses that we are to wait and remember in this time.

In our waiting and remembering, we are not alone. The spiritual readings that we have explored alongside Luke's biblical narrative have reminded us that not only are we part of a much wider community of faith but that Christians down through the ages have been seeking to give themselves to God and to be formed in faith. The spiritual classics of devotion also

---

1. Alan Kreider, *The Patient Ferment of the Early Church: The Improbable Rise of Christianity in the Roman Empire* (Grand Rapids, MI: Baker, 2016).

2. Kreider, *The Patient Ferment of the Early Church*, 122–23.

remind us that we need guides and spiritual companions on the way who will help us learn what it means to be a follower of Jesus. The spiritual readings remind us of "a community of pilgrims large enough and varied enough for all to find companionship and guidance."[3] The challenge for us all is to go beyond the mere reading of these works and even beyond the mere reading of Scripture.

This sense of going beyond a mere reading of the text is what we have tried to do in exploring the book of Acts. In looking at the texts, we have tried, in the words of Thomas Merton, to "enter into the strange and paradoxical world of meanings and experiences that are beyond us and yet often extremely and mysteriously relevant to us."[4] As we have tried to go beyond a mere reading of the text and, indeed, to enter into the narrative, we have been confronted by the reality that spiritual formation is a lifelong process of conversion and transformation. Moreover, we have examined some of the many hindrances to spiritual formation, including—but not limited to—individualism, fear of revealing our true self, lack of community, busyness, an emphasis on doctrine and belief rather than relationship, fear of silence and solitude, and a lack of accountability.

It should be said that while we might name these and many other hindrances to spiritual growth, many of us have also devised ways of not addressing these hindrances head on. Sometimes we fail to notice the blocks to spiritual growth because we assume that we understand Christian faith or that, if we are following certain rules or rituals, we are surely religious people and as such nothing more is needed. Another way of avoiding the call to give ourselves to God, according to Thomas Kelly, is that we live life at two levels rather than seeking to live out of what Kelly calls "the Divine Center." While we may order our "mental life on more than one level at once," Kelly claimed that there is another level, a deeper, "profounder level" that must be developed.[5] A key to the quest of "centering down" (as Kelly puts it) is to learn that there can be "fruitful interplay" between both levels. What is destructive to the spiritual life is when a person begins to "compartmentalize" certain parts of life and fails to remember that all of life is to be lived with an awareness of God's presence. There is no task too small, no worry too minor, and no activity that falls outside the sphere of the Divine.

---

3. Mogabgab, "Along the Desert Road," 182.

4. Thomas Merton, *Opening the Bible* (London: George Allen and Unwin, 1972), 27.

5. Kelly, *A Testament of Devotion*, 35.

In addition to compartmentalizing life, another major stumbling block to addressing hindrances to spiritual growth is what some early Christians referred to as *acedia*, which in Greek simply means the absence or lack of care. Those who spoke in terms of the "seven deadly sins" referred to this malaise as sloth, a condition characterized by apathy or listlessness. The early monks referred to it as the "noonday demon" because they often felt susceptible to the temptation to fall into such a lack of attentiveness at that time. Evagrius, an early monk whose work we have noted, described the situation of a monk who had been hindered in his prayer by *acedia* in this rather humorous way:

> The eye of the despondent one stares constantly at the window, and his mind presents visitors to him. The door creaks, and he jumps up; he hears a voice, and peers through the window, and he does not go away from there, until, exhausted, he sits down. If the despondent one reads, then yawns a great deal, and soon he sinks into sleep. He rubs his eyes, and stretches out his hands, and while his eyes wander from the book, he stares at the wall, then he turns away again, and reads a little, and when he leafs through [the book], he searches for the end of the exposition. He counts the pages, and determines the number of sheets, finds fault with the writing and the design and in the end snaps the book shut. He lays his head on it, and falls into not-too-deep sleep, and in the end hunger wakes up his soul again, and the soul [now renewed] attends to its own concerns.[6]

The cure for acedia according to Evagrius was to be steadfast and diligent and to persevere. He wrote,

> Steadfastness, and that one does everything with great care, fear of God and perseverance, [these] heal despondency. Set for yourself a goal in every task and do not rise from it until you have finished it. And pray unceasingly, and express yourself concisely, and the spirit of despondency will flee from you.[7]

Reading these thoughts from an early spiritual writer, we may be tempted to think today that what he called a spiritual problem we might simply say was a "psychological problem," or perhaps something akin to a depressive

---

6. In Gabriel Bunge, *Despondency: The Spiritual Teachings of Evagrius Ponticus on Acedia*, trans. Anthony P. Gythiel (New York: St. Vladimir's Press, 2012), 75.

7. In Bunge, *Despondency*, 96–97.

illness. If we are inclined to think that *acedia* is not a spiritual problem, we must stop and think again. Kathleeen Norris, in a book titled *Acedia and Me*, reminds us that anyone who wants to seriously reflect on the spiritual life is susceptible to what we might call the modern-day temptation to the "ease of indifference."[8]

As we have reflected on spiritual formation while studying Acts, we have been prompted not only to think about what might hinder us in seeking to go forward in faith but also to consider what we might do to encourage growth in the spiritual life. These practices include total dependence on the power of the Holy Spirit, regular worship and fellowship with others, and developing an attitude of surrender, meaning that we give up on our own ideas of what God might be doing and simply allow God to show us the way. We have noted that while we often want to take back control, we are always to let go and to seek "to will the one thing": that is, to seek to be single-minded for God.

Two other important aspects of spiritual formation, remembering and waiting (which we noted in the introduction to our conversation), should be mentioned again here, for both are critical to a spiritual life. By remembering, as we have already said, we do not mean simply recalling an event or person mentally. Rather we are speaking of memory in terms of the way that the act of remembering can actualize the past and create for others the possibility of a new experience. As noted in the introduction, the pastoral question in any discussion of memory and the spiritual life is, What happens when one can no longer remember?

Writing on dementia, while acknowledging all the complexities of understanding love and identity as a person, John Swinton has argued that losing memory does not necessarily mean that one loses self. Moreover, while a person suffering from dementia may not be able to show or express recognition of friends or family, or carry on a conversation, we should not assume that the person is no longer present to God. How care for the individual and the relationship with God is fostered further may not be clear to us. However, as Swinton claimed, the basis for our ongoing trust is that even when we may no longer remember God, God remembers us. To underscore this point, he recalled a conversation with a friend who, during her pastoral training, was assigned to a ward with patients who had severe dementia. While it was a difficult experience, the trainee minister claimed that what she had learned most came to her through the words of the hymn

---

8. Kathleen Norris, *Acedia and Me* (London: Riverhead Books, 2008), 6.

by James Montgomery. In this hymn, the first verses speak of the call for us to remember Jesus, but the last verse offers a reminder that even when we can't or don't remember God, we have a God who remembers us![9]

According to thy gracious word
in meek humility,
this will I do, my dying Lord,
I will remember thee.

Thy body, broken for my sake,
my bread from heaven shall be;
thy cup of blessing I will take,
and thus remember thee.

Gethsemane, can I forget?
Or there thy conflict see,
thine agony and bloody sweat,
and not remember thee?

When to the cross I turn mine eyes,
and rest on Calvary,
O Lamb of God, my sacrifice,
I must remember thee.

Remember Thee, and all Thy pains
and all Thy love to me
Lord while a breath, a pulse remains
I will remember thee.

And when these failing lips grow dumb,
and mind and memory flee,
when thou shalt in thy kingdom come,
then, Lord, remember me.[10]

---

9. John Swinton, *Dementia: Living in the Memories of God* (London: SCM Press, 2012/2017), 195.

10. While Swinton identifies this hymn as one that is often sung in Anglo-Catholic worship services on Maundy Thursday, it was written by James Montgomery, who was theologically trained in the Moravian Church. This is another example of hymnody that transcends doctrinal difference and unites believers of different theological persuasions. See Watson, *The English Hymn*, 304ff.

Having noted the importance of memory to individual spiritual life, we must go one step further and note that memory is also very important to the church as a whole. In 1985, sociologists critiquing the rise of American individualism stressed that what was needed in order for society to thrive were "communities of memory."[11] Communities, as they defined them, are "constituted by their past." Moreover, in order not to forget the past, a community shares in retelling its story, its "constitutive narrative," and in so doing it offers examples of men and women who have embodied and exemplified the meaning of the community. A genuine community will tell stories of exemplary individuals but also painful stories of shared suffering. In this way, "the communities of memory that tie us to the past also turn us to the future as communities of hope."[12]

Building on the idea of needing "communities of memory," Robert Wuthnow turns attention to the church as a particular type of community of memory. In this sense, contrary to what many churches might think, Wuthnow claimed that churches must be "backward looking."[13] That is to say, his thesis suggested that the church has a special mission to preserve the past. This is not just a matter of carrying on tradition for tradition's sake (as a failure to recognize mere custom for what it is). Rather, it is a matter of realizing that our identities as "Christians" depend on it.

So what stories are told? The stories of Scripture are paramount with particular emphasis on the story of Jesus: his birth, life, death, and resurrection. But, as Wuthnow points out, even that story "will not instill a deep Christian identity unless it is told and retold, related in innovative ways, and intertwined with the other individual and collective pasts that are part of every person's tradition."[14] The church, as Wuthnow suggested, must be a place where discourse, whether about the past, present, or future, is actively encouraged. "Memory comes alive and is renewed only when it is discussed."[15]

As we remember and help others remember, we also remind one another that God is both loving and patient and, indeed, a God who not only remember us but waits on us, too. In effect, as W. H. Vanstone has

---

11. Robert Bellah et.al, *Habits of the Heart* (Berkeley: University of California Press, 1985), 152ff.

12. Bellah, *Habits of the Heart*, 153.

13. Robert Wuthnow, *Christianity in the Twenty-first Century* (Oxford: Oxford University Press, 1993), 48.

14. Wuthnow, *Christianity in the Twenty-first Century*, 49.

15. Wuthnow, *Christianity in the Twenty-first Century*, 49.

pointed out, waiting is the only thing that genuine love can finally do. Reflecting on the human experience of loving another person, Vanstone wrote,

> In authentic loving there is no control of the other who is loved: that he or she will receive is beyond the power of love to ordain or know. So when our work of love is done we are destined to wait upon the outcome—to wait upon the response of acceptance or rejection, of understanding or misunderstanding, which either fulfills our own activity or makes it vain. By our activity of loving we destine ourselves, in the end, to waiting . . . .[16]

Turning his attention to the love of God, Vanstone suggests that in an act of free will, an act of absolute love,

> God Himself, of His own free initiative, "hands Himself over", makes Himself object to the world: in loving the world gives to the world the terrible power to have meaning to and for Himself. So He Who made, everlastingly makes, the world also, of His own freedom, waits upon the world, exposed to and receptive of its power meaning.[17]

This picture of a God who is always waiting and longing to be in relationship with us was captured by Luke in the Gospel account of the parable of the waiting father (Luke 15:11-32). Reflecting on this parable, which was also depicted in a painting by Rembrandt, Henri Nouwen wrote,

> The Father's love does not force itself on the beloved. Although he wants to heal us of all our inner darkness, we are still free to make our own choice to stay in the darkness or to step into the light of God's love. God is there. God's light is there. God's forgiveness is there. God's boundless love is there. What is so clear is that God is always there, always ready to give and forgive, absolutely independent of our response.[18]

God remembers us. God's love for us and for all creation is seen supremely in the life, death, and resurrection of Jesus Christ. Luke's message in the Gospel account and in Acts is that God's love is for all. In that love,

---

16. W. H. Vanstone, *The Stature of Waiting* (London: Darton, Longman and Todd, 1982), 96.

17. Vanstone, *The Stature of Waiting*, 111.

18. Henri J. M. Nouwen, *The Return of the Prodigal Son: A Story of Homecoming* (London: Darton, Longman and Todd, 1994), 78.

God waits on our response. For Luke, the good news of Jesus and our growth in the spiritual life is never merely about personal individual growth in holiness. Rather, life in relationship with God through faith in Christ is also to be lived with, and for, others.

We are to take up the cross, knowing that daily we must repent, and then, in the forgiveness of God, we resolve anew to seek to be the people God has called us to be. Thankfully, we are not alone as we make the journey, but we know the companionship of those who are fellow travellers now as well as those who are part of the wider communion of saints who already know the fullness of the love of God. As we journey onward, however, as we have been reminded in our reflections on Luke's narrative, taking up the cross of Christ demands courage, obedience, patience, single-mindedness, detachment, the ability to listen, openness to God and others, and so much more. The journey of those who seek to follow Jesus is never straightforward or without pain and suffering. Yet the joy of knowing the love of God in Christ far outweighs the trouble we may face. It is this love—the love of God that knows no bounds—that the followers of the Way must seek to proclaim boldly and "unhinderedly."

Selected Bibliography

Biblical and Theological Sources

d'Angelo, Mary Rose. "Women in Luke-Acts: A Redactional View." *Journal of Biblical Literature* 109/3 (Autumn, 1990): 441–61.

Brown, Raymond E. *A Once-and-Coming Spirit at Pentecost: Essays on the Liturgical Readings between Easter and Pentecost.* Collegeville, MN: Liturgical Press, 1994.

Bruce, F. F. "The Acts of the Apostles." In D. Guthrie et al., *The New Bible Commentary Revised.* London, 1970.

———. *Commentary on the Book of Acts.* London: Marshall, Morgan and Scott, 1954.

Brueggemann, Walter. *The Creative Word, Canon as a Model for Biblical Education*, 2nd edition. Minneapolis: Fortress Press, 2015.

Cadbury, Henry J. *The Book of Acts in History.* London: Adam and Charles Black, 1955.

———. "Some Lukan Expressions of Time (Lexical Notes on Luke-Acts VII)." *Journal of Biblical Literature* 82/3 (September 1963): 272–78. https://www.jstor.org/stable/3264629.

Caird, G. B. *The Apostolic Age.* London: Duckworth Press, 1955; revised 1975.

Cassidy, Richard. *Society and Politics in the Acts of the Apostles.* Eugene, OR: Wipf and Stock, 1987.

Child, Brevard. *Memory and Tradition in Israel.* London: SCM Press, 1967.

Chung-Kim, Esther, and Todd R. Hains. *Reformation Commentary on Scripture, New Testament VI, Acts.* Downers Grove, IL: Intervarsity, 2014.

Conzelmann, Hans. *The Theology of St. Luke.* Los Angeles: Harper, 1961.

Craddock, Fred. *Luke.* Interpretation: A Bible Commentary for Teaching and Preaching Louisville, KY: John Knox Press, 1990.

Dahl, Nils Alstrup. *Jesus in the Memory of the Early Church.* Minneapolis: Augsburg, 1976.

Davies, John D. "Inclusion in the Acts of the Apostles." *The Expository Times* 124/9 (2013): 425–32.

Davies, J. G. *The Early Christian Church: A History of the First Five Centuries.* Grand Rapids, MI: Baker Book House, 1965.

Deissmann, Adolf. *Paul: A Study of Social and Religious History.* New York: Harper and Brothers, 1957.

Dickerson, Febbie C. "Acts 9:36-43, The Many Faces of Tabitha, a Womanist Reading." In Mitzi J. Smith, ed., *I Found God in Me: A Womanist Biblical Hermeneutics Reader.* Eugene, OR: Wipf and Stock, 2015. 296–312.

Dodd, C. H. *The Apostolic Preaching and Its Development.* New York: Harper and Row, 1937.

Dunn, James D. G. *Acts of the Apostles.* Grand Rapids, MI: Eerdmans, 1996, 2016.

———. *Jesus and the Spirit: A Study of the Religious and Charismatic Experience of Jesus and the First Christian as Reflected in the New Testament.* London: SCM, 1975.

Dupertuis, Rubén René. "The Acts of the Apostles, Narrative, and History." In the *Oxford Handbook of Biblical Narrative*, ed. Dana Nolan Ferwell. Oxford: Oxford University Press, 2016.

Ferguson, Everett. "Laying on of Hands: its Significance in Ordination." *The Journal of Theological Studies* 26/1 (New Series) (1975): 1–12.

———. *Baptism in the Early Church: History, Theology and Liturgy in the First Five Centuries.* Grand Rapids, MI: Eerdmans, 2009.

Fiorenza, Elisabeth Schüssler. *In Memory of Her*. New York: Crossroads, 1983.

Joseph A. Fitzmyer. *The Acts of the Apostles*. The Anchor Yale Bible. New Haven: Yale University Press, 1998.

Garland, David E. *Acts: Teach the Text Commentary Series*. Grand Rapids, MI: Baker Books, 2017.

Garroway, Joshua. "The Pharisee Heresy: Circumcision of the Gentiles in the Texts of the Apostles." *New Testament Studies* 60/1 (January 2014): 20–36.

Gasque, W. Ward. "A Fruitful Field: Recent Study of the Acts of the Apostles." In *Interpretation, The Journal of Bible and Theology* 42/2 (April 1988): 123–24.

Gaventa, Beverly Roberts. *Acts: Abingdon New Testament Commentaries*. Nashville: Abingdon, 2003.

Goodspeed, E. J. *Introduction to the New Testament*. Chicago: University of Chicago Press, 1937.

Guthrie, D., et al. *The New Bible Commentary Revised*. Grand Rapids, MI: Eerdmans 1970, 1984.

Hays, Christopher M. *Luke's Wealth Ethics, A Study in Their Coherence and Character*. Tübingen: Mohr Siebeck, 2010.

Hauerwas, Stanley. *The Hauerwas Reader*. Ed. John Berkman and Michael Cartwright. Durham, NC: Duke University Press, 2001.

————, et al. *Truthfulness and Tragedy*. Notre Dame, IN: University of Notre Dame Press, 1977.

Hornik, Heidi J., and Mikeal C. Parsons. *Acts of the Apostles Through the Centuries*. Wiley Blackwell Bible Commentaries. Oxford: Wiley Blackwell, 2016.

Horsley, G. H. R. "Speeches and Dialogues in Acts, Short Studies." *New Testament Studies* 32 (1986): 609–64.

Jennings, Willie James. *Acts*. Belief: A Theological Commentary on the Bible. Louisville: Westminster/ John Knox, 2017

Jeremias, Joachim. *The Central Message of the New Testament*. London: SCM, 1965.

Jervell, Jacob. *The Theology of Acts*. Cambridge: Cambridge University Press, 1996.

Johnson, Luke Timothy. *Gospel of Luke*. Sacra Pagina. Collegeville: Liturgical Press, Michael Glazier, 2006.

Karris, Robert J. "Women and Discipleship in Luke," *The Catholic Biblical Quarterly* 56/1 (January 1994): 1–20.

Keener, Craig S. *Introduction and 1:1–2:47*. Volume 1 of *Acts: An Exegetical Commentary*. Grand Rapids, MI: Baker Academic, 2012.

———. *3:1–14:28*. Volume 2 of Acts: An Exegetical Commentary. Grand Rapids, MI: Baker Academic, 2013.

———. *15:1–23:35*. Volume 3 of Acts: An Exegetical Commentary. Grand Rapids, MI: Baker Academic, 2014.

———. *24:1–28:31*. Volume 4 of Acts: An Exegetical Commentary. Grand Rapids, MI: Baker Academic, 2015.

Kidd, Richard. "Memory and Communion." In *Baptists and the Communion of Saints: A Theology of Covenanted Disciples*, ed. Paul S. Fiddes, Brian Haymes, and Richard Kidd. Waco, TX: Baylor University Press, 2014.

Kucicki, Janusz. *The Function of the Speeches in the Acts of the Apostles*. Leiden: Brill, 2018.

Jennings, Willie James. *Acts*. Belief: A Theological Commentary. Louisville, KY: Westminster, 2017.

Jeremias, Joachim. *The Central Message of the New Testament*. London: SCM, 1965.

Kreider, Alan. *The Patient Ferment of the Early Church: The Improbable Rise of Christianity in the Roman Empire*. Grand Rapids, MI: Baker Academic Press, 2016.

Longenecker, Richard. "Taking up the Cross Daily: Discipleship in Luke-Acts." In Richard N. Longenecker, ed., *Patterns of Discipleship in the New Testament*. Grand Rapids, MI: Eerdmans, 1996. 50.

Marshall, I. Howard. *Acts*. Tyndale New Testament Commentaries: Leicester: Intervarsity Press, 1980; reprint, 1983.

———. *Luke, Historian and Theologian*. Exeter: Paternoster Press, 1970/1979.

Martin, Francis, ed. *Ancient Christian Commentary on Scripture, New Testament V, Acts*. Downers Grove, IL: Intervarsity Press, 2006.

Moltmann, Jürgen. *The Church in the Power of the Spirit*. London: SCM Press, 1977.

———. *Theology of Hope*. London: SCM Press, 1967/1978.

Morrill, Bruce T. *Anamnesis as Dangerous Memory: Political and Liturgical Theology in Dialogue*. Collegeville, MN: Liturgical Press, 2000.

Murphy-O'Connor, Jerome. *Paul: A Critical Life*. Oxford: Clarendon, 1996.

Nuttall, Geoffrey F. *The Holy Spirit in Puritan Faith and Experience*. Oxford: Basil Blackwell, 1946.

O'Neill, J. C. *The Theology of Acts in its Historical Setting*. London: S.P.C.K, 1961.

O'Toole, Robert F., S.J. *The Unity of Luke's Theology: An Analysis of Luke-Acts*. Eugene, OR: Wipf and Stock, 2016.

Parsons, Mikeal C. *Acts*. Grand Rapids, MI: Baker Publishing, 2008.

———. "The Place of Jerusalem on the Lukan Landscape: An Exercise in Symbolic Cartography." In *Literary Studies in Luke-Acts: Essays in Honor of Joseph B. Tyson*, ed. Richard P. Thompson and Thomas E. Phillips. Macon, GA: Mercer University Press, 1998. 155–71.

———, and Joseph B. Tyson, eds. *Cadbury, Knox and Talbert: American Contributions to the Story of Acts*. Atlanta: Scholars Press. 1992.

Parvey, Constance F. "Theology and Leadership of Women in the New Testament." In *Religion and Sexism*, ed. Rosemary Radford Reuther. New York: Simon and Schuster, 1974. 139–46.

Pelikan, Jaroslav. *Acts*. Brazos Theological Commentary. Grand Rapids, MI: Brazos Press, 2013.

Pervo, Richard I. *Acts: A Commentary*. Hermeneia: A Critical and Historical Commentary on the Bible. Minneapolis: Fortress Press, 2009.

———. *Luke's Story of Paul*. Minneapolis: Fortress Press, 1990.

———. *Profit with Delight: The Literary Genre of the Acts of the Apostles*. Philadelphia: Fortress, 1987.

Peterson, David G. *The Acts of the Apostles*. The Pillar New Testament Commentary. Grand Rapids, MI: Eerdmans, 2009.

Peterson, Eugene H. *The Contemplative Pastor: Returning to the Art of Spiritual Direction.* Grand Rapids, MI: Eerdmans, 1988.

Polhill, John B. *Acts.* Volume 26 of The New American Commentary. Nashville: Broadman Press, 1991.

Praeder, Susan Marie. "Acts 27:1-28:16: Sea Voyages in Ancient Literature and the Theology of Luke-Acts." *The Catholic Biblical Quarterly* 46/4 (October 1984): 683–706.

Raverty, Aaron, OSB. "Hospitality in the Benedictine Monastic Tradition." *Revista Interdisciplinar da Mobilidade Humana [Brasília]* (January/June 2012): 251–55.

Regev, Eyal. *The Temple in Early Christianity, Experiencing the Sacred.* New Haven/London: Yale University Press, 2019.

Reimer, Ivoni Richter. *Women in the Acts of the Apostles: A Feminist Liberation Perspective.* Minneapolis: Augsburg, 1995.

Richardson, Alan, and John Bowden, eds. *A New Dictionary of Christian Theology.* London: SCM Press, 1983.

Robinson, Joanne. *Waiting in the Christian Traditions: Balancing Ideology and Utopia.* London: Lexington Books, 2006.

Robinson, H. Wheeler. *The Christian Experience of the Holy Spirit.* London: Nisbet and Co., 1928.

Rowe, C. Kavin. *World Upside Down: Reading Acts in the Graeco-Roman Age.* Oxford: Oxford University Press, 2009.

Schmemann, Alexander. *The Eucharist.* Crestwood, NY: St. Vladimir's Seminary Press, 2003.

———. *For the Life of the World: Sacraments and Orthodoxy,* revised. Crestwood, NY: St. Vladimir's Seminary Press, 1973.

Solomon, David. "Procurator." In *Encyclopaedia Judaica.* https://www.jewishvirtuallibrary.org/procurator.

Stagg, Frank. *The Book of Acts: The Early Struggle for an Unhindered Gospel.* Nashville: Broadman, 1955.

Soards, Marion L. *The Speeches in Acts: Their Content, Context, and Concerns.* Louisville, KY: Westminster/John Knox Press, 1994.

Strelan, Rick. *Luke The Priest: The Authority of the Author of the Third Gospel.* Farnham UK: Ashgate Publishing, Ltd., 2008/2013.

Stroup, George W. *The Promise of Narrative Theology*. London: SCM Press, 1981.

Talbert, Charles H. "The Bible as Spiritual Friend." Presidential Address at National Association of Baptist Professors of Religion. November 25, 1985.

———. *Learning through Suffering: The Educational Value of Suffering in the New Testament and in Its Milieu*. Collegeville, MN: The Liturgical Press, 1991.

———. *Reading Acts, A Literary and Theological Commentary*. Revised edition. Macon, GA: Smyth & Helwys, 2005.

———. *The Way of the Lukan Jesus: Dimensions of Lukan Spirituality in Perspectives in Religious Studies*. Presidential Address, Association of Baptist Professors of Religion, Southeast. Gainesville, FL, March 18, 1982.

Tannehill, Robert C. "Acts of the Apostles and Ethics." *Interpretation: A Journal of Bible and Theology* 66/3 (July 2012): 270–82.

Thurston, Bonnie. *Women in the New Testament*. New York: Crossroads, 1998.

Trites, Allison. "Church Growth in the Book of Acts." Chapter 4 in *Vital New Testament Issues*, ed. Roy B. Suck. Eugene, OR: Wipf and Stock, 1996. 44–54.

———. "The Importance of Legal Scenes and Language in the Book of Acts." In *Novum Testamentum* 16/4 (1974): 278–84.

———. *The New Testament Concept of Witness*. Cambridge: Cambridge University Press, 1977/2004.

———. "Two Witness Motifs in Acts 1:8 and the Book of Acts." *Themelios* 7 (1970): 17–22.

Walaskay, Paul W. *Acts*. Louisville, KY: Westminster/John Knox Press, 1998.

Watson, Francis. *Paul and the Hermeneutics of Faith*. 2nd ed. New York: Bloomsbury, 2014/2016.

Wilcox, M. "The Judas-Tradition in Acts I.15-26." *New Testament Studies* 4 (1973): 438–52.

Williams, C. S. C. *A Commentary on the Acts of the Apostles*. Black's New Testament Commentaries. London: A and C Black Ltd, 1957, 2nd ed. 1964; repr., 1978.

Willimon, William H. *Acts*. Interpretation A Biblical Commentary for Teaching and Preaching. Atlanta: John Knox Press, 1988.

Williamson, Charles C. *Interpretation Bible Studies*. Reformation Commentary. Louisville, KY: Geneva Press, 2000.

Wilson, Stephen G. "Jewish-Christian Relations 70-170 C.E." In volume 3 of *Anchor Bible Dictionary*, ed. D. N. Freedman. New York: Doubleday, 1992.

Wintle, Brian, ed. *South Asia Bible Commentary*. Rajasthan: Open Doors Publications, 2015.

Witherington Ben III. *The Acts of the Apostles: A Socio-Rhetorical Commentary*. Grand Rapids, MI: Eerdmans, 2001.

————. *The Paul Quest: The Renewed Search for the Jew of Tarsus*. Leicester: Intervarsity Press, 1998.

————. *Women and the Genesis of Christianity*. Cambridge: CUP, 1990.

Young, Frances M. *Biblical Exegesis and the Formation of Christian Culture*. Cambridge: Cambridge University Press, 1997.

Sources for Spiritual Formation

Aelred of Rievaulx. *Spiritual Friendship*. Ed. Marsha L. Dutton and trans. Lawrence C. Braceland, S.J. Collegeville, MN: Liturgical Press, 2010.

Anselm. *Prayers and Meditations of St. Anselm with the Proslogian*. Trans. Sister Benedicta Ward. Harmondsworth: Penguin Books, 1973.

Appleton, George, ed. *The Oxford Book of Prayer*. Oxford: Oxford University Press, 1985.

Aquinas, Thomas. "Of Envy." Question 36 of "Treatise on Virtues." In *Summa Theologica*. https://www.sacred-texts.com/chr/aquinas/summa/sum291.htm.

Atkinson, James, ed. *The Darkness of Faith: Daily Readings with Martin Luther*. London: Darton, Longman and Todd, 1987.

Augustine. *The Confessions*. Garden City, NY: Image Books, 1960.

Baelz, Peter. *Does God Answer Prayer?* London: Darton, Longman and Todd, 1982.

Baptist Praise and Worship. Oxford: Oxford University Press, 1991.

Baxter, Richard. *Dying Thoughts upon Philippians 1:23* (1683), with an introductory essay by the Revd H. Stebbing, D.D. London: Hall, Virtue and Co.,1850.

Bellah, Robert, et al. *Habits of the Heart.* Berkeley: University of California Press, 1985.

Bernstein, Harry. *The Invisible Wall.* London: Random House, 2007.

Bethge, Eberhard. *Friendship and Resistance: Essays on Dietrich Bonhoeffer.* Grand Rapids, MI: Eerdmans, 1995.

The Book of Common Prayer, 1662.

St. Benedict. *The Rule of St Benedict.* Ed. Timothy Fry, O.S.B. New York: Vintage Spiritual Classics, 1998.

Bloom, Anthony. *School for Prayer.* London: Darton, Longman and Todd, 1970/1978.

Bondi, Roberta C. "Forgiveness, Judgmentalism, and the Sense of Self." In Andrew Weaver and Monica Furlong, eds., *Reflections on Forgiveness and Spiritual Growth.* Nashville: Abingdon Press, 2000. 27–35.

Bonhoeffer, Dietrich. *The Cost of Discipleship.* London: SCM Press, 1959.

———. *Life Together.* London: SCM Press, 1976.

Bouyer, Louis. *A History of Christian Spirituality: The Spirituality of the New Testament and the Fathers,* volume 1. Kent: Burns and Oates, 1968.

Bradley, Ian. *Colonies of Heaven: Celtic Models for Today's Church.* London: Darton, Longman and Todd, 2000.

Brother Lawrence. *The Practice of the Presence of God.* London: Hodder and Stoughton, 1984.

Brother Roger. "A Heart that Trusts" (1985). In *Brother Roger of Taizé: His Love Is a Fire: Central Writings with Extracts from His Journals.* London: Geoffrey Chapman Mowbray, 1988/1990.

Bunge, Gabriel. *Despondency: The Spiritual Teachings of Evagrius Ponticus on Acedia.* Trans. Anthony P. Gythiel. New York: St. Vladimir's Press, 2012.

Byrne, Lavinia, ed. *The Hidden Tradition: Women's Spiritual Writings Rediscovered*. London: SPCK, 1991.

Cassian, John. *Conferences*. In Nicene and Post-Nicene Fathers, Second Series, vol. 11, ed. Philip Schaff and Henry Wace. Buffalo, NY: Christian Literature Publishing Co., 1894. Revised and edited for New Advent by Kevin Knight, *New Advent*, https://www.newadvent.org/fathers/350816.htm.

Celtic Spirituality. The Classics of Western Spirituality. Trans. and introduced by Oliver Davies. New York: Paulist Press, 1999.

Day, Dorothy. *The Long Loneliness*. San Francisco: Harper Collins, 1952; repr., 1997.

Dürr, Alfred. Trans. Richard D. P. Jones. *The Cantatas of J. S. Bach*. Oxford: Oxford University Press, 2005.

Easter, Opal V. *Nannie Helen Burroughs*. New York: Garland Publishing, 1995.

Edwards, Jonathan. *A Treatise Concerning Religious Affections*. New Haven: Yale University Press, 1959.

Evagrius Ponticus. *The Praktikos and Chapters on Prayer*. Trans. John Eudes Bamberger. Trappist, KY: Cistercian Publications, 1972.

Ford, Stephanie. *Kindred Souls: Connecting Through Spiritual Friendship*. Nashville: Upper Room, 2006.

Foster, Richard. *Freedom of Simplicity*. London: Harper and Row, 1981.

Gladden, Washington. "The Church and the Social Crisis." In *Report Made to the National Council of the Congregational Church*. Thirteenth Triennial Session. October 8-17, 1907. Boston: Office of the Secretary, 1907.

Graves, Mike, and Richard F. Ward. *Craddock Stories*. St. Louis: Chalice Press, 2001.

Gray, Howard. "Detachment." In *The New SCM Dictionary of Christian Spirituality*, ed. Philip Sheldrake. London: SCM Press, 2005. 234–35.

Hammarskjöld, Dag. *Markings*. Trans. Leif Sjöberg and W. H. Auden. New York: Ballentine Books, 1964.

Heiler, Friedrich. *Prayer: A Study in the History and Psychology of Religion*. London: Oxford University Press, 1932.

Hinson, E. Glenn. "On Coping with Your Anger." *Weavings: A Journal of the Spiritual Life* 9/2 (March/April 1994): 37.

―――. "Kindlers and Purifiers of Dreams." *Weavings* 11/3 (May/June 1996): 38–45.

―――. *A Miracle of Grace.* Macon, GA: Mercer University Press, 2012.

―――. *The Reaffirmation of Prayer.* Nashville: Broadman, 1979.

―――. "Reconciliation and Resistance." *Weavings* 15/6 (November/December 2000): 46.

―――, ed. *Spirituality in Ecumenical Perspective.* Louisville, KY: Westminster/John Knox Press, 1993.

Inge, W.R. *Personal Religion and the Life of Devotion.* London: Longmans, Green and Co., 1924.

Jones, W. Paul. *The Art of Spiritual Direction: Giving and Receiving Spiritual Guidance.* Nashville: Upper Room Books, 2002.

Kelly, Thomas R. *A Testament of Devotion.* New York: Harper and Row, 1941.

à Kempis, Thomas. *The Imitation of Christ.* Harmondsworth: Penguin Books, 1952/1982.

Kierkegaard, Søren. *Purity of Heart.* New York: Harper and Row, 1938/1956.

King, Coretta Scott. *My Life with Martin Luther King Jr.* London: Hodder and Stoughton, 1969.

King, Martin Luther, Jr. "The Violence of Desperate Men." Chapter 8 in *The Autobiography of Martin Luther King Jr.*, ed. Claybourn E. Carson. New York: Grand Central Publishing, 2001.

Ledoux, Clare Marie. *Clare of Assisi: Her Spirituality Revealed in Her Letters.* Cincinnati: St Anthony Messenger Press, 1996

Leech, Kenneth. *Soul Friend: A Study of Spirituality.* London: Sheldon Press, 1977.

Lewis, C. S. *Surprised by Joy.* London: Collins, 1955/1982.

Lipsey, Roger. *Hammarskjöld: A Life.* Ann Arbor: University of Michigan Press, 2013.

MacCulloch, Diarmaid. *Silence: A Christian History*. London: Penguin, 2014.

Merton, Thomas. *Opening the Bible*. London: George Allen and Unwin, 1972.

———. *Seeds of Contemplation*. Wheathamstead: Burns and Oates, 1962.

———. *Thoughts in Solitude*. Tunbridge Wells: Burns and Oates, 1958.

———. *The Wisdom of the Desert*. New York: New Direction, 1960.

Miller, Robert Moats. *Harry Emerson Fosdick: Preacher, Pastor, Prophet*. Oxford: Oxford University Press, 1985.

Mogabgab, John S. "Along the Desert Road: Notes on Spiritual Reading." In E. Glenn Hinson, *Spirituality in Ecumenical Perspective*. Louisville: Westminster/John Knox Press, 1993.

Mother Julian. *Revelations of Divine Love*. London: Hodder and Stoughton, 1987.

Norris, Kathleen. *Acedia and Me*. London: Riverhead Books, 2008.

———. *Amazing Grace: A Vocabulary of Faith*. New York: Riverhead Books, 1998.

Nolan, Christopher. *Under the Eye of the Clock*. London: Orion Publishing/Weidenfeld & Nicolson, 1987.

Nouwen, Henri J. M. *Reaching Out: The Three Movement of the Spiritual Life*. London: Collins, 1976.

———. *The Return of the Prodigal Son: A Story of Homecoming*. London: Darton, Longman and Todd, 1994.

———. "A Spirituality of Waiting: Being Alert to God's Presence in Our Lives." *Weavings* 2/1 (January/February 1987).

O'Donohue, John. *Anam Cara*. London: Bantam Books, 1997.

O'Malley, Brendan, ed. *A Celtic Primer*. Norwich: Canterbury Press, 2002.

Palmer, Parker J. *To Know as We Are Known: A Spirituality of Education*. San Francisco: Harper and Row, 1986.

Peterson, Eugene. *Contemplative Pastor: Returning to the Art of Spiritual Direction*. Grand Rapids, MI: Eerdmans, 1989.

Rauschenbusch, Walter. *Walter Rauschenbusch: Selected Writings.* Sources of American Spirituality, ed. Winthrop S. Hudson. New York: Paulist Press, 1984.

Smith, James K. A. *You Are What You Love.* Grand Rapids, MI: Brazos Press, 2016.

Smith, K. E. *Christian Spirituality.* London: SCM Press, 2007.

Spener, Philip Jacob. *Pia Desideria.* Trans. Theodore G. Tappert. Philadelphia: Fortress Press, 1946/1974.

Steere, Douglas V. *On Listening to Another.* San Francisco: Harper and Row, 1955.

———, ed. *Spiritual Counsel and Letters of Baron von Hügel.* New York: Harper and Row, 1964.

Streeter, B. H. "Worship." In *Concerning Prayer.* London: Macmillan, 1918.

Swan, Laura. *The Forgotten Desert Mothers.* New York: Paulist Press, 2001.

Swinton, John. *Dementia: Living in the Memories of God.* London: SCM Press, 2012.

Taylor, John V. *A Matter of Life and Death.* London: SCM Press, 1986.

Teilhard de Chardin, Pierre. *Hymn of the Universe.* New York: Harper and Row, 1965.

Teresa of Avila. *The Interior Castle.* Mahwah, NJ: Paulist Press, 1979.

Thompson, Marjorie J. *Soul Feast: An Invitation to the Christian Spiritual Life.* Louisville, KY: Westminster/John Knox, 1995.

Thurman, Howard. *Deep Is the Hunger.* New York: Harper and Row, 1951; repr., Richmond, IN: Friends United Press, 2000.

———. *Disciplines of the Spirit.* New York: Harper and Row Publishers, 1963.

———. *With Head and Heart.* London: Harcourt Brace and Company, 1979.

Underhill, Evelyn. *The Letters of Evelyn Underhill.* London: Longmans, Green and Company, 1943/1944.

———. *School of Charity.* London: Longmans, Green and Co., 1934.

Vanstone, W. H. *The Stature of Waiting*. London: Darton, Longman and Todd, 1982.

von Hügel, Friedrich. *Letters to a Niece*. Ed. Gwendolyn Greene. London: Dent, 1928.

de Waal, Esther. *A World Made Whole: Rediscovering the Celtic Tradition*. London: Harper and Collins, 1991.

Watson, J. R. *The English Hymn: A Critical and Theological Study*. Oxford: OUP, 1999.

Weaver, Andrew, and Monica Furlong, eds. *Reflections on Forgiveness and Spiritual Growth*. Nashville: Abingdon Press, 2000.

Williams, Rowan. *Teresa of Avila*. London: Geoffrey Chapman, 1991.

Woolman, John. "A Plea for the Poor" (1793). In *The Journal of John Woolman and a Plea for the Poor*. Secaucus, NJ: Citadel Press, 1961.

Wuthnow, Robert. *Christianity in the Twenty-first Century*. Oxford: Oxford University Press, 1993.

Yates, Miles Lowell. *God in Us: The Theory and Practice of Christian Devotion*. Ed. W. Norman Pittenger and William H. Ralston, Jr. London: SPCK, 1960.

Index of Scriptural References

Index of Names and Subjects Related to Spiritual Formation